Realistic Compiler Generation

Foundations of Computing
Michael Garey and Albert Meyer, editors

Complexity Issues in VLSI: Optimal Layouts for the Shuffle-Exchange Graph and Other Networks , Frank Thomson Leighton, 1983

Equational Logic as a Programming Language , Michael J. O'Donnell, 1985

General Theory of Deductive Systems and Its Applications , S. Yu.Maslov, 1987

Resource Allocation Problems: Algorithmic Approaches , Toshihide Ibaraki and Naoki Katoh, 1988

Algebraic Theory of Processes , Michael Hennessy, 1988

PX: A Computational Logic , Susumu Hayashi and Hiroshi Nakano, 1989

Realistic Compiler Generation , Peter Lee, 1989

Realistic Compiler Generation

Peter Lee

The MIT Press
Cambridge, Massachusetts
London, England

Library of Congress Cataloging-in-Publication Data

Lee, Peter, 1960–
    Realistic compiler generation / Peter Lee.
         p.   cm. — (Foundations of computing)
    Bibliography: p.
    Includes index.
    ISBN 0-262-12141-7
    1. Compilers (Computer programs) 2. Programming
    languages (Electronic computers) — Semantics.   I. Title.
    II. Series.
    QA76.76.C65L44 1989   89-33174
    005.4'53—dc20   CIP

To my parents, Sung and Incha

Contents

Series Foreword

Theoretical computer science has now undergone several decades of development. The "classical" topics of automata theory, formal languages, and computational complexity have become firmly established, and their importance to other theoretical work and to practice is widely recognized. Stimulated by technological advances, theoreticians have been rapidly expanding the areas under study, and the time delay between theoretical progress and its practical impact has been decreasing dramatically. Much publicity has been given recently to breakthroughs in cryptography and linear programming, and steady progress is being made on programming language semantics, computational geometry, and efficient data structures. Newer, more speculative, areas of study include relational databases, VLSI theory, and parallel and distributed computation. As this list of topics continues expanding, it is becoming more and more difficult to stay abreast of the progress that is being made and increasingly important that the most significant work be distilled and communicated in a manner that will facilitate further research and application of this work. By publishing comprehensive books and specialized monographs on the theoretical aspects of computer science, the series on Foundations of Computing provides a forum in which important research topics can be presented in their entirety and placed in perspective for researchers, students, and practitioners alike.

Michael R. Garey
Albert R. Meyer

Foreword

When Peter asked me to write this foreword, I happily agreed. Since I have often wished that I had written my thesis on the topic of compiler generation, it is with great pleasure that I contribute at least a foreword to a book in the field.

Peter and I started working on semantics-directed compiler generation at the end of 1984, while I was on leave of absence from the University of Michigan, and working for a now-defunct small computer company. During the prior four years at Michigan I had managed to experiment extensively with two semantics systems (SIS and PSP), and develop *normal-form semantics*, which in essence is a precursor to high-level semantics, the topic of Peter's thesis. I had dreamed of building a compiler generator based on the concepts of normal-form semantics, but had almost resigned myself to the idea that this might never happen. Because of Peter's enthusiasm and programming skills, we now have the MESS system, whose performance has exceeded all my expectations. I believe that it is fair to say that MESS is the first true semantics-directed compiler generator.

I am very proud of Peter's accomplishments, and at the same time, pleased to have been able to contribute to the development of high-level semantics and MESS in a number of ways. First, my experimentation with SIS and PSP brought to light a number of fundamental engineering problems with using standard denotational semantics as a basis for compiler generation, and precipitated the development of normal-form semantics. Second, I helped Peter with the formulation of macrosemantic descriptions of common language features. Third, I developed the front-end generator FrEGe in my spare time, and for good measure threw in the specification of the code generator for the SOL/C compiler described in Chapter 7. Finally, I took great pains to steer Peter around many of the common stumbling blocks in thesis writing which I myself ran into as a student.

Fortunately for us, we both own IBM PC's, along with three excellent software packages: Turbo Pascal, TI PC Scheme, and Turbo Prolog. Without Turbo Pascal's phenomenal compilation speed, there would not be a front end generator. Without TI's excellent Scheme system, Peter would probably still be hacking on tree traversal routines. And without Turbo Prolog, there would not be a SOL/C code generator. These three packages have made it possible to develop the entire MESS system on a moderately sized personal computer. In contrast, SIS was born on a DEC-10 computer, and PSP on a VAX-11.

Let me summarize what I have learned from our research. First, the semanticist's view of compilers and the compiler writer's view of semantics can be unified. Semantics-directed compilers need not be based on the λ-calculus and β-reduction, and semantic definitions need not look abstruse and incomprehensible. Second, languages such as Scheme, ML, or even the Mathematica metalanguage are superb tools for compiler (generator) writing. Quite frankly, I find the almost superstitious misconceptions of the Pascal/C/Ada/Modula community concerning the efficiency and practicality of these "almost functional" languages rather disturbing. Finally, there are still many challenging problems to solve in this field, so the future looks quite interesting.

Supervising Peter's thesis research was fun and satisfying for me. For Peter, being finished with his thesis and this book must certainly be satisfying, and for him, let the fun begin! I hope that you, the reader, find the study of this book satisfying, and also fun.

Uwe Pleban

Ann Arbor, Michigan
January 10, 1989

Preface

This book is essentially a revised version of the doctoral dissertation I wrote at the University of Michigan, first completed in February, 1987.

My thesis can be stated as follows: Realistic compilers can be automatically generated from formal semantic descriptions. To do this requires that certain engineering concerns be taken into account, for example the readability and maintainability of the semantics. I claim that when standard software-engineering principles are properly applied to the construction of formal semantic descriptions, then it becomes possible to generate realistic compilers. Hence, we can, to some extent, have our cake and eat it too—formal specifications can at the same time serve as programming language definitions and as compiler specifications.

I hope that you, the reader, find the contents of this book to be worthwhile. Perhaps you will even be inspired to extend or bring to a real practical use some of the ideas presented here. I would be most happy to hear about it if you did!

Now, for some acknowledgements. First, I would like to make a special acknowledgement to Uwe Pleban, who was my thesis advisor at the University of Michigan. Uwe taught me about denotational semantics, compilers, and Scheme. He guided me through the ins and outs of teaching and writing, and instilled in me a healthy respect for both the theory and practice of computing. The work described in this book is really the result of our joint effort, conducted over the course of several years of stimulating, challenging, fun, and, of course, sometimes painful collaborative research. Uwe's deep interest in our research, and also in my general welfare, made my trek through graduate school much more fulfilling and less perilous than is usually the case. I feel very lucky to have had this experience, and Uwe will always have my heartfelt gratitude for that.

I would like to thank my thesis committee members, Bill Rounds, Satish Thatte, and Peter Hinman for their enthusiasm about my thesis research. Further acknowledgements go to Yuri Gurevich, Fritz Ruehr, and my sisters Patty and Janet, all while I was at Michigan; and also to the Ergo Project and the Department of Computer Science at Carnegie Mellon University for giving me the time and resources to turn this thesis into a book.

Finally, I would like to dedicate this book to my parents, Sung and Incha. This book would not have been possible without their love and support.

Peter Lee

Pittsburgh, Pennsylvania
January 15, 1989

Realistic Compiler Generation

1 Compiler Generation

The term *compilation* refers to the translation of a program written in a *source language* to a program with an equivalent meaning in a *target language*. A *compiler* is a program that performs this process for a particular pair of source and target languages. This book presents a new method for generating correct and efficient implementations of compilers.

Conceptually, compilation is accomplished in two stages, *analysis* followed by *synthesis*. In the first stage, the grammatical structure of a program is analyzed so that it can be certified as belonging to the source language. The second stage determines the meaning of the source program, and then synthesizes a target program with the same meaning. Compilation thus depends on the *structure* and *meaning* of programs, which are given by the programming language *syntax* and *semantics*, respectively. There is also a third characteristic, *pragmatics*, which describes the proper use and intended application of a language. Although pragmatics is important in the study of programming languages, it has, for the purposes of this book, little impact on the problem of compiling programs. Hence, it will be largely ignored here.

Clearly, writing a compiler requires complete knowledge of the syntax and semantics of the source and target languages. The designer of a new language must therefore find a way to describe the syntax and semantics to compiler writers. Syntax (or, more precisely, the context-free syntax) has long been described by standard formal methods— variations of the Backus-Naur Form [Naur 63] are commonplace. Semantics, on the other hand, is usually defined informally, in English rather than in a formal notation.

Informal descriptions are acceptable for some purposes. Experience shows, however, that they fail to provide the unambiguous and consistent definition of semantics required for compiler writing. For instance, numerous inconsistencies and omissions in the informal description of Pascal [Wirth 71] have been reported [Habermann 73, Lecarme & Desjardins 75, Watt 79] despite the care with which it was written. Similar problems have also been found in the definition of Algol 60 [Naur 63]. Such uncertainty makes it impossible for the compiler writer to carry out the intentions of the language designer. It is not surprising, then, that we are left in a situation in which virtually no two compilers implement exactly the same language.

In order to get out of this "mess," I, along with many others, believe that the implementation of compilers ought to be guided by *formal language definitions* consisting of formal descriptions of the syntax and semantics. Besides eliminating many of the problems of informal descriptions, the use of formal descriptions allows us to consider the development of a *semantics-directed compiler generator*.

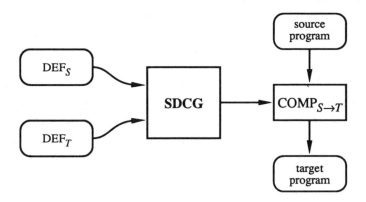

A semantics-directed compiler generator (SDCG) takes as input the formal definitions of the source language (DEF_S) and target language (DEF_T). From this, it generates a compiler ($COMP_{S \rightarrow T}$).

Figure 1.1
A Semantics-Directed Compiler Generator

As shown in Figure 1.1, such a system produces compilers from formal definitions of the source and target languages. This provides several advantages. First, some aspects of the formal definitions can be checked for consistency and correctness by the system, thereby increasing the likelihood that they accurately reflect the intentions of the language designer. Second, compilers are automatically generated from the formal definitions. Presumably, the definitions are much easier to write and debug than the typical C or Pascal (or whatever) code for a compiler. Finally, if the compiler generator is correct, then the generated compilers are guaranteed to be correct with respect to the formal definitions.

There are several known methods for formally describing the semantics of programming languages. The denotational method [Scott 71, Milne & Strachey 76, Stoy 77] has gained particularly wide acceptance among semanticists and language designers. Denotational semantics has also been a popular basis for semantics-directed compiler generation. Since 1979, a number of systems based on the direct implementation of denotational semantics have been developed. This book discusses three such systems: Mosses' Semantics Implementation System [Mosses 75, Mosses 79], Paulson's Semantics Processor [Paulson 81, Paulson 82], and Wand's Semantic Prototyping System [Wand 84]. These systems are all based on fundamentally the same strategy, which I call the *classical approach* to semantics-directed compiler generation. They are important because they demonstrate the possibility of automatically generating compilers for non-trivial languages from formal semantic descriptions.

Beyond the issues of correctness, the generated compilers must also (1) carry out the translation of source programs to target programs efficiently and (2) produce efficient target programs. I use the term *performance characteristics* to refer collectively to these two aspects of compiler efficiency. Unfortunately, the classical systems generate compilers with performance characteristics that are several orders of magnitude worse than those exhibited by handwritten compilers.

1.1 A New Approach

I believe that the classical approach to compiler generation inherently leads to compilers with poor performance characteristics. This, I believe, is due to fundamental problems with traditional denotational semantics[1] as a language for specifying compilers. The techniques used in the denotational method lead to poorly engineered semantic specifications that *define*, but do not satisfactorily *describe*, programming languages. This effectively precludes any possibility for efficient implementation, and furthermore makes the semantic specifications unnecessarily hard to comprehend and debug.

In order to overcome these problems, I have developed a new style of semantic description called *high-level semantics*. Its development has been guided by the following principles:

- *Engineering*: It ought to be straightforward to construct and debug good semantic specifications.

- *Philosophy*: The fundamental concepts embodied by a language should appear explicitly in its semantic description. Semantic concepts not fundamental to the language should be left out.

- *Implementation*: It should be possible to derive efficient compilers from the semantic specifications, provided that the language being described is amenable to compilation.

---

[1]I say *traditional* denotational semantics because I am referring not only to the mathematical basis of the approach, but also to the notation, writing style, and "tricks of the trade" used in denotational specifications. This traditional style is discussed in more detail in Chapters 3 and 4.

In this book I present evidence that, in a high-level semantics, the third principle is compatible with the first two. Thus, unlike traditional denotational semantics, high-level semantics is suitable for both defining the functional meaning of programming languages as well as describing compiler implementations. The high-level approach also allows for considerably improved "semantics engineering," resulting in formal specifications that are more descriptive and intelligible than traditional specifications. Moreover, *realistic* compilers can be automatically generated from high-level specifications in a straightforward manner. By "realistic," I mean that the compilers have the following properties:

- They compile nontrivial sequential programming languages into target code that can be directly executed on machines with conventional architectures.

- Their internal structure is similar to that exhibited by handwritten compilers: they have a multipass structure and perform the usual compile-time computations, such as type checking, during compilation.

- Their performance characteristics compare favorably to those of handwritten compilers.

In order to demonstrate the viability of this new approach, I have implemented a semantics-directed compiler generator called MESS which embodies the principles of high-level semantics. MESS has been used to generate a compiler for a language with recursive procedures, reference and value parameters, multidimensional flexible array parameters, and the usual Pascal-like control structures, among other things. To my knowledge, this is the first time a realistic compiler for such a complex language has been generated completely from formal specifications. The target programs produced by the compiler compare favorably with those produced by several commercially available, handwritten compilers in both size and speed.

1.2   A Preview of the Book

There are, I believe, three main advantages of high-level semantics over previously developed approaches. First, high-level descriptions are easier to write and comprehend than traditional denotational specifications. Second, realistic compilers can be straightforwardly generated from high-level descriptions. Finally, the high-level approach forms a useful basis for reasoning about programs.

Of these three claims, only the first two are treated in this book. Thus, this book has less to do with the theoretical foundations of high-level semantics, and more with formal specification techniques and the automatic generation of realistic compilers. A more theoretically oriented treatment of high-level semantics is left to future work.

With this caveat stated, I can now present, in full, MESS and the high-level approach to semantic description. I begin by reviewing, in the next two chapters, the previous approaches to compiler generation. The contents of the remaining chapters are summarized below.

Chapter 4. Traditional denotational semantics is a poor language for compiler specification. This is due to several fundamental problems that lead to semantic specifications that are poorly engineered (in a software-engineering sense) and also practically eliminate any possibility for efficient implementation. These problems can be summarized as follows:

1. Traditional specifications are written in Scott's language LAMBDA (with more or less syntactic sugar). This essentially amounts to writing an interpreter in a primitive assembly language for a λ calculus machine, with all of the usual engineering problems of coding in assembly language. The implementation of such low-level specifications requires the costly emulation of a λ-calculus machine.

2. The actual semantics of a programming language is inextricably intertwined with details of the underlying semantic models, such as the structure of environments and store, the use of direct or continuation styles, and so on. This usually necessitates a complete reformulation of the semantic specification should any aspect of the model change. In a classically generated compiler, this can cause the phenomenon of *overreduction* to occur, making it extremely difficult for the compiler to discover the presence of even the simplest basic operations in a program.

3. Programming language concepts are rarely expressed directly in a traditional denotational semantics. Instead, they are explicated in terms of a small set of low-level mechanisms. Thus, important semantic distinctions, for instance between variables and formal parameters, are either ignored or expressed in highly cryptic terms. This impairs the comprehensibility of the semantic specifications and makes it impossible for a compiler generator

to choose implementation strategies that might exploit these distinctions in order to improve performance.

4. Semantic concepts not fundamental to the language being described are often overspecified, thus making semantic specifications less abstract than desirable. This restricts a compiler generator to a specific, and often simplistic, implementation model.

5. An essential part of the design of most programming languages is the distinction between its static and dynamic aspects. However, this distinction is blurred in traditional specifications. This makes it difficult or impossible for a compiler generator to determine those aspects of a language that should be analyzed at compile time.

Chapter 5. A new approach called *high-level semantics* overcomes these problems by considering the issues of readability, clarity, and implementability of semantic descriptions. The result is a flexible technique for semantic description that can be efficiently implemented in a straightforward manner. In practice, high-level specifications are also easier to write, comprehend, and debug than traditional specifications. The salient characteristics of the high-level approach can be summarized as follows:

1. *Description in terms of action-based operators.* As with traditional denotational semantics, semantic equations are used to supply the constructs of a language with their denotations. However, in a high-level semantics the denotations are expressed in terms of a semantic algebra of action-based operators rather than the λ-calculus. The operators yield various kinds of *actions*, akin to the actions of Mosses' abstract semantic algebras [Mosses 82, Mosses 84].

2. *Exposition of implementation structures.* The operators of a semantic algebra are chosen to directly reflect both fundamental language concepts as well as fundamental implementation concepts. This improves the comprehensibility of the semantic descriptions. Furthermore, an efficient implementation can be obtained by interpreting the operators as templates of intermediate code for a code generator.

3. *Separability.* The semantic equations and the semantic algebra are defined in separate specifications called the *macrosemantics* and *microsemantics*, respectively. Semantic model details are used only in providing an interpretation

for the algebra, and thus appear only in the microsemantics. This provides a clean separation of the actual language semantics from the underlying model details.

4. *Interchangeability of microsemantic definitions.* The only information shared between the macrosemantics and microsemantics is the signature of the semantic algebra defined by the microsemantics. This provides a modularity that guarantees the invariance of the macrosemantics under different interpretations of the microsemantic operators. As an example, a microsemantics is presented with interpretations based on traditional denotational models, abstract machine models, and a code-generator specification.

5. *Distinction between static and dynamic language components.* The separation between macrosemantics and microsemantics is also used to distinguish between the static and dynamic aspects of a language. Compile-time objects are defined in the macrosemantics, whereas runtime objects are defined in the microsemantics. In this respect, high-level descriptions are similar to the two-level metalanguages described in [Nielson & Nielson 86].

6. *Extensibility.* It is usually straightforward to add new operators to a semantic algebra. Doing so may require rewriting of parts of the microsemantics, but always leaves the macrosemantics intact. The portions of the microsemantics requiring modification are easy to identify.

7. *Readability.* High-level specifications are written in a readable notation based on the Standard ML language [Harper 86].

Chapters 6 and 7. The suitability of the high-level approach for semantics-directed compiler generation is demonstrated by the MESS system. MESS generates realistic compilers for nontrivial languages from high-level semantic specifications. It has been used to generate a compiler for a language called SOL/C that features recursive procedures, value and reference parameters, multidimensional flexible array parameters, and the usual Pascal-like control structures. The performance characteristics of the generated SOL/C compiler compare favorably with those exhibited by commercially available, handwritten compilers.

2 Tools for Practical Compiler Generation

I use the term *handwritten* to describe compilers constructed by the usual manual methods. This terminology is not very precise, however, since significant portions of handwritten compilers are often implemented with the aid of *compiler-writing tools*. These tools automatically transform the formal specification of some phase of compilation into a corresponding piece of a compiler.

This chapter gives a brief overview of the various types of compiler-writing tools commonly used in implementing practical compilers.

2.1 The Idealized Structure of a Compiler

In the previous chapter, compilation was characterized as a process of analysis followed by synthesis. Customarily, these two steps are further divided into several phases which can be viewed as the structural components of an *idealized compiler*.

The first phase is the *syntax analyzer*, **SA**, which has the functionality

$$\textbf{SA} \in \text{EXT}_{PL} \rightarrow \text{AST}_{PL}$$

where EXT_{PL} is the domain of external textual representations of source programs in the programming language PL, and AST_{PL} is the domain of their abstract internal representations. The syntax analyzer examines the syntactic structure of a source program, and builds an *abstract syntax tree* representation of it. This phase is sometimes called the *syntax checker*, or *parser*.

The second phase is the *static semantic analyzer*:

$$\textbf{SS} \in \text{AST}_{PL} \rightarrow \text{AST}_{PL}^{+}$$

Here, AST_{PL}^{+} is the domain of extended abstract tree representations of PL programs. This phase analyzes an abstract syntax tree in order to collect the statically determinable information about a program. For example, type constraints on identifiers might be gathered from abstract syntax tree nodes representing the program declarations. Tree nodes containing references to the identifiers can then be "decorated" with this type information, thereby extending the tree. This allows the semantic analyzer to enforce context-sensitive constraints which, for most modern programming languages, deal mostly with the issue of type correctness. Thus, this phase is sometimes called the *type checker*.

The *translation phase*, **TR**, has the functionality

$$\textbf{TR} \in \text{AST}_{PL}^{+} \rightarrow \text{INT}_{PL}$$

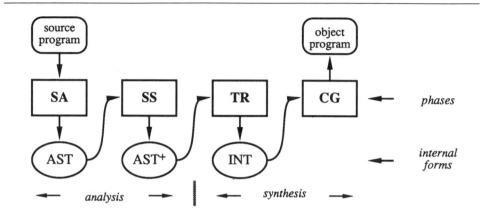

An idealized compiler is divided into four phases. The two analysis phases are semantic analysis (**SA**) and static semantic analysis (**SS**). The two synthesis phases are translation (**TR**) and code generation (**CG**). Each phase operates in turn, transforming a source program into a succession of internal representations, finally resulting in an object program.

Figure 2.1
The Structure of an Idealized Compiler

where INT_{PL} is the domain of intermediate internal representations of *PL* programs. This phase translates extended abstract syntax trees into *intermediate representations* that are amenable to direct conversion to code for the target machine. Hence, it essentially analyzes the runtime behavior, or dynamic semantics, of a program.

Finally, the *code generator* is as follows:

$$\mathbf{CG} \in INT_{PL} \rightarrow REP_M(I \rightarrow O)$$

$REP_M(I \rightarrow O)$ is the domain of representations of functions from domains I to O, expressed as programs in *M*-machine code, where *M* is either a hardware or software (virtual) machine. I and O are typically the domains of input and output files, respectively, or initial and final target-machine configurations. The code generator translates intermediate representations into object programs consisting of code that can be directly executed by the target machine.

The functional composition of these four phases yields $COMP_{PL}$, a compiler for *PL*:

$$\mathrm{COMP}_{PL} = \mathbf{SA} \circ \mathbf{SS} \circ \mathbf{TR} \circ \mathbf{CG} \in \mathrm{EXT}_{PL} \rightarrow \mathrm{REP}_M (\mathrm{I} \rightarrow \mathrm{O})$$

Of course, this is just one possible version of the idealized compiler—other versions might differ in the details. Syntax analysis, for instance, is often split into three phases: lexical analysis, parsing, and tree building. Still, the basic tasks of the four phases presented here are well enough accepted that similar descriptions can be found in almost any textbook on compiler construction, for example [Aho *et al.* 86], [Barrett & Couch 85], or [Waite & Goos 84].

2.2   The Structure of Real Compilers

Actual implementations of compilers realize the idealized structure in many different ways. A *multipass compiler*, for instance, is structured as a sequence of *passes*, with each pass implementing one or more phases, or part of a phase. The passes operate in turn, making transformations on successive internal forms, some of which represent elements of the domains described above.

It is not unusual to implement several phases in a single pass. For example, the **SS** and **TR** phases are often combined into one pass that performs static semantic analysis and translation in parallel. In a *single-pass compiler* all of the phases are implemented in one pass. This generally results in very fast compilation, but not all languages can be compiled this way.

Optimization phases are often inserted in order to improve the efficiency of the object code. Machine-independent optimizations are carried out on intermediate representations, in between the translation and code generation phases. This typically involves a process called data flow analysis [Kennedy 81] in which information about a program's use of data is collected. This information can then be used to trigger meaning-preserving transformations on an intermediate representation in an effort to gain improvements in efficiency. Machine-dependent optimizations, such as peephole optimizations [McKeeman 65, Davidson & Fraser 80], are conducted by a phase that operates on the machine code at the very end of compilation.

Compiler optimization clearly has a strong connection to formal semantics. Researchers have just barely begun to explore this connection, however, and at present, very little is known about it. The research presented in this book also stops short of considering optimization issues. It seems that the methods proposed here will be useful in building optimization phases, but this has yet to be substantiated.

2.3   Compiler Generation Tools

The idealized compiler structure reveals the basic elements of the compilation, which provides a useful decomposition of the problem of *automatic compiler generation* into smaller, more manageable subproblems. Solutions to several of these subproblems have already been pursued with a great deal of success, with the result that various types of *compiler writing tools* are now commonly used to generate portions of compilers automatically.

These tools are "automatic" in the sense that they generate implementations of portions of compilers from *formal specifications*. The essential feature of a formal specification is that the phase of compilation or aspect of a programming language under consideration is described *directly*—not by some algorithm for translation. Furthermore, formal specification techniques are usually based on well-established mathematical principles, thus allowing the specifications to be understood and reasoned about in terms of these principles. In practice, formal specifications are also easier to write and less prone to error than standard code.

Parser generators

The most common type of compiler generation tool is the *parser generator*. This tool generates the parsing component of a compiler from a grammar specifying the language syntax. The parsers often employ the highly efficient LALR(1) parsing technique [DeRemer 69]. An example of such a system is FrEGe [Pleban 87] which automatically produces LALR(1) parsers capable of recovering from syntax errors in the source input.

Some parser generators provide "hooks" in the syntax specifications for interfacing with other parts of a compiler. The YACC system [Johnson 75], for example, allows "action routines" to be attached to the productions in the grammar so that the generated parsers can perform compiling actions beyond syntax analysis. The action routines, however, do not formally specify these compiling actions—they must in fact be hand-coded in the C programming language [Kernighan & Ritchie 78].

Front-end generators

Another type of compiler generation tool is the *front-end generator*. The term *front end* refers to the portion of a compiler that performs both syntactic analysis and static semantic analysis. Front-end generators typically process attribute grammars [Knuth 65, Madsen 80], which are useful for specifying the context-sensitive constraints of a programming language together with its context-free syntax.

With an attribute grammar the parse of a program results in an attributed parse tree. Each node of the tree is decorated with attributes whose values describe the properties of that node. The values of the attributes are computed according to rules specified in the attribute grammar. Evaluating a rule may require the values of other attributes in the tree. Thus, computing the attribute values—a process called *attribute evaluation*—demands that a correct sequence of evaluation be found.

Unfortunately, determining such a sequence for general attribute grammars has exponential time complexity [Jazayeri *et al.* 75]. Therefore, the problem is usually simplified by restricting the class of acceptable grammars. For example, a popular attribute evaluation strategy, called alternating-pass evaluation [Jazayeri & Walter 75], restricts the grammars to those that can be evaluated in a fixed number of alternating passes over the tree (*i.e.*, a left-to-right pass, followed by a right-to-left pass, and so on). The front-end generator, Linguist-86 [Farrow 82, Farrow 84] is based on this strategy. Systems employing other efficient attribute evaluation strategies include GAG [Kastens *et al.* 82] and HLP [Raiha 80].

Code generator generators

A code generator matches patterns in the intermediate representation, emitting the appropriate machine instructions after each successful match. At the same time, it allocates machine resources such as registers.

Glanville and Graham have developed a method for implementing the pattern matching via LR parsing [Glanville & Graham 78]. Instructions are emitted after each reduction by the parser. In essence, the code generators are specified as syntax-directed translation schemes. As such, this approach focusses mainly on instruction selection and largely ignores the problem of register allocation. The most significant contribution of this approach is the idea that linear intermediate representations should be in prefix form rather than the more typical postfix or tuple forms. The suitability—indeed, the preferability—of prefix-form intermediate representations was not widely recognized before this work.

One problem with the Graham-Glanville approach is that the grammars tend to produce numerous shift-reduce and reduce-reduce parsing conflicts which must be resolved before a code generator can be generated. Ganapathi eliminates this problem by allowing semantic attributes to influence the actions of the parser [Ganapathi 80]. Parsing conflicts can thus be resolved by interrogating the values of certain attributes during, rather than before, code generation.

Bird has applied these techniques to implement code generators for production compilers [Bird 82]. He argues that certain constraints imposed by common machine architectures, for instance on the use of registers in multiplication operations, cannot be satisfactorily dealt with by purely syntactic transformations. He thus advocates the use of semantic values propagated in the attributes to provide such information.

The code generators produced by these methods produce machine code with quality comparable to that produced by handwritten code generators. From a theoretical standpoint, however, the problem of generating code generators automatically is far from solved. A code generator translates from one language to another, and this translation must be shown to preserve the semantics of the source language. This unfortunately involves unwieldy and often intractable congruence proofs that have never, to my knowledge, been conducted for practical code generators. Hence, for the time being, the correctness of the code generators produced by these methods must be taken for granted, and an assumption made that the methods will be properly justified whenever the necessary theoretical tools are developed.

2.4   Semantics-Directed Compiler Generation

The tools described above aid in the development of handwritten compilers. They cover three of the four basic phases of compilation. The only phase not yet considered is the translation phase. Translation is the central and most difficult issue in compiling because it has the strongest connection to the formal semantics of the source language. The remainder of this book is concerned with the problem of automatically generating the translation phase.

2.5   Summary

The four basic phases of an *idealized compiler* are as follows:

1. *Syntax analyzer*: Transforms source programs into abstract syntax trees.

2. *Static semantic analyzer*: Decorates the abstract syntax trees with statically determinable semantic information.

3. *Translator*: Translates the decorated syntax trees to intermediate representations.

4. *Code generator*: Translates the intermediate representations to target machine
   code.

Compiler-writing tools are widely available for automatically generating efficient
implementations of all phases, except for the translation phase. Translation is
the central and most difficult issue in compiling because it has the strongest
connection to the formal semantics of programming languages.

The problem of automatically generating the translation phase of a compiler is
addressed by *semantics-directed compiler generation*, the subject of the next chapter.

3 Semantics-Directed Compiler Generation

Several systems have been developed that generate compilers from formal semantic descriptions. Of particular interest here are those based on the direct implementation of denotational semantics. This chapter examines the principles of operation underlying these and related systems.

3.1 Methods for Formal Description of Semantics

Several methods have been devised for formally describing the semantics of programming languages. They can be grouped into three major categories: *operational*, *axiomatic*, and *functional* semantics.

Operational semantics

In an operational semantics, a language is defined by an interpreter. Often, the interpreter takes the form of an abstract machine, in which case the language semantics is specified as an algorithm for translating source programs into abstract machine code. The "execution" of this code on the abstract machine traces out a sequences of states, and this sequence is taken to be the meaning of the program. Presumably the machine is so simple that there is no chance of misunderstanding *its* semantics.

A number of techniques for this type of semantic description have been developed and successfully applied to widely used languages. For example, the programming language Algol 68 was defined operationally, via the so-called van Wijngaarden grammars [van Wijngaarden *et al.* 75]. Another similar technique is the Vienna Definition Language [Wegner 72], which was used to define PL/1.

For some languages, the operational semantics is specified most conveniently by writing an interpreter for the language in the language itself; hence the defined language is also the defining language. These *metacircular interpreters* are especially convenient for languages well suited for writing interpreters, such as Lisp [McCarthy *et al.* 65]. The semantics of the Lisp dialect, Scheme, for instance, was originally defined by an interpreter written in Scheme [Steele & Sussman 78].

An interesting problem with this approach (described in [Stoy 77, page 180]) is that a metacircular interpreter might fail to confirm or deny fundamental assumptions that are made about the language semantics. For example, the metacircular interpreter for Scheme does not define an evaluation order for the language; whatever order is assumed for Scheme is carried over to its semantics (and *vice versa*). In [Reynolds 72], Reynolds explains how this problem can be avoided

by using the functional device of continuations to specify the order of evaluation explicitly, in a manner independent of the evaluation order of the defining
language.

The operational approaches to semantics are appealing because they are easy
to understand and straightforward to implement. However, no standard formal basis exists for these methods—every new description might define a new
machine or language on which to base the semantics. This makes it extremely
difficult to compare languages. Even worse, the meanings of programs are given
only indirectly, by executing complete programs on an abstract machine or interpreter. The meaning of a fragment of a program, or of a particular construct
in a language, is thus difficult to obtain.

Axiomatic semantics

Axiomatic approaches to semantics were developed primarily for program verifi-
cation [Floyd 67]. Hence, they are designed to support reasoning about particular
properties of programs.

In an axiomatic semantics, axioms and deduction rules from mathematical
logic are specified for each construct in a language. These allow assertions to be
made about what is true after the execution of a language construct relative to
what was true before (provided that the execution terminates). The nature of the
assertions depends on the kinds of properties described by the axioms and rules.
For example, a semantics might be constructed so as to allow assertions to be
made about the output properties of the language constructs, thereby allowing
one to prove that two programs produce the same output.

An axiomatic method developed by Hoare [Hoare 69] has been used to describe the semantics of a subset of Pascal [Hoare & Wirth 73]. Unfortunately,
the usefulness of this method is severely limited by its inability to deal easily
with common language features such as side effects and scoping. A more fundamental problem with these approaches, at least as far as compiler generation
is concerned, is that an axiomatic specification restricts one to reasoning about
particular *properties* of programs—there is no stipulation that these properties
correspond to program *meanings*. Hence, the prospects for generating compilers
from axiomatic descriptions seem quite remote.

Functional semantics

Functional approaches to semantic description are characterized by their use of
valuation functions. These functions map the constructs of a language directly to

their meanings, which are usually abstract mathematical objects such as numbers, functions, or terms in an algebra. The mappings are specified recursively; in other words, the meaning of a construct is derived from the meanings of its subconstructs. Valuation functions thus directly determine the meanings of entire programs, fragments of programs, or particular constructs of languages. In contrast with the operational methods, no translation or interpretation is necessary.

The most completely developed form of functional semantics is the *denotational method* [Scott 71, Milne & Strachey 76]. In a denotational semantics, the meaning, or *denotation*, of a program is given as an object belonging to a well-defined mathematical domain. The valuation functions are normally written as a collection of equations, with each equation specifying the denotation of a language construct in terms of the λ-calculus.[1] It is also possible to write a denotational semantics in the form of an attribute grammar [Mayoh 78]. A wide variety of programming languages have been defined denotationally, including Algol 60 [Mosses 74], Algol 68 [Henhapl & Jones 82], Pascal [Tennent 77], portions of Ada [Donzeau-Gouge 80], SNOBOL [Tennent 73], Lisp [Muchnick & Pleban 82], and Prolog [van Emden & Kowalski 76].

Another functional approach is algebraic semantics, in which the meanings of programs are given as terms in an abstract algebra. The use of algebraic concepts makes available a considerable body of mathematical knowledge [Burstall & Landin 69, Morris 73]. One form of algebraic semantics, called initial-algebra semantics [ADJ 78], has received a good deal of attention in recent years. However, to my knowledge initial-algebra semantics has not been used to describe the semantics of a nontrivial programming language.

Mosses has observed that denotational descriptions are, in some sense, "too concrete," due to the intertwining of model details with the actual semantics of the language. Thus, he proposes a new approach to semantics in which program meanings are given in terms of *abstract semantic algebras* (ASA's) [Mosses 82, Mosses 84]. The operators in an ASA belong to an algebraic sort of *actions*, which may produce and consume values, have side effects on the store, and so on. The properties of the operators are defined axiomatically (*i.e.*, in the same manner as abstract data types, by equational specifications). More importantly, the operators are chosen so as to directly reflect the "fundamental" concepts embodied by the programming language.

---

[1] Actually, the denotations are given in terms of a syntactic extension of Scott's language, LAMBDA, [Scott 71] which may be viewed as a typed λ-calculus. More will be said about this later in this chapter.

The need for semantic modeling "devices" is completely eliminated by the equationally specified algebras. For example, the associativity of a statement-sequencing operator for an imperative language can be expressed directly (by a single equation) in an ASA specification; there is no need to resort to devices such as continuations to model flow of control. In this sense, ASA-based descriptions are more "abstract" than denotational (or algebraic) descriptions since semantic model details (like continuations) can be ignored. This provides a kind of modularity that protects semantic descriptions from the nearly total rewriting normally required when the underlying model changes. Also, it becomes possible to provide models in a variety of ways without affecting the semantic descriptions. This is accomplished by using alternative methods for specifying the algebras [Bohlbro & Schwartzbach 82].

More recently, Mosses and Watt have extended the idea of ASA's by developing a highly descriptive notation for expressing the semantics. This new method, called *action semantics* [Mosses & Watt 86], has been used to describe the semantics of Pascal [Mosses & Watt 87] and ML [Watt 88]. We shall see in Chapter 5 that the ideas underlying abstract semantic algebras and action semantics have had a significant influence on the development of high-level semantics.

3.2   Classical Compiler Generation

The semantics-directed compiler generator shown in Figure 1.1 (on page 2) requires formal definitions of both the source and target languages in order to produce a compiler. The problem of properly relating the two language definitions is quite daunting, however. It becomes necessary, therefore, to simplify matters by choosing a fixed target language. Fortunately, this simplification is easily tolerated since language designers and semanticists are usually not so interested in the target language—their interests lie with the source language, independent of any particular target.

For the remainder of this chapter, a class of semantics-directed compiler generators will be considered in which the fixed target is a reducer for the λ-calculus, and the source language descriptions are written using the denotational method. These systems generate the core component of a compiler that performs both static semantic analysis and translation. This component produces a λ-calculus intermediate code that can be directly interpreted by a β-reducer.

As shown in Figure 3.1, I call these the *classical semantics-directed compiler generators*. A compiler generated by such a system is called a *classical compiler*, which

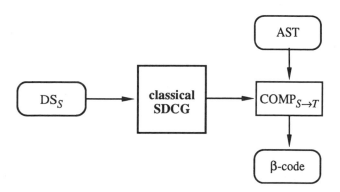

A classical semantics-directed compiler generator takes as input the denotational description of the source language (DS_S). From this it generates a compiler component ($COMP_{S \to \lambda}$) that translates abstract syntax trees to λ-calculus code for a β-reduction machine.

Figure 3.1
A Classical Semantics-Directed Compiler Generator

performs *classical compilation*. Classical compiler generation is based on the direct implementation of denotational semantics.

3.3   The Structure of Denotational Descriptions

Denotational specifications are very much like programs written in a high-level functional language. It is natural, therefore, to view denotational semantics as a programming language and then study the problem of its efficient implementation. This is, in fact, the basic idea behind classical compiler generation, and hence this will be the approach taken for the rest of this chapter. The theoretical basis for denotational semantics is not explained here. For this the reader is referred to the seminal paper by Scott [Scott 71] and to the textbooks by Milne [Milne & Strachey 76], Stoy [Stoy 77], and Schmidt [Schmidt 86]. Tennent [Tennent 76] and Gordon [Gordon 79] also provide introductions to the subject.

Meanings in denotational semantics

In denotational semantics, the meanings of programs are drawn from *semantic domains*. A considerable amount of mathematical theory has been developed, primarily by Scott [Scott 71], in order to characterize the nature of these domains. In this theory, a language called LAMBDA is defined for specifying elements of the universal domain $\mathbf{P}\omega$, where $\omega = \{n \mid n \geq 0\}$ (and $\mathbf{P}\omega = 2^\omega$). A denotational semantics maps programs to terms in LAMBDA, which ultimately denote elements in $\mathbf{P}\omega$.

The LAMBDA language is not very expressive. Thus, some syntactic sugar is usually added. The behavior of the syntactic extensions may be described by writing theorems in the LAMBDA theory. Alternatively, one may view the extended language as a typed λ-calculus which can be easily given a semantics in terms of LAMBDA. Here, I follow the latter approach and assume that the meanings denoted by programs are written as expressions in a typed λ-calculus.[2] Section 3.5 gives a brief overview of the λ-calculus. See [Hindley *et al.* 72] for a complete treatment of the subject.

The specification of valuation functions

Recall that valuation functions are used to map programs to their meanings. A valuation function is written as a collection of *semantic equations*, with each equation mapping a particular syntactic construct to its meaning in the λ-calculus.

The structure of the syntactic constructs is given by the *abstract syntax* of the language being described. As a simple example, consider the following specification of the abstract syntax for a tiny language of addition expressions:

Syntactic domains
    B $\in$ **Bas**   (basic values)
    E $\in$ **Exp**   (addition expressions)

Abstract syntax
    E ::= B $\mid$ E$_1$ + E$_2$

Two syntactic domains are declared. The first, **Bas**, is a predefined domain of syntactic constructs, for example integer numerals, representing basic literal values. **Exp** is a new domain of addition expressions, the structure of which is

---

[2] For the remainder of this book, the λ-calculus, when referred to, is "typed."

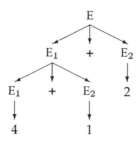

Abstract syntax trees are commonly drawn graphically. The tree shown here is for the addition expression, '4 + 1 + 2'.

Figure 3.2
An Abstract Syntax Tree

defined by the two grammar rules. B and E are declared to be metavariables taking values from the domains **Bas** and **Exp**, respectively

The first rule of the abstract syntax specifies that the domain **Bas** is contained in **Exp**; an addition expression may be simply the representation of a basic value. The second rule specifies that an addition expression also may consist of two distinct instances of addition expressions (referred to as E_1 and E_2) combined by the *noise string*, +. Together, these rules specify the two syntactic constructs of the language. The syntax is called "abstract" because syntactic details not needed for semantic analysis, such as the associativity of +, are not specified in the grammar. Elements of the syntactic domains are usually called *abstract syntax trees* since they can be drawn as trees, as shown in Figure 3.2.

A valuation function is defined by specifying a semantic equation for every syntactic construct in the language.

    Semantic functions
      $\mathcal{B} : \textbf{Bas} \rightarrow \textbf{B}$
      $\mathcal{E} : \textbf{Exp} \rightarrow \textbf{B}$

      $\mathcal{E}[\![B]\!] \quad\quad = \mathcal{B}[\![B]\!]$
      $\mathcal{E}[\![E_1 + E_2]\!] = \mathcal{E}[\![E_1]\!] \oplus \mathcal{E}[\![E_2]\!]$

The valuation function $\mathcal{E}$ converts syntactic expressions (from domain **Exp**) to values in the predefined domain **B** of basic values. Thus, the meanings of addition expressions are drawn from the domain **B**. It is important to note that

B (in boldface) is a *semantic* domain containing basic mathematical values such as integers. This must be kept distinct from B, which is a metavariable ranging over **Bas**, the domain of *syntactic* representations of basic values, in this case integer numerals. (Distinguishing names by type face is a confusing but common practice in denotational semantics.)

In the two equations, the syntax brackets, ⟦ ⟧, delimit the syntactic entities. The meaning of a syntactic construct appearing on the left-hand side of an equation is given by the (λ-)expression on the right-hand side. In the first equation, the meaning of a tree representing a basic value is derived by applying the $\mathcal{B}$ function. $\mathcal{B}$ is a predefined valuation function that converts syntactic entities to their corresponding semantic values. The second equation derives the meaning of an addition expression by adding the meanings of the two subconstructs via the semantic operator $\oplus$, which presumably adds two integers.

The two equations together define the valuation function $\mathcal{E}$ for the expression language. This function determines the meaning of a sentence in the language by a straightforward traversal of its abstract syntax tree. For example, deriving the meaning of '4 + 1 + 2' is accomplished by a top-down recursive traversal as follows. First, the $\mathcal{E}$ function is applied to the entire tree:

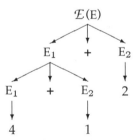

Drawing abstract syntax trees like this is not very compact,[3] so the syntax brackets are used instead to refer to abstract syntax tree representations of pieces of source text. Thus, the above is written as follows:

$$\mathcal{E}⟦4 + 1 + 2⟧$$

This expression is evaluated by repeated expansion according to the semantic equations, as follows:

---

[3] Not to mention the typesetting difficulties involved!

$$\mathcal{E}[\![4 + 1]\!] \oplus \mathcal{E}[\![2]\!]$$
$$\Rightarrow \quad \mathcal{E}[\![4]\!] \oplus \mathcal{E}[\![1]\!] \oplus \mathcal{B}[\![2]\!]$$
$$\Rightarrow \quad \mathcal{B}[\![4]\!] \oplus \mathcal{B}[\![1]\!] \oplus 2$$
$$\Rightarrow \quad 4 \oplus 1 \oplus 2$$

The resulting λ-expression is then simplified to obtain the program's "answer":

$$4 \oplus 1 \oplus 2 \Rightarrow 7$$

In the above, the semantic values (integers) are written in italics in order to distinguish them from the corresponding syntactic numerals. The valuation results in an integer (from domain **B**) denoting the meaning of the addition expression. Of course, $\mathcal{E}$ is so simple that it always results in an integer. For more realistic languages, the valuation function generally produces a higher-order function (*i.e.*, a λ-abstraction) that models the input/output behavior of a program.

This example is also unusual in that only one semantic valuation function, $\mathcal{E}$, is defined. Usually several are defined, one for each category of constructs in a language such as commands, expressions, declarations, and so on. This helps to organize a semantic specification and improve its readability.

The semantic metalanguage

The notation, or *semantic metalanguage*, of denotational semantics is traditionally based on λ-notation with Greek letters for variable names. This is a trademark of the so-called "Oxford-school" notation of Milne [Milne & Strachey 76]. For example, the semantics of statement sequencing in a subset of Pascal might be specified by the following equation:

$$C[\![\Gamma_1 \; ; \; \Gamma_2]\!]\rho\theta = C[\![\Gamma_1]\!]\rho \; \{ \; C[\![\Gamma_2]\!]\rho\theta \; \}.$$

Here, Γ_1 and Γ_2 are metavariables ranging over the syntactic domain of commands, or statements. In this case they represent the two constituents of the construct, '$\Gamma_1 \; ; \; \Gamma_2$.' The two semantic metavariables, ρ and θ, together represent the current semantic context. The environment, ρ, is the static portion of this context which provides denotations for program variables and other identifiers. The dynamic portion, θ, is a *continuation* function providing the computational future, or "the remainder of the program execution." The appearance of these variables on the left-hand side of the semantic equation is a shorthand for their appearance as λ-variables on the right-hand side:

$$C[\![\Gamma_1 \; ; \; \Gamma_2]\!] = \lambda\rho. \; \lambda\theta. \; C[\![\Gamma_1]\!]\rho \; \{ \; C[\![\Gamma_2]\!]\rho\theta \; \}.$$

As usual, parentheses are used to override the normally left-associative application of functions. The curly braces, { }, are like parentheses but are customarily used to enclose expressions that result in continuations. Right-associative function application is also expressed via the semicolon operator. This is used mainly for expressions involving continuations, which are often applied in a right-to-left order. For example, the two expressions, '$C[\![\Gamma_2]\!]\rho\theta$' and '$\theta$', both result in continuations. Hence the equation can be written as

$$C[\![\Gamma_1 \; ; \; \Gamma_2]\!]\rho\theta = C[\![\Gamma_1]\!]\rho \; ; \; C[\![\Gamma_2]\!]\rho \; ; \; \theta.$$

which lends itself to the following intuitive reading:

> The meaning of '$\Gamma_1 \; ; \; \Gamma_2$', given the environment, ρ, and current continuation, θ, is Γ_1, followed by Γ_2, and finally followed by the remainder of the program execution, θ.

Continuations model the flow of control in a program. The use of semicolons to express their right-associative nature thus corresponds with the programmer's conventional understanding of semicolon as a sequencing operator.

Readers unfamiliar with denotational semantics may find this notation rather cryptic. This is, in fact, a frequently heard criticism of the method.[4] However, practitioners of the denotational approach use these symbols in a consistent manner. For example, Γ is nearly always used to represent statements, ρ to represent environments, θ to represent continuations, and so forth. This traditional writing style also covers the specific techniques used for modeling common and fundamental language concepts. The use of environments and continuations is not mandated by the denotational method, but appears in most descriptions. As one becomes accustomed to these conventions, denotational descriptions become much less mysterious.

Still, denotational specifications are difficult to read and write, even for experienced semanticists, primarily because the standard λ-notation is not very expressive. In particular, manipulating elements of semantic domains typically involves many projection and injection operations which, in large specifications, are invariably misused or forgotten.

Much of this difficulty can be alleviated by choosing a more expressive notation. For this, I choose a notation based on the Standard ML programming

---

[4]The expression, "It's all Greek to me," seems appropriate here.

language [Harper 86]. The equation for statement sequencing is thus written as follows:

```
C [[ stmt1 ";" stmt2 ]] = fn env. fn cont.
    C [[stmt1]] env {C [[stmt2]] env cont}.
```

Like ML, this notation allows higher-order functions and polymorphic types. Standard alphanumeric identifiers are used instead of Greek or script letters. The syntax brackets, ⟦ ⟧, are written as `[[ ]]`, and noise strings in the abstract syntax are delimited by double-quotes ("). Functional abstraction is expressed by `fn` instead of λ.

As before, semicolons may be used to express right-associative function application, and λ-variables may be moved to the left-hand side of the equation:

```
C [[ stmt1 ";" stmt2 ]] env cont -
    C [[stmt1]] env ; C [[stmt2]] env ; cont.
```

The differences between this notation and Standard ML are described in Appendix H. I am essentially using Standard ML as a syntactically-sugared version of LAMBDA.

3.4 An Example of Denotational Semantics

As a complete example, let us consider a denotational description for a "toy" programming language called ToyPL (pronounced *toy*-pee-ell). Although ToyPL is unrealistically simple, it suits the present illustrative purposes. The main purpose of this example is to show the structure and notation of denotational descriptions and the manner in which the meanings of programs are derived from them. The specific techniques used for modeling various language concepts are not explained here. For these technical details the reader is referred to [Gordon 79, Ch. 6]. The following ToyPL semantics is based on Gordon's denotational description of the language SMALL.

A complete denotational specification consists of five parts.

1. The *abstract syntax* section. This defines the structure of the syntactic domains.

2. The *semantic domains* section. This defines the structure of the semantic domains.

3. The *auxiliary functions* section. This defines utility functions that may be invoked by the semantic equations.

4. The *semantic functions* section. This defines the functionalities of the semantic valuation functions.

5. The *semantic equations* section. This gives the equations that define the semantic valuation functions.

Abstract syntax

The *abstract syntax* section for the ToyPL semantics is as follows:

```
abstract syntax

    prog -> decl "begin" stmt "end"

    decl -> "var" id |
            "const" id "=" int |
            decl1 ";" decl2.

    stmt -> id ":=" expr |
            stmt1 ";" stmt2.

    expr -> int |
            id |
            expr1 "+" expr2.
```

This section serves two purposes. First, it defines the syntactic domains of the language. These are named by the nonterminals of the abstract syntax, in this case, prog, decl, stmt, and expr. Multiple distinct occurrences of the same domain name in the right-hand side of a rule are distinguished by numeric suffixes, for example stmt1 and stmt2 in the second rule for stmt. Some syntactic domains are predefined, for example IDENT and INTEGER, the syntactic domains of identifiers and integer numerals, respectively. The (nonterminal) names id and int are predefined to be syntactic metavariables ranging over these domains.

The second purpose of this section is to define the "shape" of the abstract syntax trees. The source program fragment,

```
a := a + 2
```

is represented, according to the abstract syntax specification, by the tree shown in Figure 3.3. Instead of this graphical form, I will write these trees in a Lisp-like s-expression format, as follows:

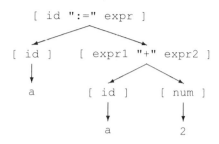

The abstract syntax tree for 'a := a + 2'.

Figure 3.3
An Abstract Syntax Tree

```
([id ":=" expr]
   ([id] a)
   ([expr1 "+" expr2]
      ([id] a) ([num] 2)))
```

Semantic domains

The *semantic domains* section for ToyPL is given after the abstract syntax. It gives equations for defining the various kinds of semantic domains in the language. Usually, the equations define the structure of the values, environments, stores, and continuations that are used to model the meanings of programs.

Let us start by presenting the *value domains* for ToyPL:

```
semantic domains

   DV = union unbound |            (* Denotable values *)
               variable of LOC |
               constant of RV.
   LOC = INT.
   RV = SV.

   SV = union uninit |             (* Storable values *)
               integer of INT.

   EV = DV.                        (* Expressible values *)
```

Note that `INT` is the predefined semantic domain of integers, which is quite distinct from `INTEGER`, the predefined syntactic domain of integer numerals.

The domain equations are very much like a collection of mutually recursive type definitions in the language Standard ML, where equations with right-hand sides prefixed by `union` correspond to ML `datatype` declarations, and the other equations to ML `type` abbreviations. (ML, however, does not allow type abbreviations to participate in a system of mutually recursive definitions.) More information about how domain equations are expressed in this notation may be found in Appendix H.

In a denotational semantics, the values operated on by language constructs are traditionally grouped into three categories. The first is the category of *denotable* values. These are the values that may be named by identifiers in the language. The definition of `DV` specifies that a ToyPL identifier may either denote a variable (*i.e.*, a location) or a constant, or be unbound.

Storable values are those that may be assigned to variables. In ToyPL these include the integers, plus an additional "unitialized" value. The *expressible* values are those that may result from the evaluation of expressions. The domain equations for ToyPL specify that these are exactly the denotable values, although in most common languages there are more denotable values than expressible values. (Pascal procedures, for instance, are denotable but not expressible.)

Next, the domains of environments and stores:

```
ENV = ID -> DV.                          (* Environments *)

STORE   = MEMORY * INPUTFILE * FREELOC. (* Stores *)
MEMORY  = LOC -> SV.
FREELOC = LOC.
```

The denotations of the identifiers in a program are traditionally maintained in a structure called the *environment*. The equation above shows that an environment is a function that maps identifiers to their denotations. Note the use of the predefined domain, `ID`. This domain of *semantic* identifiers is carefully distinguished from `IDENT`, the domain of *syntactic* identifiers (used in the abstract syntax). This distinction is relatively unimportant in theoretical applications and thus frequently ignored. This is also true of the similar distinction between `INT` and `INTEGER`. In a compiler generator, however, this distinction, which effectively separates the *abstract syntax tree* of an identifier from its actual *semantic value*, can be exploited by a compiler generator. This point is discussed further in Chapter 5.

The *store* (also called the program *state*) is primarily a mapping from locations to storable values. It also contains the input file and a counter for keeping track of the next unallocated location in the store.

Finally, the continuation domains:

```
CONT  = STORE -> ANSWER.   (* Command continuations *)
ECONT = EV -> CONT.        (* Expression continuations *)
DCONT = ENV -> CONT.       (* Declaration continuations *)

ANSWER = union halt |      (* Final program answers *)
                error |
         output of RV * ANSWER.
```

Continuations are used for modeling the flow of control in a program. They can be used to model even the most general control-flow constructs, such as **goto** and first-class continuations. Continuations can at first seem quite mind boggling. Complete explanations of this device may be found in any of the previously cited introductory texts on denotational semantics.

ToyPL has only one control-flow construct: the sequencing of statements. Hence, its semantics could be described in the so-called *direct* style which does not involve the use of continuations. The *continuation* style is used in this example because it is more relevant to practical languages. Also, since there is no possibility of aliasing of variables in ToyPL, the indirect access of values in the store through locations is not really necessary. In other words, a store model in which identifiers were bound directly to storable values instead of locations would work just as well. Again, locations are incorporated into the semantics in order to illustrate the traditional style for more realistic programming languages.

The semantic domains provide a great deal of information about the language being described. For instance, it is clear that ToyPL does not support procedures, since procedure values are neither expressible nor denotable. Also, one might surmise from the use of continuations that escapes from loops and **goto**'s might be possible (even though in this case they are not). This informative aspect of the semantic domains section is important and useful.

Auxiliary functions

Utility functions are specified in the *auxiliary functions* section. These functions are used in the semantic equations as "subroutines" for performing common operations. The auxiliary functions for the ToyPL semantics follow. Note that the notation, `[a => b] f`, denotes the function `f` perturbed to map `a` to `b`.

```
auxiliary functions

   (* err : CONT - The error continuation. *)
   err = { fn store. error }.

   (* quit : CONT - The final continuation. *)
   quit = { fn store. halt }.        .

   (* initStore : INPUTFILE -> STORE
    * Given an input file, create an initial store. *)
   initStore input = ( (fn loc. uninit), input, 0 ).

   (* initEnv : ENV
    * Create an empty environment. *)
   initEnv = fn id. unbound.

   (* bind : ID -> DV -> ENV
    * Create an environment with the given id bound to the
    * given value. *)
   bind id value = fn i. if i = id then value else unbound.

   (* combine : ENV -> ENV -> ENV
    * Update the first environment with the bindings of the
    * second environment. *)
   combine env1 env2 = fn id.
      let dv1 = env2 id in
         if dv1 = unbound then env1 id else dv1
      end.

   (* isLoc : ECONT -> ECONT (= ECONT -> EV -> CONT)
    * Check that the value is a variable and if so, pass it
    * on to the continuation. *)
   isLoc econt =
      { fn var. case var of
         variable (_) => econt var |
          _              => err }.

   (* isRvalue : ECONT -> ECONT (= ECONT -> EV -> CONT)
    * Check that the value is a constant, and if so, pass it
    * on to the continuation. *)
   isRvalue econt =
      { fn val. case val of
         constant (_) => econt val |
          _              => err }.
```

```
(* contents : ECONT -> ECONT (= ECONT -> EV -> ECONT)
 * Check that the value is a variable, and if so, retrieve
 * its contents from the store and pass it on
 * to the continuation. *)
contents econt =
    { fn ev. { fn store.
        case ev of
            variable (loc) =>
                let (mem, _, _) = store in
                    ( case mem loc of
                        uninit => error |
                        value  => econt value store )
                end |
            _ => error } }.

(* update : LOC -> CONT -> ECONT
         (= LOC -> CONT -> EV -> CONT)
 * Store the value in the given location, and pass the
 * resulting store on to the continuation. *)
update loc cont =
    { fn ev. { fn store.
        let (mem, input, freeLoc) = store in
            case ev of
                constant (val) =>
                    cont (([loc => val] mem), input, freeLoc) |
                _ => error
        end } }.

(* ref : ECONT -> ECONT (= ECONT -> EV -> CONT)
 * Allocate the next free location in the store,
 * initialize it with the given value and pass it
 * and the new store on to the continuation. *)
ref econt =
    { fn ev. { fn store.
        let (mem, input, freeLoc) = store.
            newVar = variable (freeLoc).
            newStore = (mem, input, freeLoc + 1)
        in
            update freeLoc (econt newVar) ev newStore
        end } }.
```

```
(* deref : ECONT -> ECONT (= ECONT -> EV -> CONT)
 * Dereference the value by first checking to see if it
 * is a variable.  If so, then pass its value on to the
 * continuation.  Otherwise, pass on the value itself. *)
deref econt =
    { fn ev. { fn store.
        case ev of
            variable (_) => contents econt ev store |
            _            => econt ev store } }.
```

Auxiliary functions are often written as *continuation transformers*. The function deref, for instance, takes a continuation as an argument and produces a new one. This turns out to be convenient in traditional denotational specifications.

Semantic functions

Following the auxiliary functions, the functionalities of the valuation functions are defined:

```
semantic functions

    P : prog -> INPUTFILE -> ANSWER.    (* Programs *)
    D : decl -> ENV -> DCONT -> CONT.   (* Declarations *)
    C : stmt -> ENV -> CONT -> CONT.    (* Commands *)
    R : expr -> ENV -> ECONT -> CONT.   (* R-values *)
    E : expr -> ENV -> ECONT -> CONT.   (* Expressions *)
```

The valuation functions map elements of the syntactic domains to their meanings. For instance, P maps programs (from the syntactic domain prog) to their meanings (in the semantic domain INPUTFILE -> ANSWER).

Semantic equations

Finally, the semantic equations:

```
semantic equations

    P [[ decl "begin" stmt "end" ]] input =
        D [[decl]] initEnv { fn env. C [[stmt]] env quit }
            (initStore input).

    D [[ "var" id ]] env dcont =
        { ref { fn newVar.
            dcont (bind id newVar) } (constant uninit) }.
```

```
D [[ "const" id "=" int ]] env dcont =
   R [[int]] env { fn ev. dcont (bind id ev) }.

D [[ decl1 ";" decl2 ]] env dcont =
   D [[decl1]] env { fn env1.
      D [[decl2]] (combine env env1) { fn env2.
         dcont (combine env (combine env1 env2)) } }.

C [[ id ":=" expr ]] env cont =
   E [[id]] env { isLoc { fn (variable loc).
      R [[expr]] env ; update loc ; cont } }.

C [[ stmt1 ";" stmt2 ]] env cont =
   C [[stmt1]] env ; C [[stmt2]] env ; cont.

R [[ expr ]] env econt =
   E [[expr]] env ; deref ; isRvalue ; econt.

E [[ int ]] env econt = econt (constant (integer int)).

E [[ id ]] env econt =
   if (env id) = unbound then err
   else econt (env id).

E [[ expr1 "+" expr2 ]] env econt =
   R [[expr1]] env { fn (constant (integer v1)).
      R [[expr2]] env { fn (constant (integer v2)).
         econt (constant (integer (v1 + v2))) } }.
```

In this ML-like notation, the $\mathcal{B}$ function is not used to convert the syntactic representation of a basic-value construct to its corresponding semantic value. Instead, this conversion is expressed simply by writing the construct name without the syntax brackets ([[ ]]). For example, in the equation for constant integer expressions above (*i.e.*, the equation for E [[int]]), the integer value of the syntactic construct, int, is referred to on the right-hand side by writing it without the brackets. The construct, id, is treated similarly in the equation for references to variables (E [[id]]). A construct name enclosed within the brackets refers to the syntactic construct rather than the semantic value. So, E [[int]] is an element of the syntactic domain, INTEGER, and int (not within brackets) is an element of INT. Chapter 5 explains how this allows a compiler generator to retrieval lexical information, or whatever other information is included in abstract syntax tree structures, perhaps to mark the textual position of a static semantic error. This capability is, in fact, exploited by the MESS described in Chapter 6.

It is customary in denotational semantics to focus attention almost exclusively on the *dynamic semantics*. The dynamic semantics involves the actions and runtime effects of the language constructs, which is dependent on runtime entities such as input files. The *static semantics*, on the other hand, does not depend on runtime values. It deals with the static aspects of a language, most of which are normally processed at compile time.

Typically, little attention is paid to static semantics since the main interest of semanticists has historically been with the dynamic aspects of languages. For example, in the equation for variable declarations (D [["var" id]]) no check is made to ensure that the variable has not already been declared. Specification of static semantics is not precluded by the denotational method—it is simply ignored in order to avoid clutter. When it is necessary (or not too inconvenient), static semantics *is* specified in traditional denotational descriptions. In the equation for references to variables, for instance, a simple check is made to ensure that the identifier does indeed denote a memory location—in other words, that the identifier has been properly declared. The handling of environments throughout the semantics may also be considered a part of the static semantics, since in ToyPL environments can be statically determined.

Obviously, a semantic description must completely specify the static semantics if practical compilers are to be derived. Unfortunately, the "incidental" inclusion of static semantics in denotational descriptions has the effect of blurring the distinctions between the static and dynamic components of a language. This severely complicates the task of generating a realistic compiler.

3.5   Implementing Denotational Semantics

Let us now consider how the ToyPL semantics might be implemented. In general, the denotational description of a language *PL*, written in some formalized notation $\hat{\lambda}$ (such as the ML-like metalanguage), defines a valuation function:

$$\mathcal{D}^{\hat{\lambda}}_{PL} : \text{AST}_{PL} \rightarrow rep^{\hat{\lambda}}(\text{I} \rightarrow \text{O})$$

The valuation function $\mathcal{D}^{\hat{\lambda}}_{PL}$ maps abstract syntax trees of *PL* programs to representations of functions from inputs to outputs, also written in $\hat{\lambda}$ notation. Extracting $\mathcal{D}^{\hat{\lambda}}_{PL}$ from the denotational description is accomplished simply by viewing the semantic equations as the specification of a syntax-directed translator from abstract syntax trees to $\hat{\lambda}$ terms.

Since both the valuation function, $\mathcal{D}^{\hat{\lambda}}_{PL}$, and the meanings it derives for programs, $rep^{\hat{\lambda}}(I \rightarrow O)$, are expressed in $\hat{\lambda}$, the denotational semantics can be *directly implemented* by implementing the $\hat{\lambda}$ language. This is the basic principle of classical compiler generation.

As an example, consider the following ToyPL program:

```
var a;
begin
    a := a + 2
end
```

Syntax analysis results in the following abstract syntax tree:

```
([decl "begin" stmt "end"]
    (["var" id] a) ([id ":=" expr]
                        ([id] a) ([expr1 "+" expr2]
                                    ([id] a) ([num] 2))))
```

Now, a syntax-directed translation of this tree proceeds as follows. First, the main valuation function, P, is applied to the entire program tree:

```
P [[ "var" a ";" "begin" a ":=" a "+" 2 "end" ]]
```

Expansion of this application of P according to the appropriate semantic equation results in the following expression:

```
fn input0. D [["var" a]] initEnv
                    { fn env0. C [[a ":=" a "+" 2]] env0 quit }
                    (initStore input0)
```

Through α-conversion (discussed below), a 0 suffix has been added to the λ-variables, input and env, in order to avoid the possibility of name clashes. This systematic renaming of variables is easily performed automatically.

Expansion of the application of the valuation function D results in:

```
fn input0.
    { fn env1. fn dcont1.
        { ref { fn newVar1.
            dcont1 (bind *a* newVar1) } (constant uninit) } }
    initEnv
    { fn env0. C [[a ":=" a "+" 2]] env0 quit }
    (initStore input0)
```

Note that the semantic value of [[a]] is written as *a*.

Eight more expansions according to the semantic equations result in the following expression:

```
fn input0.
    { fn env1. fn dcont1.
        { ref { fn newVar1.
            dcont1 (bind *a* newVar1) } } (constant uninit) } }
    initEnv
    { fn env0.
        { fn env2. { fn cont2.
            { fn env3. { fn econt3.
                if (env3 *a*) = unbound then err
                else econt3 (env3 *a*) } }
            env2
            { isLoc
                { fn (variable loc2).
                    { fn env4. { fn econt4.
                        { fn env5. { fn econt5.
                            { fn env6. { fn econt6.
                                { fn env7, { fn econt7.
                                    if (env7 *a*) = unbound then err
                                    else econt7 (env7 *a*) } }
                                env6
                                { deref { isRvalue econt6 } } } } }
                            env5
                            { fn (constant (integer v15)).
                                { fn env8. { fn econt8.
                                    { fn env9. { fn econt9.
                                        econt9 (constant (integer 2)) }
                                    }
                                    env8
                                    { deref { isRvalue econt8 } } } } }
                                env5
                                { fn (constant (integer v25)).
                                    econt5
                                    (constant (integer
                                            (v15 + v25))) } } } }
                        env4
                        { deref { isRvalue econt4 } } } } }
                    env2
                    { update loc2 cont2 } } } } }
            env0
            quit }
        (initStore input0)
```

This expression represents the meaning of the program.[5] In the context of compiler generation, this top-down expansion of valuation-function applications is a syntax-directed translation of the abstract syntax tree into ML. The expansions correspond to the process of compilation, and the resultant expression is the "target" code for the program, assuming that the target machine is an evaluator for the ML-like semantic metalanguage. A standard implementation of ML could, in fact, be used as the target machine.[6] This direct implementation strategy requires only textual substitution (with α-renaming) and is thus an easy way to derive compilers from denotational descriptions.

There is a serious problem with this simple approach, however: computations normally performed at compile time are "frozen" in the program meanings. For example, the allocation of memory for the variable a is expressed (somewhere) in the ML target code expression above. Also, environment "lookups" (*i.e.*, expressions of the form $\text{env}_i*\text{a}*$) appear in the target code even though a compiler would normally be expected to perform these lookups at compile time. In fact, *all* of the static semantics processing for the program is expressed in the target code, and therefore must be recomputed every time the program is executed.

Classical compilers solve this problem by using *partial evaluation*.

Partial evaluation

The syntax of the pure λ-calculus is as follows:

$$
\begin{aligned}
E ::= \;&v &&\text{variables} \\
| \;&\text{fn } v.\; F &&\lambda\text{-abstractions} \\
| \;&E\; E' &&\text{applications} \\
| \;&(\,E\,) &&\text{parenthesized } \lambda\text{-expressions}
\end{aligned}
$$

In the λ-calculus, partial evaluation, or reduction, is based on a set of *rewrite rules*. The α-rule has already been encountered. It is specified as follows:

$$(\text{fn } \text{x}.\; E_{\bar{y}}) \;\Rightarrow\; (\text{fn } \text{y}.\; [\text{y}/\text{x}]\, E_{\bar{y}})$$

$E_{\bar{y}}$ represents an arbitrary λ-expression containing no free occurrences of the variable y. The term *free occurrences* refers to those variables not bound by λ-

---

[5] Applications of auxiliary functions, for example ref and isLoc, have not been expanded, although in principle they ought to be. I have elected not to do so for the sake of brevity.

[6] Actually, using a Standard ML implementation is not strictly correct since ML is evaluated in applicative order rather than normal order. In practice, however, applicative order seems to work, especially when the semantics is written with continuations [Paulson 81].

abstraction. For example, in (fn x. E), occurrences of x are not free. The
notation,

$$[\text{y}/\text{x}]\ E$$

denotes the substitution of all free occurrences of the identifier x in E by y.

Rewrite rules are applied by finding a subexpression matching the left-hand
side of a rule and then rewriting it according to the right-hand side. The matched
subexpression is called a *redex*.

In addition to the α-rule, there are two other fundamental rewrite rules that
specify *reductions*, or *simplifications*, of λ-expressions. One is the β-rule:

$$(\text{fn x. } E')\ E'' \Rightarrow ([E''/\text{x}]\ E')$$

The expression E'' is textually substituted for all free occurrences of x in E', with
the final result being the new E'. Reduction by the β-rule is analogous to function
application in a functional programming language.

Finally, there is the η-rule:

$$(\text{fn x. } M_{\bar{x}}\ \text{x}) \Rightarrow M_{\bar{x}}$$

In the pure λ-calculus, the α-, β- and η-rules are all that are needed to reduce
any λ-expression. The ML-like notation is considerably more expressive than
the λ-calculus, however. Hence, many other rewrite rules must be specified.
Typically these are given informally, for example:

$$E' + E'' \Rightarrow \quad \textit{the sum of } E' \textit{ and } E''$$
$$\textit{when } E' \textit{ and } E'' \textit{ are numbers}$$

A partial evaluator simplifies an expression by scanning it for a redex, and
then reducing by the appropriate rewrite rule. This process is repeated until
no further redexes can be found, at which point the expression is said to be in
normal form. For some expressions the normal form can never be reached. The
confluence property (see [Barendregt 81]) ensures that the normal form, if it exists,
is unique regardless of the order in which the rewrite rules are applied.

It can happen that a particular reduction order will fail to arrive at the normal
form for an expression that has one. A reduction strategy that is guaranteed
to attain the normal form if it exists is the *normal order*, or *call-by-name*, reduction strategy: consistently reduce only the "leftmost, outermost" redex in an
expression. In functional programming languages this amounts to delaying the

evaluation of arguments to functions until their values are actually needed. The application of a nonstrict function to an argument involving a nonterminating computation can then be successfully evaluated in the case that the argument's value is never needed.

In practice, normal-order reduction is often implemented by using a *call-by-need* reduction strategy [Vuilleman 73]. This strategy simulates normal-order reduction by maintaining an environment of variable bindings. When the β-rule is applied, no explicit textual substitution of x by E'' is performed. (Note that x and E'' refer to the metavariables in the β-rule definition given above.) Instead, an entry binding x to E'' is added to the environment. The result of β-reduction is then a *closure* consisting of the original expression, E', paired with a *closing environment* containing bindings for the free variables in E'.

The call-by-need strategy tends to be more efficient than simple normal-order reduction because multiple occurrences of the variable x in E' will all refer to the same single copy of E'' in the environment. Thus, E'' will be reduced at most one time, rather than once for every occurrence of x in E'. Also, explicit construction of closures as code-environment pairs can sometimes be avoided by allocating environments on a stack, with each pending reduction simply referring to the stack frame where its part of the environment begins.

The allocation of environments on a stack is not possible when a β-reduction results in a λ-abstraction containing references to free variables. This is analogous to an expression producing an anonymous, or higher-order, function in a functional language, and also closely related to the so-called "funarg" problem in Lisp [Moses 70]. When this happens, closures must be constructed explicitly, thus incurring a significant performance penalty.

Digression: Evaluation strategies for programming languages

Most programming language implementations do not support partial evaluation. Hence, they normally use other evaluation strategies.

Lazy evaluation [Friedman & Wise 76, Henderson & Morris 76] is similar to the call-by-need strategy in that the evaluation of an argument is delayed until its value is needed. It differs, though, in the case that only a component of an argument's value is required. Then, the argument is evaluated only as much as is necessary to obtain the value of the component; a call-by-need reducer, on the other hand, evaluates the argument completely. For data constructors such as the CONS function of Lisp, lazy evaluation allows one to express computations involving data structures with potentially infinite numbers of elements.

Although the call-by-need strategy is a considerable improvement in efficiency over simple normal-order reduction, it is still unacceptably inefficient for practical languages. Thus, *applicative-order*, or *call-by-value*, reduction, in which the "leftmost, innermost" redex is chosen, is often used instead. This corresponds to the immediate evaluation of function arguments, also called *eager evaluation*. Because call-by-value evaluation may fail, unnecessarily, to reach a normal form, it is theoretically "unsafe." However, it is typically an order of magnitude faster than the other reduction strategies [Hughes 82].

Static semantics processing via partial evaluation

After several reductions of the target code expression on page 38, the following expression is obtained:

```
fn input0.
   ( { deref { isRvalue
         { fn (constant (integer v15)).
            { deref { isRvalue
               { fn (constant (integer v25)).
                  { deref { isRvalue
                     { update 0 quit } } }
                  (constant (integer (v15 + v25))) } } }
            (constant (integer 2)) } } }
      (variable 0)
   )
   ( ([0 => uninit] (fn loc. uninit)), input0, 1 )
```

Notice that all references to environments have disappeared and that the memory location allocated for the variable a has been completely computed as 0. Thus, this expression no longer contains any direct references to *a*. Also, all of the context-sensitive constraints have been enforced. For example, the static semantic checks for the declaration of the variable a,

```
   if (env3 *a*) = unbound then err
   ...
```

have been reduced away.

At this point all of the usual compile-time computations have been performed, and so this expression now represents the computations which would normally be present in an object program produced by a handwritten compiler. But it is still not in normal form! Simplification can continue by expanding the applications of deref and isRvalue:

```
fn input0.
   case ((([0 => uninit] (fn loc. uninit)) 0) of
       uninit =>
          error |
       value  =>
         ( { isRvalue
              { fn (constant (integer v15)).
                 { deref { isRvalue
                    { fn (constant (integer v25)).
                       { deref { isRvalue
                          { update 0 quit } } ;
                          (constant (integer(v15 + v25))) } } }
                    (constant (integer 2)) } }
           value
           ( (([0 => uninit] (fn loc. uninit)), input0, 1 )
         )
```

Then, in the next reduction step, the case test expression,

```
   case ((([0 => uninit] (fn loc. uninit)) 0) of ...
```

reduces to the value uninit from the domain SV of storable values. The case expression then signals the occurrence of a program error. The partial evaluator has essentially *predicted*, at compile time, the occurrence of the runtime error caused by the reference to an uninitialized variable.

Of course, the output of a program in general is not predictable since it may depend on runtime values (such as input files). Operations on runtime values, for instance a "read input file" operation, in fact should not be reduced at compile time. Classical semantics systems provide mechanisms for declaring which auxiliary functions represent runtime operations. The contents and update auxiliary functions in the ToyPL semantics, for example, might be declared as runtime operations. The partial evaluator would then avoid reducing these operations, thereby deferring their reduction to runtime. (Interestingly, all ToyPL programs can be completely evaluated at compile time since ToyPL programs can never depend on runtime values.)

A compiler that reduces static computations during compilation is said to have the *partial evaluability property*. The name derives from the fact that a partial evaluation mechanism is required in order perform the compile time reductions. An ML evaluator does not support partial evaluation and hence would not provide the desired result—it would simply treat a target code expression as a higher-order function, holding off reduction until provided with an input file. In hand-written compilers, a language-specific partial evaluation mechanism is in a sense

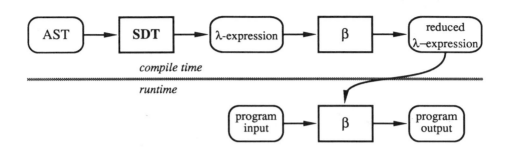

This figure shows the typical process of compilation by a classically generated compiler. A denotational description specifies a syntax-directed translator (SDT) which is used to translate abstract syntax trees to their meanings. These are then reduced at compile time via partial evaluation (β) as far as possible. The reduced meaning is taken as the target code for the program, which is executed by performing further reductions in the presence of the input file.

Figure 3.4
Classical Semantics-Directed Compilation

"built in" by the compiler writer, in the form of *ad hoc* code for processing the static semantics.

3.6   Existing Classical Compiler Generators

Several classical compiler generators have been implemented. Three systems of particular interest are Mosses' Semantics Implementation System (SIS) [Mosses 75, Mosses 79], Paulson's Semantics Processor (PSP) [Paulson 81, Paulson 82], and Wand's Semantic Prototyping System (SPS) [Wand 84]. All three generate compilers based on the direct implementation of denotational semantics as described in the previous section. This principle of operation is summarized in Figure 3.4.

Mosses' Semantics Implementation System

In SIS, a front end and an "encoder" are specified in order to generate a compiler. The front end is specified in an extension of Backus-Naur Form called GRAM. SIS converts GRAM specifications into two-pass SLR(1) parsers with routines for building abstract syntax trees. The rest of the compiler, or encoder, is specified by semantic equations written in a language called DSL. DSL specifications are translated by SIS into LAMB, which is a version of Scott's language LAMBDA. Interpretation of LAMB expressions is provided by a reducer employing the call-by-need reduction strategy. SIS is implemented in the language BCPL [Richards & Whitby-Stevens 79].

In terms of Figure 3.4, the boxes marked "β" correspond to SIS's LAMB reducer. SIS is absolutely faithful to the classical compilation strategy—hence the translator (*i.e.*, the box marked "SDT") is itself a LAMB expression which is reduced when applied to an abstract syntax tree.

SIS has been used for both teaching and research purposes. However, several shortcomings of the system are reported in [Bodwin *et al.* 82]. The most serious is SIS's inefficiency—the compilers generated even from very small specifications require vast amounts of CPU time. Also, SIS lacks a type checker for the DSL language. This makes it extremely difficult to debug the semantic specifications.

Paulson's Semantics Processor

PSP processes *semantic grammars* which combine extended attribute grammars with the semantic domains of denotational semantics and a typed λ-calculus metalanguage. The system consists of three components. The first of these is the grammar analyzer, GA. It reads a semantic grammar and produces a language description file (LDF) containing LALR(1) parse tables and attribute-dependency information. The second component is the univeral translator, UT. After reading an LDF, the UT becomes a compiler. The compiler first parses a source program and constructs a directed acyclic graph (DAG) of its attribute dependencies. The DAG is then simplified, mainly by β-reduction, and compiled into stack code for an SECD machine [Landin 64].[7] The third component of PSP is an SECD machine simulator which applies the stack code to an input file, thereby executing the program. All three components of PSP are written in standard Pascal.

The box marked "SDT" in Figure 3.4 corresponds to PSP's attribute evaluator. The compile time "β" box is the DAG simplifier, whereas the runtime box is the SECD machine. Use of the SECD machine improves efficiency in two ways. First, it uses applicative-order evaluation. Although theoretically unsafe, experience has shown that applicative-order reduction works well in classical compilers, particularly when the semantic specifications are written in the continuation style.

---

[7]SECD stands for Stack, Environment, Control, and Dump. It is essentially a stack machine capable of manipulating closures.

Second, the SECD machine, since it is used only for runtime reduction, doesn't need to worry about partial evaluation. Thus, evaluation occurs in "one fell swoop" rather than through a series of symbolic reductions on a program graph.

PSP is efficient and provides a type checker for the semantic grammars. It has been used to generate compilers for large subsets of Pascal and FORTRAN.

Wand's Semantic Prototyping System

In SPS, the semantic equations in a denotational description are viewed as the specification of a "transducer" that maps abstract syntax trees to lambda expressions in Scheme. An implementation of the transducer is generated by extracting a YACC specification from the semantic equations. The result is a compiler that translates abstract syntax trees to Scheme code.

A partial evaluator for Scheme is not provided by SPS. Hence, the generated compilers lack the partial evaluability property. In terms of Figure 3.4, this means that there is no "β" process at compile time. The runtime "β" box corresponds to a Scheme evaluator.

SPS is written in a variety of languages taken from the UNIX toolbox [Ritchie & Thompson 74]. It is efficient and provides strong polymorphic type checking of the semantic specifications.

Performance of the classical systems

The compilers generated by PSP and SPS are considerably more efficient than those generated by SIS. Both Paulson [Paulson 81] and Pleban [Pleban 84] report that PSP-generated compilers run 25 to 50 times slower than handwritten compilers, and that the SECD target code runs 500 to 1,000 times slower than ordinary compiled code. In order to make a direct comparison of SIS and PSP, Pleban has used each system to generate a compiler for a small language. Wand has also generated a compiler for the same language using SPS[Wand 84]. The following table gives the execution times for the various systems and generated compilers.

Task	SIS	PSP	SPS
compiler generation	108	2.89	
program compilation	7.91	2.26	6
program execution	4.12	0.02	0.18

All timings are given in seconds. The timings for SIS were taken on an Amdahl 470/V6, which is a large mainframe computer. The PSP timings were taken on an Amdahl 580, which at the time was reportedly 25% faster than the 470 model. The SPS timings were recorded on a VAX-11/780, which is approximately ten times slower than the Amdahl 580. No compiler generation time was reported for SPS. The following table takes into account these differences in machine speed:

Task	SIS	PSP	SPS
compiler generation	29.9	1	
program compilation	2.80	1	0.27
program execution	165	1	0.90

The figures in this table have been normalized around the PSP timings. Discounting the performance of SIS (which seems to have been very poorly engineered), it can be seen that the PSP and SPS timings are quite similar. In Chapter 6, I report on my own experiments with PSP-generated compilers. In all cases, the object programs produced by these classically generated compilers run about three orders of magnitude slower than the corresponding object programs produced by handwritten compilers.

3.7 Nonclassical Compiler Generation

The classical approach to semantics-directed compiler generation is useful and appealing because of its generality—a classical system can implement *any* denotational description. Other approaches have also been developed, however. For the most part, these alternative strategies use algebraically oriented semantic specification techniques in order to improve the object code efficiency, possibly at the expense of generality.

Sethi, for example, has developed a compiler generator based on a notation called *Plumb* [Sethi 81]. In this notation, function composition is expressed by the pipe operator, written as "|", as in the UNIX operating system [Ritchie & Thompson 74]. Primitive operators are provided by his system for modeling common runtime actions, for example, `plus` and `fetch`. A Plumb semantics for control-flow constructs, when applied to a program, yields a graph structure. The graph is then reduced via β-reduction, with the predefined runtime operators treated as uninterpreted symbols. This results in a "closure-free" graph in which the nodes are runtime operations and the edges represent continuations, or flow of control through the program. A handwritten code generator can then be used to linearize the graph into target code which looks like ordinary, closure-free stack-machine code. Using this system, Sethi has generated a compiler for a subset of the C language containing all of its control structures.

Performance is improved by Sethi's system in two ways. First, since closure-free postfix code is produced, there is no need to simulate a machine that must handle closures, such as the SECD machine. The lack of closures comes largely from the fact that continuations are represented as edges in a program graph and can thus be compiled into jumps. Secondly, the runtime primitives supplied by the system make certain assumptions about the underlying semantic models. These assumptions limit the generality of the system, but allow a code generator to choose efficient implementation strategies. For example, the store operations supplied by Plumb are based on the assumption that the store is single-threaded. This allows an implementation of the store as a global array instead of as a partial function.

Unfortunately, the limits imposed by these assumptions are quite severe. The introduction of data structures or procedures into a language, for example, has the effect of introducing closures into the target code. When this happens, Sethi's system becomes essentially similar to the classical systems. Appel has extended Sethi's idea to handle some of these language constructs [Appel 85]. The extensions, however, tend to make the language definitions less formal, and more like *ad hoc* compiler specifications. Still, these approaches demonstrate that efficient target code can be produced by treating the fundamental runtime operators as uninterpreted symbols. The MESS system uses a similar technique in generating efficient implementations of high-level descriptions.

Wand has devised a technique for deriving stack machine code from standard denotational descriptions [Wand 82]. The basic idea of his approach is to eliminate λ-variables from the semantic equations via the introduction of special combinators. Once this is done, the denotation of a program can be represented as a graph with the combinators as internal nodes and expressions representing primitive operations at the leaves. A series of meaning-preserving transformations applied to the graph restructures it into a right-linear form which is then converted into closure-free stack-machine code.

This technique may be hard to automate; introduction of the combinators seems to require a considerable amount of expertise on the part of the semanticist. Also, the effectiveness of the method seems to depend in large measure on the way in which the original semantics is written. Still, the idea of eliminating λ-abstractions via application of combinators is important and, as we shall see, is incorporated into high-level semantics.

Two other systems of note that are based on algebraically oriented descriptive techniques are CERES [Jones & Christiansen 82] and Perluette [Gaudel 81]. Since both are similar in spirit to MESS, a discussion of these systems is deferred until after the description of MESS.

Finally, a novel approach has been taken by Jones *et al.* [Jones *et al.* 85]. They have implemented a partial evaluator called **mix** which, when given a program and one (of possibly several) input parameters, will produce a "residual" program. The residual program completes the evaluation of the original program when given the remaining input parameters. In the case that the two inputs to **mix** are an interpreter for a programming language and a program written in that language, the residual program corresponds to a target program. In other words, applying **mix** to an interpreter and a source program effects the compilation of the source program.

The **mix** program can itself be analyzed by **mix**. Thus, when **mix** is applied to **mix** and an interpreter, a residual program is obtained which partially evaluates source programs into residual programs. In other words, a compiler is automatically generated. This idea can be taken even one step further by applying **mix** to **mix** and **mix**. The result: the automatic generation of a compiler generator.

The elegance of this approach is striking. It remains to be seen, however, whether this use of partial evaluation will lead to the generation of practical compilers.

An important characteristic common to all of the nonclassical methods (except for the **mix** approach) is that they attempt to eliminate explicit references to continuations, stores, and other semantic modeling devices from the semantic descriptions. In the next chapter, I argue that this is essential for improving the runtime efficiency of the object programs.

3.8 Summary

Classical semantics-directed compiler generation is based on the direct implementation of denotational semantics. This principle of operation can be summarized as follows:

1. The semantic equations in a denotational description are viewed as the specification of a syntax-directed translator from abstract syntax trees to λ-expressions.

2. Compilation proceeds by translating a program to its λ-expression meaning, and then reducing the λ-expression as much as possible. Reduction is accomplished via partial evaluation.

3. The reduced λ-expressions are taken as final target programs, to be further reduced when applied to an input file.

The three classical semantics systems, SIS, PSP, and SIS, all generate compilers based on this principle. Although these systems have been successful in generating compilers for nontrivial programming languages, the object programs they produce run about three orders of magnitude slower than corresponding target programs produced by handwritten compilers.

The reasons for this inefficiency are explored in the next chapter.

4 Problems with Using Denotational Semantics

The performance characteristics[1] exhibited by classically generated compilers are much worse than those exhibited by handwritten compilers. In this chapter, I argue that this is a consequence of several fundamental problems with traditional denotational semantics as a language for specifying compilers. The nature of these problems implies that poor performance is an intrinsic feature of the classical compilation strategy, and not simply a shortcoming of the currently known methods for implementing β-reduction in the λ-calculus.

As explained earlier, the word *traditional* refers to a particular style of writing customarily used in denotational semantics. In addition to providing a standard notation, this traditional style embodies certain techniques, or "tricks of the trade," for modeling common semantic concepts. The problems described here have to do with this traditional writing style—they are not fundamental to the denotational method itself. In fact, the next chapter will show that high-level descriptions may be based on the same mathematical foundations as denotational descriptions.

The following criticisms, therefore, have little to do with the theoretical basis of the denotational method. Instead, I claim that denotational descriptions, as traditionally written, are poorly engineered (in a software-engineering sense), and are based on a conceptual framework that is usually inappropriate for clearly describing semantics. In other words, the specifications *define*, but do not satisfactorily *describe*, programming languages. This has the effect of eliminating any possibility for efficient implementation. Furthermore, the specifications become much less descriptive, and hence much less useful, than they ought to be.

The following sections describe the shortcomings of traditional denotational semantics as a language for specifying compilers. The impact of each problem on the automatic generation of compilers is also discussed.

4.1 The Use of a Low-Level Notation

Denotational descriptions are written in a version of Scott's language LAMBDA, with more or less syntactic sugar. This amounts to writing in a low-level assembly code for a λ-calculus machine, with all of the usual software-engineering problems that accompany assembly-language programming. Some abstraction and encapsulation of the "code" is obtained by defining auxiliary functions, but this provides only a superficial improvement, akin to using the macro facility

---

[1] Recall that the term *performance characteristics* refers to the efficiency of both the compiler and the object programs it produces.

provided by most assemblers.

Every aspect of a denotational semantics is expressed in terms of just λ-abstraction and application. This total dependence on λ-notation forces a classical system to emulate a reduction machine for the λ-calculus, which leads to inefficiencies at both compile time and runtime.

At compile time, a partial evaluation of the semantics must be performed. Typically, this means that a λ-expression must be symbolically β-reduced, as described in the previous chapter (page 39), or else statically analyzed to determine its partial reduction, as done in the **mix** system [Jones *et al*. 85]. Although partial evaluation has not been shown to be inherently inefficient, practical techniques have yet to be devised. PSP-generated compilers run 25 to 50 times slower than handwritten compilers, often spending over 60% of their time performing symbolic β-reductions on the program graph [Lee & Pleban 86]. It is clear that partial evaluation exacts a severe penalty on compile time performance.

Partial evaluation is unnecessary at runtime. Furthermore, there is apparently little risk in using applicative-order instead of normal-order evaluation, particularly when the semantics is written in the continuation style [Paulson 81]. More efficient runtime reduction can thus be accomplished by translating λ-abstractions into strict functions, as is done, for example, in programming languages like ML and Scheme.

The PSP system, for instance, uses an SECD machine for runtime evaluation. The generated compilers translate reduced λ-expressions into linear stack code for an SECD machine, which then performs an efficient applicative-order evaluation. The SPS system is similar in its use of a Scheme evaluator for the runtime reductions. Compared to SIS's call-by-need reducer, both the SECD machine and Scheme are quite efficient. Nevertheless, experiments indicate that the object programs produced by PSP and SPS-generated compilers run 500 to 1,000 times slower than those produced by handwritten compilers.

This inefficiency is due in part to the large number of closures that must be handled during evaluation. Most of the λ-variables in a denotational semantics are bound to entities such as continuations, stores, and environments, all of which are modeled by λ-abstractions. Also, many λ-abstractions are written in the semantic equations. (Recall from the discussion in Chapter 3, page 41, that anonymous λ-abstractions can force a β-reducer to construct closures explicitly.) As can be seen in the λ-expression on page 42, these abstractions may survive the compile time reductions, thus leading to the handling of closures at runtime.

Significant progress has been made recently toward the efficient implementation of higher-order functional languages [Kranz *et al*. 86], and further improvements are likely to reduce greatly the impact of closures on runtime performance. A more fundamental source of inefficiency, then, is attributable to the modeling of environments and stores via the composition of λ-abstractions. An example of this appears in the auxiliary function `update` from page 34, repeated here:

```
update loc cont =
    { fn ev. { fn store.
        let (mem, input, freeLoc) = store in
            case ev of
                constant (val) =>
                    cont ( ([loc => val] mem), input, freeLoc) |
                    _ => error
        end } }.
```

The actual modification of the store is performed by the subexpression,

```
[loc => val] mem
```

which is a shorthand for the following:

```
fn l. if l = loc then val else mem l
```

It is now evident that every update results in a new closure being "wrapped" around the store. Retrieval of an element of the store then involves the application of a (possibly large) number of these closures. This obviously incurs an enormous overhead since components of such structures cannot be retrieved directly.

4.2   The Lack of Separability

A second problem with traditional denotational semantics has to do with the *lack of separation* between the actual semantics of a language and the model-dependent details underlying it. This problem was first observed by Mosses, and it has led him to argue that model-dependent details should be completely eliminated from semantic descriptions. He thus proposes to abandon the present form of denotational semantics, with its dependence on λ-notation, in favor of *abstract semantic algebras* [Mosses 82].

Abstract semantic algebras

Mosses cites several problems with traditional denotational descriptions. First, the fundamental concepts embodied by a programming language are rarely reflected explicitly in the semantics. An example of this is given in [Pleban & Lee

87], which considers the semantics of procedure call and return in traditional
denotational descriptions. The restoration of the caller's environment after return from a procedure is expressed only implicitly; a considerable amount of
analysis of the semantics is required in order to see that the proper environment
is indeed restored. Furthermore, the manner in which fundamental semantic
concepts, like procedure call, are expressed varies from one description to another. Some aspects of the semantics are often left unspecified or only informally
described.

A second problem is that the use of λ-notation complicates formal reasoning
about programs, since higher-order functions have to be manipulated. Finally,
when the addition of new language features brings about a change to the underlying semantic models, the semantic specifications usually require extensive
rewriting.

As an illustration of this last problem, consider the following fragment of a
semantics for statement sequencing and assignments in ToyPL, written in the
so-called "direct" style:

```
semantic domains

    STATE = Ide -> EV.

semantic functions

    C : stmt -> ENV -> STATE -> STATE.
    E : expr -> ENV -> STATE -> EV.

semantic equations

    C [[ stmt1 ";" stmt2 ]] env state =
       C [[stmt2]] env ( C [[stmt1]] env state ).

    C [[ id ":=" expr ]] env state =
       [ id => E [[expr]] env ] state.
```

Instead of using continuations, flow of control is modeled directly. Also, the state
of the program is modeled simply by mapping identifiers directly to expressible
values instead of store locations. From this choice of semantic models, one can
infer that ToyPL supports neither escapes from loops nor aliasing of identifiers.
If these features are later added to the language, the semantics must be written
with continuations and a store, as was done in the semantics on page 34. The
relevant semantic equations are repeated here:

```
semantic functions

    C : stmt -> ENV -> CONT -> CONT.
    E : expr -> ENV -> ECONT -> CONT.
    R : expr -> ENV -> ECONT -> CONT.

semantic equations

    C [[ stmt1 ";" stmt2 ]] env cont =
        C [[stmt1]] env ; C [[stmt2]] env ; cont.

    C [[ id ":=" expr ]] env cont =
        E [[id]] env { isLoc { fn (variable loc).
            R [[expr]] env ; update loc ; cont } }.
```

The simple models used in the direct semantics are not adequate for expressing the semantics of jumps and aliasing. Thus, more sophisticated models involving continuations and stores must be introduced. The unfortunate effect of this change of models is that the *entire* semantics must be rewritten.

In order to avoid these problems, Mosses has proposed a new method for semantic description in which abstract semantic algebras (ASA's) are used instead of λ-notation. An ASA is an algebra of *actions*, and is called "abstract" because the properties of the operators in the algebra are specified equationally. Model details, for instance the use (or non-use) of continuations to model flow of control, are thus absent from ASA-based semantic descriptions.

The operators in an ASA are chosen to represent basic semantic concepts typically expressed only indirectly in traditional denotational descriptions.[2] For example, in the two (continuation-style) semantic equations shown above, the semicolon operator seems to express the semantic concept of sequencing. Of course, this is nothing more than syntactic trickery. (Recall from the discussion on page 26 that this semicolon actually denotes right-associative application.) With ASA's, however, sequencing is actually expressed by a semantic operator. Thus, the two equations may be written with ASA's as follows:

```
semantic functions

    C : stmt -> ACTION.
    E : expr -> ACTION.
```

---

[2]Later in this chapter I argue that many of these traditional semantic concepts do not actually represent concepts that are fundamental to the languages being described.

```
semantic equations

    C [[ stmt1 ";" stmt2 ]] =
        C [[stmt1]] $ C [[stmt2]].

    C [[ id ":=" expr ]] =
        ( find [[id]], rvalue (E [[expr]]) ) ! store.
```

Devices such as continuations, stores, and environments are completely absent
from this example. These model details are essentially hidden in the abstract
semantic algebra over which the operators $ (sequencing), find (environment
look-up), rvalue (R-value coercion), (_ , _) (tupling), _ ! _ (piping, *i.e.*, value
propagation), and store (store update) are defined. The operators produce actions that may consume and produce values, have side effects on the store, and
establish bindings in the environment.

When writing semantic descriptions based on ASA's, no assumptions about
model details (*e.g.*, how the program state is modeled, whether the semantic
domains correspond to the direct or continuation style, *etc.*) may be made. The
semantics is thus "abstracted" from the underlying models, and protected from
massive rewriting should aspects of these models change.

The direct implementation of abstract semantic algebras

Mosses has undertaken the development of a *basic* abstract semantic algebra
containing operators for the fundamental semantic concepts of Algol-like programming languages [Mosses 84]. Watt has implemented a variant of this basic
ASA in the language ML [Watt 84].

The main idea of Watt's implementation is to define the domain of actions as
follows:

```
semantic domains

    ACTION = union action of (ENV * STORE * VALUE list) ->
                             (ENV * STORE * VALUE list).
```

This definition of ACTION captures the idea that actions consume and produce
values, and may also have side effects on the store and environment. This is sufficient for modeling the features of many sequential programming languages. The
operators are then implemented in a straightforward manner as action transformers. The pipe operator, for example, is implemented simply by function
composition:

```
auxiliary functions

   infix !;

   (action a1) ! (action a2) = action (a2 o a1)
```

The principle of separability

The *principle of separability* dictates that model details must be encapsulated in a semantic algebra (and hence factored out of the "main" part of the language semantics). A semantics that adheres to this principle is called a *separated* semantics. ASA-based semantic descriptions are separated.

In traditional denotational descriptions, separability is destroyed by the intertwining of the language semantics with details of semantic models. Lack of separability forces the semanticist to choose a semantic model *in advance* of writing the language semantics. If the choice of model turns out not to be adequate, the entire semantics usually must be rewritten.

The impact of lack of separability on compiler generation

A lack of separability makes it extremely difficult to generate compilers that produce efficient object programs. To see why this is so, consider the classical compilation of the following ToyPL program fragment:

```
...   a := 1 ; b := 2 ...
```

The meaning of this fragment is determined by applying the valuation function C from the ToyPL semantics given on page 34:

```
C [[a := 1 ; b := 2]]
```

This expands into

```
{ fn env. fn cont.
    C [[a := 1]] env { C [[b := 2]] env cont } }
```

and then into the following:

```
{ fn env. fn cont.
    E [[a]] env { isLoc { fn (variable loc).
      R [[1]] env { update loc {
        E [[b]] env { isLoc { fn (variable loc).
          R [[2]] env { update loc cont } } } } } } } }
```

At this point the simple concept of the sequencing of two statements has been completely obscured. Complete expansion of semantic valuations results in the following:

```
{ fn env. fn cont.
   if (env *a*) = unbound then err
   else { isLoc { fn (variable loc).
           { deref { isRvalue {
               { update loc {
                   if (env *b*) = unbound then err
                   else { isLoc { fn (variable loc).
                             { deref { isRvalue {
                                 { update loc cont } } } }
                             (constant (integer 2)) } }
                         (env *b*) } } } } }
           (constant (integer 1)) } }
   (env *a*) }
```

A compiler generator is now left with the task of "discovering" that this λ-term expresses the assignment of two integer constants. The direct reduction of this expression would, of course, be considerably less efficient than two store instructions on a conventional computer.

Some analysis of this λ-expression might be possible after a few reductions are performed. For example, consider the portion of this λ-term which represents the meaning of the second assignment statement, b := 2:

```
if (env *b*) = unbound then err
else { isLoc { fn (variable loc).
        { deref { isRvalue {
            { update loc cont } } } }
        (constant (integer 2)) } }
      (env *b*)
```

After several reduction steps, the following is obtained:

```
if (env *b*) = unbound then err
else case (env *b*) of
        variable (_) =>
            { fn (variable loc).
                { fn store.
                    { update loc cont }
                    (constant (integer 2))
                    store } }
            (env *b*) |
        _ => err
```

The retrieval of the location allocated for the variable b in the subexpression, (env *b*), is now in plain view. Furthermore, the subexpression,

```
{ fn store.
  { update loc cont }
  (constant (integer 2))
  store }
```

is clearly the assignment of the constant 2 into the retrieved location for b.

It is conceivable that a "smart" code generator could be instructed to find patterns of subexpressions like this so that a single store instruction could be emitted in this case. Such a code generator would have to analyze the semantics in order to ensure that the store is *single-threaded*; in other words, that it will not be necessary to restore previous incarnations of the store arbitrarily. Schmidt provides a list of sufficient criteria for single-threadedness in denotational specifications [Schmidt 85]. Unfortunately, many traditional specifications may fail to meet these criteria, and there are no known algorithms for transforming a multi-threaded semantics into a single-threaded one.

There is also another complication: how did the reducer know to stop reducing at this point? Since only the update function is involved in the pattern for the code generator, the other auxiliary functions have been reduced away. It is not likely that a reducer could be instructed to do this automatically, especially since other functions, say deref, might also be involved in code generation patterns. Complicating matters even further, it is possible to reduce partially the application of update. A few reduction steps results in the following:

```
if (env *b*) = unbound then err
else case (env *b*) of
     variable (_) =>
        { fn (variable loc).
          { fn store.
            let (mem, input, freeLoc) = store in
               cont ( ([loc => (integer 2)] mem),
                      input, freeLoc )
            end } }
        (env *b*) |
     _ => err
```

The presence of the store-update operation is now obscured by the partial reduction of the application of the update function.

After expanding the perturbation of the function, mem, the following is obtained:

```
if (env *b*) = unbound then err
else { fn (variable loc).
        { fn store.
           let (mem, input, freeLoc) = store in
              cont
              ( ( fn l. if l = loc then (integer 2)
                            else mem l ),
                 input, freeLoc )
           end } }
   (env *b*)
```

All hope of discovering the simple operation of storing an integer constant is now lost. At this point, the evaluation of this rather complicated expression (with the implementation problems cited in the previous section) is forced upon us, and just in order to perform the single environment lookup and store update. This obviously has a detrimental effect on runtime performance.

Compile-time performance has also been degraded since, in essence, *too many compile-time reductions have been performed.* The lack of separability has caused useful high-level information to be reduced down to a low-level "mish-mash" of semantic model details. This is called the phenomenon of *overreduction*.

4.3   The Loss of Semantic Distinctions

Consider the semantics of variable declarations in ToyPL:

```
D [[ "var" id ]] env dcont =
  { ref { fn newVar.
      dcont (bind id newVar) } (constant uninit) }.
```

The inner workings of this equation can be exposed by expanding the application of the ref auxiliary function, and then performing a few reductions, to obtain:

```
D [[ "var" id ]] env dcont =
  { fn store.
     let (mem, freeLoc, input) = store.
        newVar = variable freeLoc.
        newStore = (mem, freeLoc + 1, input)
     in
        update freeLoc (dcont (bind id newVar))
             (constant uninit) newStore
     end }.
```

It is now possible to see that `ref` extracts the next free location from the store and forms it into a new variable, `newVar`. The variable name, `id`, is then bound to this new variable and passed on to the remainder of the program execution, `dcont`. In general, an expression of the form,

```
{ ref { fn loc. ...
```

allocates a new variable from the store and passes it along for processing in the λ-variable `loc`.

Now consider the semantics of blocks and procedures with single call-by-value parameters:

```
abstract syntax

    decl  -> "procedure" id1 "(" id2 ")" block.
    block -> decl "begin" stmt "end".

semantic domains

    DV = union unbound |
                variable of LOC |
                constant of RV |
                procedure of PROC.

    PROC = CONT -> ECONT.          (* Procedure objects *)

semantic functions

    B : block -> ENV > CONT -> CONT.

semantic equations

    B [[ decl "begin" stmt "end" ]] env cont =
      D [[decl]] env { fn localEnv.
          C [[stmt]] (combine env localEnv) cont }.

    D [[ "procedure" id1 "(" id2 ")" block ]] env dcont =
      let proc = fn returnCont.
          { deref { ref { fn paramLoc.
            { B [[block]] (combine env (bind id2 paramLoc))
                returnCont } } } }
        in
          dcont (bind id1 (procedure proc))
        end.
```

In order to allow for procedures, a `procedure` denotation has been added to the domain DV of denotable values. A procedure object from the domain PROC takes a "return" continuation, and from this produces an expression continuation. The expressible value taken by this expression continuation is the actual argument value for the procedure.

In the equation for procedure declaration, the λ-variable `paramLoc` receives the new variable allocated by `ref`. The parameter name `id2` is then bound to this variable inside the procedure body. Thus, formal value parameters are in every respect identical to simple variables. Inspection of the semantic equation for blocks reveals that a block's local environment, `localEnv`, is derived by the same semantic valuation function D also used for deriving nonlocal environments. Hence, local variables, like procedure parameters, are also not distinguished from nonlocal variables.

This blurring of semantic distinctions is characteristic of what is called the *minimalistic semantic explication* of traditional specifications [Pleban & Lee 87]. In other words, traditional descriptions are written in as minimal terms as possible in order to simplify the semantics. The word *minimal* means that the semantics is expressed in terms of a small collection of semantic concepts. Minimalistic explication complicates the problem of compiler generation because the structures appropriate for realistic compilation are not explicitly reflected in the semantics. In the example above, no distinction is made between variables and formal parameters. This is unfortunate since realistic compilers do actually implement these variables in different ways.

In traditional denotational semantics, realistic implementation models are obtained manually by augmenting the reference semantics (called the *standard semantics* in [Milne & Strachey 76]) by a progression of increasingly implementation-oriented semantic descriptions (such as the *store semantics* and *stack semantics*). Then, these definitions must be related to one another through tortuous congruence proofs.

4.4   Overspecification of Semantics

Curiously, minimalistic semantic explication also leads to the overspecification of aspects of the language semantics. For example, the lack of distinction between local, nonlocal, and formal parameter variables might be viewed as a *stipulation* that all three classes of variable be implemented in exactly the same way.

Indeed, the use of stores and locations to express the semantics of ToyPL variables is itself an overspecification. ToyPL does not support pointers or aliasing; hence, there is no need for locations. More fundamentally, the storage model used in the ToyPL semantics specifies a specific (and unwieldy) *implementation* model. A compiler generator is required to be faithful to this model since the model can not be distinguished from elements of the actual language semantics, due to lack of separability. Implementation-oriented semantic descriptions, for instance those based on store and stack semantics, specify even more elaborate storage models, and thus in this respect are even more overspecified.

As an example consider again the allocation of storage for procedure parameters. Partial reduction of the `ref` application in the semantic equation for procedure declaration yields the following:

```
D [[ "procedure" id1 "(" id2 ")" block ]] env dcont =
    let proc =
        fn returnCont. { deref
            { fn ev. { fn store.
                let (mem, freeLoc, input) = store.
                    newVar = variable freeLoc.
                    newStore = (mem, freeLoc + 1, input)
                in
                    update
                        freeLoc
                        { B [[block]]
                            (combine env (bind id2 newVar))
                            returnCont }
                        cv
                        newStore
            end } } }
    in
        dcont (bind id1 proc)
    end.
```

A new store, `newStore`, is constructed in which the counter for the next free location has been incremented to reflect the allocation of storage for the procedure parameter. This new store is passed to the `update` function, which first stores the actual parameter value `ev` into the allocated location, and then passes the resulting store on to the remainder of the program execution, `returnCont`. Thus, every call to a procedure causes a fresh storage location to be allocated for the parameter. A similar analysis reveals that a procedure's local variables are also allocated fresh locations upon every invocation.

Although this is obviously inefficient, the fact that the storage for parameters and local variables can be reclaimed upon procedure exit is not revealed by the

semantics. Arduous proofs of congruence are required in order to justify the
reuse of local storage. In a sense, the semantics *stipulates* that storage should
never be reclaimed.

From a philosophical perspective, this semantics is less than satisfying because
it answers a question about the language that is normally left unspecified: do
local variables retain their values from one invocation of a procedure to the next?
This question is not only given a definite answer (no), but the semantics even
goes so far as to specify that local variables should be mapped onto previously
unused storage locations upon every invocation.

Similarly, the order of evaluation of expressions in parameter lists and compound expressions is often meant to be left unspecified. Traditional denotational
descriptions, however, specify particular orders of evaluation. For example, the
semantics of ToyPL addition expressions is as follows:

```
E [[ expr1 "+" expr2 ]] env econt =
   R [[expr1]] env { fn (constant (integer v1)).
      R [[expr2]] env { fn (constant (integer v2)).
         econt (constant (integer (v1 + v2))) } }.
```

The second expression is "frozen" until the the first expression has been completely evaluated. The intention of the designer of this language might very well
have been to leave this order of evaluation unspecified. However, the semantics specifies a left-to-right evaluation order. In [Stoy 77, page 235], a technique
is presented for encapsulating the order of evaluation in a semantic primitive
which is left unspecified. A compiler based on the semantics above, however,
has little choice but to faithfully (and blindly) follow the specification, regardless
of the implementation consequences.

4.5   The Lack of a Static/Dynamic Distinction

An essential part of the design of many programming languages is the distinction between its static and dynamic components. However, this distinction is
blurred in traditional semantic descriptions. This makes the semantic specifications less descriptive, and complicates the task of determining which portions
of a semantics can be statically evaluated. This difficulty is illustrated in the
following example. Suppose a static check is added to the equation for variable
declarations in ToyPL, as follows:

```
D [[ "var" id ]] env dcont =
   if env id = unbound then
      { ref { fn newVar.
         dcont (bind id newVar) } (constant uninit) }
   else
      err.
```

Before `ref` is applied to allocate a new variable, the check,

```
env id = unbound
```

ensures that the variable name has not already been declared.

In principle, this check is statically evaluable since ToyPL variables can be allocated at compile time. However, if procedures are added, as was done in Section 4.3, then ToyPL variables can no longer be allocated at compile time, and so this check can not be statically evaluated. The static evaluability of this check has changed, even though the semantic equation in which it appears has not changed.

It seems the only way to ensure that the static components are evaluated at compile time is to manually identify the runtime operations, and then use a partial evaluator. But as was pointed out earlier, partial evaluation is a major source of inefficiency in classical compilers.

Nielson and Nielson advocate distinguishing between compile-time and run-time entities in a denotational semantics [Nielson & Nielson 86]. They propose a two-level metalanguage in which the compile time domains are clearly delineated from the runtime domains. A semantics written in such a metalanguage derives program meanings that can be given various interpretations. The term, *two-level*, refers to the idea of composing the metalanguage with an interpretation. Interpretations may take various forms, depending upon the application. A "coding" interpretation, for instance, might evaluate the compile-time entities and then generate machine code for the runtime entities, thereby obtaining realistic compilation. We shall see that high-level semantic descriptions are, in some sense, also two-level.

4.6 Summary

It is not (currently) possible to automatically generate realistic compilers from traditional denotational semantics, due to the fundamental problems described in this chapter.

In addition to the implementation difficulties, these problems lead to poorly engineered semantic descriptions that are needlessly difficult to write and comprehend. The descriptions *define*, but do not satisfactorily *describe*, the semantics of programming languages.

The next chapter describes a new style of semantic definition, called *high-level semantics*, which overcomes these problems.

5 High-Level Semantics

I now present a new style of semantic description, called *high-level semantics*, that overcomes the problems described in the previous chapter. Unlike the traditional denotational approach, the high-level technique is suitable for both defining the functional meaning of programming languages as well as describing realistic compiler implementations.

5.1 An Overview of High-Level Semantics

The basic ideas of high-level semantics will be illustrated by a small example.

A semantic algebra of actions

Recall the syntactic structure of integer and addition expressions in ToyPL:

```
abstract syntax

    expr -> int | expr1 "+" expr2.
```

Each component of a program can be thought of as expressing some kind of *action*, or dynamic effect. An entire program then expresses an aggregate action consisting of all of the component actions. Expressions in ToyPL denote actions that produce expressible values. In a high-level semantics, this notion is captured by postulating the existence of a domain of *value-producing actions*, which I call VACTION:

```
action domains

    VACTION - unspecified.
```

Here, the VACTION domain has been declared in a part of a high-level specification called the *action domains* section. I have, for the moment, chosen not to specify the structure of VACTION. Instead, an informal (and intuitive) understanding of the notion of a value-producing action will be relied upon.

There is a direct analogy between these actions and those of Mosses' abstract semantic algebras. The action domains presented here correspond to Mosses' algebraic sort of actions; elements of the action domains correspond to terms in an abstract semantic algebra. Just as with ASA's, *semantic operations* are defined on actions to represent the fundamental concepts embodied by a language. For the ToyPL expressions, the following declarations in the *operators* section are needed:

```
operators

    Integer : INT -> VACTION is
    Integer =  unspecified.

    Add : VACTION * VACTION -> VACTION is
    Add =  unspecified.
```

By convention, the names of semantic operators are written with the first letter capitalized. The `Add` operator combines two value-producing actions into a new value-producing action. The new action presumably produces the sum of the values produced by the two constituent actions. `Integer` coerces an integer constant into an action that simply produces the same integer value. Only the names and functionalities of the operators have been specified, as once again only an informal understanding of their operational implications is given.

The domain `VACTION`, along with `Add` and `Integer`, define a *semantic algebra* of value-producing actions. For the moment, however, only the *signature* of this algebra has been defined. An *interpretation* for the algebra has been given only informally. The signature, however, provides enough information to allow us to write equations describing the semantics of integer expressions in ToyPL. A complete definition of the semantic algebra will be given separately, thereby enforcing separability of the semantics from model-dependent details.

Macrosemantics and microsemantics

As in a denotational semantics, high-level descriptions define semantic valuation functions via semantic equations. The valuation function for ToyPL expressions has the following functionality:

```
semantic functions

    E : expr -> ENV -> VACTION.
```

The valuation function `E` maps a ToyPL expression and environment to an action representing the dynamic effect of the expression. The semantic equations, then, are as follows:

```
semantic equations

    E [[ int ]] env = Integer (int).

    E [[ expr1 "+" expr2 ]] env =
        Add (E [[ expr1 ]] env, E [[ expr2 ]] env).
```

The metavariable env represents an environment which maps identifiers to their static denotations. The structure of environments in a high-level semantics is discussed it in detail in the next section.

There are several things to note about this semantic specification.

- Expressions no longer denote λ-terms. Instead, they denote value-producing actions which are elements of the VACTION domain. The elements of this domain can be viewed as terms in a semantic algebra of actions. For reasons that will be explained later, I call these *prefix-form operator terms*, or POTs.

- Model details such as stores and continuations are absent from the equations. Hence, the semantics adheres to the principle of separability. As we shall see, semantic model details are now used only for providing an interpretation for the semantic operators.

- The fundamental concepts embodied by the constructs of a language (in this case, constant integer values and addition) are expressed directly by the semantic operators.

- Overspecification of semantic aspects has been avoided. For example, the order of evaluation of the summands in an addition expression have not been specified since Add does not specify an order of evaluation.

- The dynamic components of the language are completely encapsulated by the semantic operators. Thus, except for the operators, the semantic equations express only static aspects of the language, for instance the handling of environments.

This model-independent portion of a semantic specification is called the *macrosemantics*. An interpretation for the operators is provided by a *microsemantics*. One possible (and very simple) microsemantic specification is as follows:

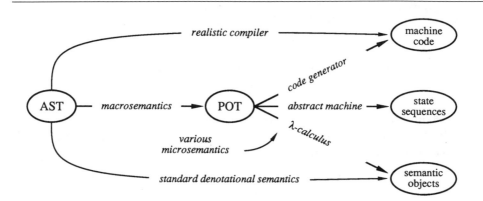

In a high-level semantics, the macrosemantics supplies a meaning to a program (AST) in the form of a prefix-form operator term (POT). An interpretation for POTs can then be given in a number of different styles.

Figure 5.1
High-Level Semantics

```
action domains

    VACTION = STATE -> INT.

operators

    Integer : INT -> VACTION is
    Integer i = fn state. i.

    Add : VACTION * VACTION -> VACTION is
    Add (v, v') = fn state. (v state) + (v' state).
```

The microsemantics declares action domains and operators like the macrosemantics, but in this case the algebra is completely defined.

The interchangeability of semantic interpretations

Other forms of interpretation, perhaps based on more powerful or nonstandard models, can be substituted for the one given above. This is depicted in Figure 5.1, where three different, yet compatible, microsemantic specifications are shown. According to the principle of separability, only the signature of the algebra defined by the microsemantics (*i.e.*, the names and functionalities of the operators) is shared between a macrosemantics and microsemantics. Thus, any two microsemantic specifications that define semantic algebras with the same signatures are interchangeable. A microsemantics might be based on traditional denotational models, with the operators defined in terms of the λ-calculus in either the direct or continuation styles. In this case the composition of macrosemantics and microsemantics constitutes a standard denotational semantics. Alternatively, the operators might be defined operationally by providing an abstract machine capable of interpreting the POTs. Finally, a compiling interpretation for the semantic algebra can be given by providing a code generator that treats the POTs as intermediate code.

The relation to compiling

Figure 5.1 also shows that a macrosemantics specifies a translation from abstract syntax trees to prefix-form operator terms.[1] This translation is a static computation since a POT represents the total dynamic effect of a program. For compiling, this means that a macrosemantics specifies all of the compile-time computations involved in translating an abstract syntax tree to an intermediate representation (in the form of a POT). The microsemantics, then, provides a way to interpret the POTs at runtime.

An example language: HypoPL

The following sections present more of the details of high-level semantics by examining excerpts from the macrosemantic and microsemantic descriptions for a hypothetical programming language. The language, called HypoPL, is an extension of ToyPL featuring strong type checking, recursive procedures with a single value parameter, input/output statements, and while loops. I will begin by considering the high-level semantics of the ToyPL subset of HypoPL. Then, I will demonstrate the extensibility of high-level descriptions by adding escapes from loops, one-dimensional arrays, and procedures.

A traditional denotational description for HypoPL is given in Appendix A. Appendix B gives the complete macrosemantic specification for HypoPL, and Appendix C presents several microsemantic specifications.

---

[1] It's true. In high-level semantics, all programs go to POT.

5.2   The Macrosemantics

Let us begin with the macrosemantics of expressions in HypoPL. Consider first
the literal expressions:

```
abstract syntax

    expr -> "true" | "false" | int.
```

HypoPL expressions may result in either integer or boolean values. To model
this, a domain of types is defined:

```
semantic domains

    TYPE = union int_type | bool_type.
```

Then, the functionality of the semantic valuation for expressions is declared as
follows:

```
semantic functions

    E : expr -> ENV -> (TYPE * VACTION);
```

The valuation function E takes a HypoPL expression and an environment, and
then returns a pair consisting of the type of the expression and the value-
producing action it denotes. (The structure of environments is discussed later.)
The type component represents the static meaning of the expression, whereas the
action component represents the dynamic meaning.

As before, the structure of the VACTION domain is left unspecified. Indeed, the
principle of separability dictates that the macrosemantics must not depend on
the internal structure of this domain.

The semantic equations for literal expressions are thus expressed as follows:

```
semantic equations

    E [[ "true" ]] env  = (bool_type, Boolean (true)).

    E [[ "false" ]] env = (bool_type, Boolean (false)).

    E [[ int ]] env     = (int_type, Integer (int)).
```

The two microsemantic operators, Boolean and Integer, have the following
signatures:

domain	syntactic	semantic
identifiers	IDENT	ID
integers	INTEGER	INT
booleans	BOOLEAN	BOOL
reals	NUMBER	REAL
characters	CHARACTER	CHAR
strings	CHARSTRING	STRING

This table shows the correspondence between the names of the domains of syntactic constructs and semantic values. Elements of any of the semantic value domains except ID may be supplied as arguments to microsemantic operators. Elements of ID must first be coerced into semantic names from domain NAME.

Figure 5.2
Correspondence Between the Names of Syntactic and Semantic Domains

```
operators

    Boolean : BOOL -> VACTION.
    Integer : INT  -> VACTION.
```

These operators coerce basic values into the corresponding value-producing actions.

Syntactic constructs and semantic values

Microsemantic operators represent purely dynamic actions. Thus, an argument supplied to an operator must be either (1) an element of an action domain, or (2) a basic semantic value. Any other type of argument value is an error. Recall from page 23 that semantic values are traditionally obtained from syntactic constructs via application of a "basic value" valuation, commonly referred to as $\mathcal{B}$. In our notation, $\mathcal{B}$ is implicitly applied whenever the syntax brackets are left off; for example, [[int]] is the syntactic construct (the numeral) from the domain INTEGER, whereas int is the corresponding semantic value (the integer) from the domain INT. (This was discussed on page 35.)

This distinction between semantic values and syntactic constructs is a fine point, but semantically important. In the next chapter we shall see that it also allows for the specification of high-quality recovery from semantic errors.

Figure 5.2 gives the names of the primitive syntactic and semantic domains, and shows how they correspond. By convention, metavariables in abstract syntax expressions are named after their corresponding semantic value domains. For example, int is used as a metavariable ranging over the syntactic domain INTEGER since it represents, when the syntax brackets are left off, an element of the semantic domain INT. By the same reasoning, the name of the syntactic metavariable for the IDENT domain is id, since the corresponding semantic value domain is named ID.

Identifiers are normally considered to be strictly syntactic entities. In other words, unlike other syntactic constructs such as integers, there is no obvious conceptual difference between the syntactic construct of an identifier and its semantic counterpart. In compiler generation, however, it is quite reasonable to maintain such a distinction for identifiers. The semantic counterpart of an identifier is thus referred to as a *semantic identifier*. By first mapping syntactic identifiers to semantic identifiers, it becomes possible to construct all of the semantic domains from primitive or compound semantic domains. This avoids the anomaly in traditional denotational semantics of having the syntactic domain IDENT be also a primitive semantic domain.

A semantic identifier often is not considered to be a basic semantic value like an integer—languages such as Pascal, for instance, do not allow one to compute with identifiers. Thus, semantic identifiers are not permitted as arguments to microsemantic operators. To obtain a notion of identifiers as computable objects (as in Lisp), a semantic identifier must first be coerced into a *semantic name* from the domain NAME. This coercion is accomplished by application of one of the predefined functions, name or alphaName, described later.

In Algol 68 parlance, semantic identifiers correspond to *external objects*, whereas semantic names correspond to *internal objects*. Semantic names can be viewed as locations in a store, although their exact structure is hidden from the macrosemantics in order to preserve separability. In a sense, the mapping from syntactic identifiers to semantic names is a "cross-over point" between static and dynamic aspects of variables and other named entities in a program.

In terms of compilation, the syntactic construct of an identifier is a leaf node in an abstract syntax tree. The leaf node may contain, in addition to the identifier itself, lexical information such as the line and column number of its occurrence in the source text. A semantic identifier, then, can be thought of as the identifier itself, without the lexical information, which is perhaps useful as a key into a symbol table. Syntactic identifiers are always unique, but two distinct syntactic identifiers may represent the same semantic identifier. Finally, semantic names are essentially abstract names for the denotable, storable, and expressible values in the semantics. For a compiler, these name the addressable objects. For block-structured languages like Pascal, semantic names might be combined with the block-level numbers in order to obtain abstract textual addresses.

Static and dynamic semantics

We can now consider the macrosemantics of addition expressions.

```
abstract syntax

   expr -> expr1 "+" expr2 .
```

The following equation expresses the semantics of this construct:

```
E [[ expr1 "+" expr2 ]] env =
   let (t1, vA1) = E [[ expr1 ]] env
   and (t2, vA2) = E [[ expr2 ]] env
   in
        (int_type, Add (vA1, vA2))
   end.
```

The meaning of each summand is obtained by recursive application of E, and then their actions are combined into a new action by the Add operator. Addition always results in an integer type.

This equation neglects to express the static semantic constraints of HypoPL, in particular that the types of the summands must both be of type integer. As mentioned earlier, this disregard for static semantics is common in denotational descriptions. However, a language description should completely specify both the static and dynamic semantics, and in addition this is required for compiler generation. Adding the static semantics here is straightforward:

```
E [[ expr1 "+" expr2 ]] env =
   let (t1, vA1) = E [[ expr1 ]] env
   and (t2, vA2) = E [[ expr2 ]] env
   in
        if (t1 = int_type) andalso (t2 = int_type) then
           (int_type, Add (vA1, vA2))
        else
           bottom:(TYPE * VACTION)
   end.
```

Now, if one of the summands fails to have an integer type, the valuation results in bottom. This is a predefined identifier which represents the bottom element

(traditionally written as ⊥) of whatever domain is specified, in this case (TYPE
* VACTION).

The effect of bottom is, of course, unpredictable. Semantically, this is acceptable since meanings are not defined for incorrect programs. In the context of
compiler generation, however, bottom is not very "friendly"—one would like
for a compiler to continue with compilation in a predictable fashion after detecting an error. Thus, a better way to write the semantics is as follows:

```
E [[ expr1 "+" expr2 ]] env =
   let (t1, vA1) = E [[ expr1 ]] env
   and (t2, vA2) = E [[ expr2 ]] env
   in
       if (t1 = int_type) andalso (t2 = int_type) then
          (int_type, Add (vA1, vA2))
       else
          exprError [[ ... ]] "Can only add integers."
   end.
```

The expression, [[...]], is a shorthand for referring to the entire abstract
syntax tree specified on the left-hand side of the equation. The auxiliary function
exprError marks the source text corresponding to the given abstract syntax tree
and issues the specified diagnostic message. Then, it yields a predictable value,
specifically:

```
(int_type, Integer (0))
```

This allows an implementation of the semantics to recover from static semantic
errors in a predictable manner. In addition, it provides a convenient way to
document the static semantic constraints in a language.

The semantics of variables

Static denotations for identifiers are retained in an environment, defined by the
following domain equations:

```
semantic domains

   ENV - ID -> MODE.

   MODE = union noneM |
                 constM of CONST |
                 varM of VAR.
```

```
CONST = INT.
VAR = NAME * TYPE.
TYPE = union int_type | bool_type.
```

The environment associates identifiers with modes. A mode is either a constant or a variable. Constant modes carry an integer-value denotation, whereas variable modes have a semantic name and type. The NAME domain is described below.

It is interesting to note that these are the only semantic domains for the HypoPL macrosemantics (at least until arrays and procedures are added). Domains for dynamic, or runtime, entities such as stores and continuations (*e.g.*, STORE and CONT in the traditional denotational semantics for HypoPL) are never present in a macrosemantics. This has several consequences. First, in contrast with traditional specifications, environments now maintain only static information about identifiers. In particular, a free-location pointer is no longer embedded in the environment. Environments can thus be completely evaluated at compile time. Second, the distinction between the static and dynamic components of a language is automatically maintained. Third, the problem of overspecification is avoided. The storage model, for instance, cannot possibly be overspecified since a store domain is not even defined in the specification.

Environments are built up as HypoPL declarations are elaborated. Consider the declarations of integer variables:

```
abstract syntax

    decl -> "int" id.
```

In order to express the semantics of declarations, *declaration* (or *binding*) *actions* and *type-producing actions* are required.

```
action domains

    DACTION = declaration actions.
    TACTION = type-producing actions.

operators

    (* Bind the name to a variable of the given type *)
    DeclSimpleVar : NAME * TACTION -> DACTION.
```

```
(* Produce the dynamic integer type value *)
IntType : TACTION.
```

As with the value-producing actions, the structure of the domains of declaration and type-producing actions are left unspecified for the time being. The De-clSimpleVar operator yields an action which binds a semantic name to a type. IntType produces the type "integer."[2] The macrosemantics of integer variable declarations can thus be expressed by defining the valuation function D:

```
semantic functions

    D : decl -> ENV -> (ENV * DACTION).
```

The valuation function D produces a pair consisting of a new environment and a declaration action. The environment can be viewed as the static component of the meaning of a declaration, whereas the action is the dynamic component.

The semantics of integer variable declarations, then, is defined as follows:

```
auxiliary functions

    notDeclared (id:ID, env:ENV) : BOOL = ((env id) = noneM).

    addAssoc (id:ID, mode:MODE, env:ENV) : ENV =
       ([id => mode] env).

semantic equations

    D [[ "int" id ]] env =
       if notDeclared (id, env) then
          let (* Obtain a semantic name *)
              varName = name (id).
              (* Construct the mode for the new variable *)
              mode = varM (varName, int_type).
              (* Add the new declaration to the environment *)
              newEnv = addAssoc (id, mode, env)
          in
              (newEnv, DeclSimpleVar (varName, IntType))
          end
       else
          declError env [[id]] "Identifier already declared.".
```

---

[2] This is somewhat imprecisely stated. It would be better to say that IntType *yields an action that* produces a semantic value corresponding to the type "integer." I ask the reader to tolerate this minor sloppiness.

Elaboration of a variable declaration proceeds by first performing a static semantic check to ensure that the variable has not already been declared within
the current block. Then, the identifier is coerced into a semantic name, and a
mode descriptor for the new variable is constructed. A new environment in
which the identifier is bound to the new mode is returned as static component
of the denotation. The dynamic-action component is obtained by applying the
DeclSimpleVar and IntType operators.

As was mentioned earlier, identifiers are not allowed as arguments to microsemantic operators. Instead, semantics names from the domain NAME are obtained
by applying the name primitive, and the names are then supplied to the operators. NAME thus serves as the cross-over point between the static and dynamic
meanings of identifiers, and is the only predefined domain which is available in
both macrosemantic and microsemantic specifications. Conceptually, semantic
names refer to cells in an idealized store.

If the variable has already been declared, the auxiliary function declError
is called on to handle the static semantic error. The syntactic construct of the
identifier, [[id]], and not the semantic identifier, id, is supplied to the error
routine since the syntactic construct contains lexical information which might be
useful for marking the exact point of the error.

The semantics of references to variables can now be defined as follows:

```
operators

    (* Produce the L-value of the named variable *)
    Var : NAME * TACTION -> VACTION.

    (* Coerce the L-value into an R-value *)
    Rvalue : VACTION -> VACTION.

auxiliary functions

    typeAction (t:TYPE) : TACTION =
      case t of int_type  => IntType |
                bool_type => BoolType.

    lookup (id:ID, env:ENV) : MODE = env id.

semantic functions

    L : expr -> ENV -> (TYPE * VACTION);  (* L-values *)
    E : expr -> ENV -> (TYPE * VACTION);  (* R-values *)
```

```
semantic equations

  L [[ id ]] env =
    case lookup (id, env) of
      noneM =>
        exprError [[id]] "Variable not declared." |
      varM (varName, t) =>
        (t, Var (varName, typeAction t)) |
      _ =>
        exprError [[id]] "Object cannot be assigned.".


  E [[ id ]] env =
    case lookup (id, env) of
      constM (n) => (int_type, Integer (n)) |
      _ => let (t, lA) = L [[ ... ]] env in
              (t, Rvalue (lA))
           end.
```

Variables may be referenced in either L-value or R-value contexts. The corresponding denotations are provided by the valuation functions L and E, respectively. In the equation for L, application of the `lookup` function obtains the mode of the identifier. If a variable mode is found, the `Var` operator is used to produce the variable's L-value. For R-value contexts, the `Rvalue` operator yields an action which coerces an L-value into an R-value.

There is a complete absence of model-dependent details, in particular stores and locations, in the semantics. Instead of locations, identifiers are mapped onto semantic names in the macrosemantics, and from these the microsemantic operators derive L-values. This is analogous to what happens in a realistic compiler. For example, a Pascal compiler maps identifiers to textual addresses consisting of a block number and offset. Then, at runtime, the textual addresses are mapped to particular storage locations, typically via a display mechanism.

Deriving POTs from programs

Before the meanings of entire programs can be considered, the imperative actions must be introduced.

```
action domains

  IACTION = imperative actions
```

Imperative actions produce no values, but simply have an effect on the state of a program. Now, the valuation function P, which provides denotations for HypoPL programs, can be given.

```
operators

   (* Open the input and output files, then do the action *)
   Prog : STRING * STRING * IACTION -> IACTION.

   (* Establish bindings for the action *)
   Block : DACTION * IACTION -> IACTION.

abstract syntax

   prog -> "program" id "(" string1 "," string2 ")" "is" block.

   block -> decl "begin" stmt "end".

auxiliary functions

   emptyEnv : ENV = fn id. noneM.

semantic functions

   P : prog -> OUTPUTFILE.        (* programs *)
   B : block -> ENV -> IACTION.   (* blocks *)

semantic equations

   P [[ "program" id "(" string1 "," string2 ")" "is"
          block ]] =
     let programBody = B [[ block ]] emptyEnv in
        execute (
           Prog (string1, string2, programBody) )
     end.

   B [[ decl "begin" stmt "end" ]] env =
     let (env', dAs) = D [[ decl ]] env in
        Block (dAs, S [[ stmt ]] env')
     end.
```

The Prog operator controls the execution of a program. It yields an action which first opens the specified input and output files, and then performs the given imperative action. Finally, it performs whatever "clean up" action is necessary, for instance closing the files.

Every microsemantic specification must define a function called `execute`:

```
execute : IACTION -> OUTPUTFILE.
```

This function is used by the macrosemantics to coerce imperative actions (or whatever type of action is appropriate for program meanings) into program answers, which in this case are output files. Conceptually, `execute` triggers the execution of an imperative action. We will discuss the `execute` function in more detail in the next section.

A few more semantic equations, and then we will have enough to be able to step through the derivation of the meaning of a program.

```
operators

    (* Perform the imperative actions in sequence *)
    StmtSeq : IACTION * IACTION -> IACTION.

    (* Do nothing *)
    NullStmt : IACTION.

    (* Assign the R-value (produced by the second action) to
       the L-value (produced by the first action *)
    Assign : VACTION * VACTION -> IACTION.

abstract syntax

    stmt -> stmt1 ";" stmt2 |
            expr1 ":=" expr2.

semantic functions

    S : stmt -> ENV -> IACTION.          (* statements *)

semantic equations

    S [[ stmt1 ";" stmt2 ]] env =
       StmtSeq (S [[ stmt1 ]] env, S [[ stmt2 ]] env).

    S [[ ]] env = NullStmt.

    S [[ expr1 ":=" expr2 ]] env =
       let (ltype, lA) = L [[ expr1 ]] env
       and (rtype, rA) = E [[ expr2 ]] env
       in
```

```
            if ltype = rtype then Assign (lA, rA)
            else stmtError [[ expr1 ]]
                           "Type mismatch in assignment."
     end.
```

These equations specify the macrosemantics of statement sequences and assignments. Now, we can consider the meaning of the following HypoPL program:

```
program example ("stdin", "stdout") is
int a;
begin
    a := 1;
    a := a + 2
end;
```

First, the valuation function P must be applied to the entire program:

```
P [[ program example ("stdin", "stdout) is
        int a; begin a := 1; a := a + 2 end ]]
```

Expansion of P results in the following expression·

```
lct programBody =
    B [[ int a; begin a :- 1; a :- a + 2 end ]] emptyEnv
in
    exccute (
        Prog ("stdin", "stdout", programBody) )
end.
```

Prog is a microsemantic operator whose interpretation is as yet unspecified.
Hence, it must be treated as an irreducible entity. (Note that exccute, although
not an operator, is also irreducible since it too is defined in the microsemantics.)
The next step in the evaluation is therefore the application of B:

```
let programBody =
    let (env', dAs) = D [[ int a ]] emptyEnv in
        Block (dAs, S [[ a := 1; a := a + 2 ]] env')
    end
in
    execute (
        Prog ("stdin", "stdout", programBody) )
end.
```

Again, Block can not be reduced since it is an operator. Application of the
valuation function D expands into

```
let programBody =
   let (env', dAs) =
      if notDeclared (*a*, emptyEnv) then
         let varName = name (*a*).
             mode = varM (varName, int_type).
             newEnv = addAssoc (*a*, mode, emptyEnv)
         in
             (newEnv, DeclSimpleVar (varName, IntType))
         end
      else declError env [[a]]
                    "Identifier already declared."
   in
      Block (dAs, S [[ a := 1; a := a + 2 ]] env')
   end
in
   execute (
      Prog ("stdin", "stdout", programBody) )
end.
```

and this can then be reduced to

```
execute (
   Prog (
      "stdin", "stdout",
      Block (
         DeclSimpleVar (a, IntType),
         S [[ a := 1; a := a + 2 ]] newEnv ) ) )
```

where *a* is the semantic name yielded by the application of name to *a* and *newEnv* is an environment which maps the syntactic identifier *a* to its mode:

```
[*a* => varM (a, int_type)] (fn id. noneM)
```

A considerable amount of simplification has taken place, but once again the application of a microsemantic operator, in this case DeclSimpleVar, cannot be reduced.

Finally, expansion of the application of S and complete reduction results in the following:

```
execute (
   Prog (
      "stdin", "stdout",
      Block (
```

```
DeclSimpleVar (a, IntType),
StmtSeq (
   Assign (Var (a, IntType), Integer 1),
   StmtSeq
      Assign (Var (a, IntType),
               Add (Rvalue (Var (a, IntType)),
                     Integer 2) )
      NullStmt) ) ) )
```

This final term consists solely of microsemantic operators and basic semantic values. Because it resembles a prefix-form tree, I call it a *prefix-form operator term*, or POT. This POT represents the model-independent meaning of the program. Semantic model details still need to be supplied in order to define the meanings of the operators in a microsemantics, but this can be done without disturbing the macrosemantics thus far developed.

Implications for compiler generation

As was the case with classical compiler generation, deriving the meaning of a program corresponds to the process of compilation. However, efficient implementation of this process is relatively straightforward. This is due to two characteristics of high-level specifications. First, since the specifications preserve both separability and the distinction between static and dynamic language components, a partial evaluator is not needed for semantic evaluation. After each expansion of an application of a semantic valuation function, a complete reduction of the resultant term can be performed. Second, separability brings about a drastic reduction in the number of anonymous λ-expressions appearing in the semantics. This causes a corresponding reduction in the number of closures which must be handled during evaluation of the semantics.

The net result of these two characteristics is that the derivation of POTs from high-level descriptions can be implemented very efficiently. Realistic implementation structures are exposed by preserving semantic distinctions that are normally blurred in traditional denotational semantics, and also by avoiding over-specification. In fact, since POTs can be easily written in prefix form, it is possible to regard them as a prefix-form intermediate representation to be processed by an automatically generated code generator. We shall see in the next two chapters that object programs can be generated from POTs that are remarkably competitive with object programs produced by hand-crafted compilers.

5.3   The Microsemantics

An interpretation for the semantic algebra is provided by a microsemantics. By *interpretation*, I mean quite literally that a microsemantics provides a direct means for "executing" a POT. A variety of styles of specification are possible. For example, following Mosses' abstract semantic algebra approach, the behavior the operators can be defined equationally. Since equational specifications are not presently suitable as a basis for automatic implementation, I prefer to write microsemantic specifications in one of the styles depicted in Figure 5.1 (page 70): (1) as a λ-calculus-based definition, (2) as an abstract machine definition, or (3) as a (formally specified) code generator definition.

Appendix C gives examples of microsemantic specifications in each of these styles. This section presents excerpts of these specifications.

The structure of high-level specifications

We have already seen that macrosemantic specifications are structurally similar to denotational specifications. The main difference is that a macrosemantics has two additional sections for specifying the signature of the semantic algebra: `action domains` and `operators`. The former declares the names of the action domains, whereas the latter defines the names and functionalities of the operators.

Microsemantic specifications also have `action domains` and `operators` sections, except that here the structure of the action domains and operators must be defined completely. The signature specified in the macrosemantics must be compatible with the signature defined by the microsemantics.

The λ-calculus-based specification of microsemantics

A microsemantics can be specified in terms of the λ-calculus, using standard denotational models. First, the dynamic semantic domains are defined.

```
semantic domains

    DENV = STORE * INPUTFILE * ANSWER.

    STORE = NAME -> DEN.

    DEN = union noValue |
                intValue of INT |
                boolValue of BOOL.
```

```
EV = union lval of NAME | rval of DEN.

TYPE = union intT | boolT.

CONT  = DENV -> ANSWER.     (* Command continuations *)
DCONT = CONT.               (* Declaration continuations *)
ECONT = EV -> CONT.         (* Expression continuations *)

ANSWER = OUTPUTFILE.
```

Loosely speaking, an action transforms a given semantic context into a new context. Here, the semantic context is modeled by continuations. Semantic names are bound to their runtime denotations in a dynamic environment, which serves essentially the same purpose as the store in a traditional denotational semantics.

The action domains are defined as follows:

```
action domains

IACTION = CONT -> CONT;    (* Imperative actions *)
DACTION = DCONT -> CONT;   (* Declarative actions *)
VACTION = ECONT -> CONT;   (* Value-producing actions *)
TACTION - TYPE;            (* Type-producing actions *)
```

As was mentioned earlier, every microsemantic specification must define an auxiliary function called execute. The purpose of execute is to "wrap up" a semantics by coercing an action into an answer, in essence triggering the execution of a POT. With continuations, this is defined as follows:

```
auxiliary functions

(* The final continuation *)
val finalCont : CONT =
   fn (_, _, answer):DENV. close_output answer.

(* The initial dynamic environment *)
val initialDenv : DENV = (fn name. noValue,
                          bottom:INPUTFILE,
                          bottom:OUTPUTFILE).

(* The mandatory "execute" function *)
execute (program:IACTION) : ANSWER =
   program finalCont initialDenv.
```

Finally, the operators can be defined. A few examples are presented below:

```
auxiliary functions

   getDen (name:NAME, (store, _, _):DENV) : DEN =
      store (name).

   update (lv:LVALUE, rv:DEN, (store, i, a):DENV) : DENV =
      ([lv => rv]store, i, a).

operators

   Integer: INT -> VACTION is
   Integer (n) = fn econt. econt (rval (intValue n)).

   Add : VACTION * VACTION -> VACTION is
   Add (vA1, vA2) = fn econt.
      vA1 { fn (rval (intValue v1)).
         vA2 { fn (rval (intValue v2)).
            econt (rval (intValue (v1 + v2))) } }.

   DeclSimpleVar : NAME * TACTION -> DACTION is
   DeclSimpleVar (_, _) = fn dcont. dcont.

   IntType : TACTION is
   IntType = intT.

   Var : NAME * TACTION -> VACTION is
   Var (name, _) = fn econt. econt (lval name).

   Rvalue : VACTION -> VACTION is
   Rvalue (vA) = fn econt.
      vA { fn (lval lv).
         { fn denv.
            econt (rval (getDen (lv, denv))) denv } }.

   Block : DACTION * IACTION -> IACTION is
   Block (declA, bodyA) = fn cont.
      declA { fn denv. bodyA cont denv }.

   StmtSeq : IACTION * IACTION -> IACTION is
   StmtSeq (iA1, iA2) = fn cont. iA1 ; iA2 ; cont.

   NullStmt : IACTION is
   NullStmt cont = cont.
```

```
Assign : VACTION * VACTION -> IACTION is
Assign (lA, rA) = fn cont.
    lA { fn (lval lv).
      rA { fn (rval rv).
         { fn denv. cont (update (lv, rv, denv)) } } }.
```

A POT can be viewed as an expression in ML. (See for instance the POT on page 84.) In this case, the operators are simply ML functions. This is akin to Watt's strategy of directly implementing abstract semantic algebras [Watt 84]. The complete continuation-style microsemantics, as well as an equivalent specification written in the direct style, are given in Appendix C.

This microsemantics employs standard denotational models. The dynamic environment, for instance, is the traditional store. Type information is completely ignored in the DeclSimpleVar and Var operations. DeclSimpleVar is essentially a no-op, as the semantic name is used directly as the "location" of a variable.

The composition of the HypoPL macrosemantics with this microsemantic specification can be viewed as a well-engineered traditional denotational specification. Just as with denotational semantics, λ-calculus-based microsemantic specifications can be written in a more implementation-oriented manner, perhaps by using stack semantic models [Milne & Strachey 76]. The problem of demonstrating the congruence of the different semantic descriptions is now somewhat simplified by the fact that those portions of the semantics that depend on the stack models are encapsulated in the microsemantics.

The abstract machine specification of microsemantics

Another approach to microsemantic specification is to provide an abstract machine which is able to interpret the POTs. The composition of the macrosemantics with such a machine is then an operational semantics for the language.

If the POT of page 84 is written as an s-expression,

```
(execute
  (Prog "stdin" "stdout"
    (Block (DeclSimpleVar a0 (IntType))
           (StmtSeq
              (Assign (Var a0 (IntType)) (Integer 1))
              (StmtSeq
                (Assign (Var a0 (IntType))
                        (Add (Rval (Var a0 (IntType)))
                             (Integer 2)))
                (NullStmt))))))
```

then it becomes clear that we can write a Lisp or Scheme program to interpret
POTs. Such a program might take the following form:

```
(define (am pot)
  (case (car pot)
    (Integer
      (cadr pot))
    (Add
      (+ (am (cadr pot)) (am (caddr pot))))
    (DeclSimpleVar
      (begin
        (vector-set! *map* (hash (cadr pot)) *next-free*)
        (set! *next-free* (1+ *next-free*))))
    (IntType
      nil)
    (Var
      (vector-ref *map* (hash (cadr pot))))
    (Rvalue
      (vector-ref *memory* (am (cadr pot))))
    ((Block StmtSeq)
      (begin (am (cadr pot)) (am (caddr pot))))
    (NullStmt
      nil)
    (Assign
      (vector-set! *memory* (am (cadr pot))
                   (am (caddr pot))))

    ... ))


(define *memory* (vector 1000 'uninitialized))
(define *map* (vector 1000 'free))
(define *next-free* 0)

(define (hash name) ...)
```

This abstract machine conducts a recursive traversal of a POT during interpretation. Semantic names are hashed by the function `hash` into a memory map,
`*map*`, which then gives an index into the storage structure, `*memory*`. (For illustrative purposes, I have assumed that the hash function is perfect.) Using a
vector instead of a closure to represent the store allows the abstract machine to
be considerably more efficient than the λ-calculus-based microsemantic specifications.

Another way to write an abstract machine interpreter in Scheme is to define a
function or macro for each microsemantic operator.

```
(define (Integer n) n)

(define (Add v1 v2) (+ v1 v2))

(define (DeclSimpleVar name type)
  (begin
    (vector-set! *map* (hash name) *next-free*)
    (set! *next-free* (1+ *next-free*)))))

(define (IntType) nil)

(define (Var name type)
  (vector-ref *map* (hash name)))

(define (Rvalue loc)
  (vector-ref *memory* loc)

(macro Block
  (lambda (e)
    (let ((decl (cadr e))
          (body (caddr e)))
      `(begin
         ,decl
         ,body))))

(alias StmtSeq Block)

(define (NullStmt) nil)

(define (Assign lhs rhs)
  (vector-set! *memory* lhs rhs))
```

With this abstract machine, the POT is itself treated as a Scheme program rather than a data structure to be interpreted. Notice the use of a macro to define the Block and StmtSeq operators. The order of argument evaluation is not specified in Scheme, and so a macro must be used to ensure that the sub-POTs are interpreted in the correct order.

The third microsemantic specification given in Appendix C is a complete abstract machine written in this style.

The code generator specification of microsemantics

The fact that a POT is in prefix form allows it to be viewed as the intermediate representation for a program, which can then be processed by a table-driven code generator in order to produce machine code. The fourth microsemantic specification in Appendix C exploits this fact. The operators in the semantic algebra are taken as templates of intermediate code which are translated into assembly code for the Intel iAPX8086 microprocessor.

The code generator allocates registers on a statement-by-statement basis, with all expression values computed in register **ax** and all L-values computed in register **bx**. Registers **cx**, **si**, and **di** are used as a stack for spilling the contents of **ax**, and when these are all in use, **ax** is spilled onto the machine stack. Throughout the code generator specification, special cases are checked in order to avoid extraneous move instructions.

This simple code generation model turns out to be sufficient for generating code that compares favorably with the code produced by handwritten compilers. Compared to the intermediate representations typically employed by handwritten compilers, the operators appearing in the POTs are relatively high level and expressive. It appears that this is conducive to the generation of high-quality machine code.

Towards a standard semantic algebra

The combination of a macrosemantics with a microsemantics constitutes a complete description of the semantics of a programming language. However, I advocate a methodology for semantic description in which languages are defined by combining a macrosemantics with a *collection* of compatible microsemantic specifications. This high-level approach provides several advantages. First, it imposes a discipline which forces the semanticist or language designer to think in terms of fundamental language concepts rather than low-level modeling tricks. Second, the resulting language definitions become more useful and usable. For most purposes, the macrosemantics provides a suitable standard of reference. When more detailed information is needed, the most appropriate form of microsemantic specification can be selected for study. Third, having a collection of microsemantic definitions affords a great deal of flexibility in choosing an efficient implementation strategy.

Unfortunately, this flexibility does not come without cost—the congruence between the various microsemantic definitions must be established by manual methods. This is a severe problem, but can be greatly simplified if a standard set of operators which are useful for a large class of programming languages is developed. Then, a proof of congruence need be made only once. This is essentially a semantics-based approach to the so-called "universal compiling language," or UNCOL, problem.

The semantic algebra presented here attempts to capture the fundamental concepts embodied by sequential, Algol-like languages. I have chosen operators that maintain important semantic distinctions, while at the same time avoiding overspecification. I believe that operators chosen by these criteria result in more descriptive semantic specifications, and also allow for efficient implementation.

5.4 Extending High-Level Semantic Specifications

In traditional denotational semantics, the addition of a new language feature often requires a complete reformulation of the semantics. For example, in a traditional, direct-style semantics for HypoPL, the addition of escapes from loops causes the entire specification to be rewritten. In a high-level semantics such extensions require only the addition of new equations to the macrosemantics. All other changes are isolated in the microsemantics.

In some cases, the addition of a language feature does not cause a wholesale reformulation of the semantics, but merely an extension. For example, adding escapes from loops to a continuation-style denotational semantics requires revision of only a subset of the semantic equations. Unfortunately, it is often difficult to identify those equations needing modification. In a continuation-style microsemantic specification, identifying the operators which must be changed in order to support the new language feature is much easier.

Adding escapes from loops

As a first example of language extension, consider the task of adding escapes from loops to the macrosemantics and continuation-style microsemantics for HypoPL. First the macrosemantics of **while** loops:

```
S [[ "while" expr "do" stmt ]] env =
    let (t, vA) = E [[ expr ]] env in
        case t of
            boolType => While (vA, S [[ stmt ]] env) |
            _ => stmtError [[ expr ]]
                        "WHILE expression must be Boolean."
    end.
```

The `While` operator represents the standard looping action:

```
While : VACTION * IACTION -> IACTION is
While (testA, bodyA) = fn cont.
   testA { fn (rval (boolValue testVal)).
      if testVal then bodyA { While (testA, bodyA) cont }
      else cont }.
```

The macrosemantics of loop escapes is given as follows:

```
S [[ "exit" ]] env = Exit.
S [[ "continue" ]] env = Continue.
```

The meaning of an `exit` statement is simply the imperative action generated by the `Exit` operator. Similarly, the meaning of the `continue` statement is the `Continue` action. To model these features in the microsemantics, a new "loop label" environment, LENV must be introduced:

```
semantic domains

    LENV = LOOP_LABEL -> CONT.
    LOOP_LABEL = union noLabel | loopTop | loopBottom.
```

Loop environments map the labels `loopTop` and `loopBottom` to continuations which represent the entry and exit points of loops. Then, the structure of imperative actions is changed as follows:

```
action domains

    IACTION = LENV -> CONT -> CONT;
```

This of course affects the `While` operator, which must now be defined as follows:

```
While : VACTION * IACTION -> IACTION is
While (testA, bodyA) = fn lenv. fn cont.
   testA { fn (rval (boolValue testVal)).
      let loop = While (testA, bodyA) lenv in
         if testVal then
            bodyA ([loopExit => cont]
                   [loopTop => loop cont] lenv)
                  (loop cont)
         else cont
      end }.
```

Here, the body action for the loop, bodyA, is applied to a loop environment in which loopExit has been bound to the exit continuation, and loopTop to the continuation representing the next iteration of the loop. The Exit and Continue operators can thus be defined as follows:

```
Exit : IACTION is
Exit = fn lenv. fn cont. lenv loopExit.

Continue : IACTION is
Continue = fn lenv. fn cont. lenv loopTop.
```

What else in the microsemantics needs to be rewritten? Since only the IACTION domain has been changed, only those operators dealing with imperative actions need modification. These operators are easy to identify since their functionalities are explicitly declared. From the excerpt on page 87, only the following modifications are necessary:

```
Block : DACTION * IACTION -> IACTION is
Block (declA, bodyA) = fn lenv. fn cont.
    declA { fn denv. bodyA lenv cont denv } }.

StmtSeq : IACTION * IACTION -> IACTION is
StmtSeq (iA1, iA2) = fn lenv. fn cont.
    iA1 lenv ; iA2 lenv ; cont.

NullStmt : IACTION is
NullStmt lenv cont = cont.

Assign : VACTION * VACTION -> IACTION is
Assign (lA, rA) = fn lenv. fn cont.
    lA { fn (lval lv).
       rA { fn (rval rv).
          { fn denv. cont (update (lv, rv, denv)) } } }.
```

In general, the only operators requiring modification are those that deal with the semantic domains affected by the extension.

The static semantics of loop escapes

So far, the static semantics of loop escapes has been ignored. However, **exit** and **continue** statements must occur only within the body of a loop. There are a number of ways to add this static semantic check to the macrosemantics. One way is to add an "in-loop flag" to the static environment:

```
ENV    = ASSOC * INLOOP.
ASSOC  = ID -> MODE.
INLOOP = BOOL.
```

Within the body of a loop, the current environment has this flag set to true. The loop semantics can then be written as follows:

```
S [[ "while" expr "do" stmt ]] env =
   let (t, vA) = E [[ expr ]] env in
      case t of
         boolType =>
            let (assoc, _) = env.
                loopEnv = (assoc, true)
            in
               While (vA, S [[ stmt ]] loopEnv)
            end |
         _ =>
            stmtError [[ expr ]]
                       "WHILE expression must be Boolean."
   end.

C [[ "exit" ]] env =
   let (_, inLoop) = env in
      if inLoop then Exit
      else stmtError [[...]] "EXIT outside of loop."
   end.

C [[ "continue" ]] env =
   let (_, inLoop) = env in
      if inLoop then Continue
      else stmtError [[...]] "CONTINUE outside of loop."
   end.
```

The other semantic equations that depend on the structure the environment must also be changed to accomodate the addition of the new flag. In HypoPL, this includes just the equations describing the semantics of variable declarations.

Adding arrays

Adding new data structures to a language in high-level semantics is also straight-forward. As an example, consider the addition of one-dimensional, zero-based arrays to HypoPL. To do this, the macrosemantics must be extended with array modes.

```
semantic domains

    MODE = union noneM |
                constM of CONST |
                varM of VAR |
                arrayM of ARRAY.

    ARRAY = NAME * UPPERBOUND.
    UPPERBOUND = INT.
```

The static denotation for an array consists of the array's semantic name and upper index bound.

Declaration of integer arrays is handled in the following manner:

```
operators

    (* Bind the array, with the given index bounds, in the
       dynamic environment. *)
    DeclArrayVar: NAME * UPPERBOUND list * TACTION -> DACTION.

semantic equations

    D [[ "array" id "[" int "]" ]] env =
        if notDeclared (id, env) then
            let arrayName = name (id).
                mode = arrayM (arrayName, int).
                newEnv = addAssoc (id, mode, env)
            in
                (newEnv, DeclArrayVar (arrayName, [ub], IntType))
            end
        else
            declError env ast "Identifier already declared.".
```

The name of the array is bound to a static array denotation in the environment, and the DeclArrayVar operator is then used to specify the creation of the new array. Notice that this operator takes a *list* of upper bounds—hence it handles multidimensional arrays even though they aren't allowed in HypoPL. In this case, the restriction to one dimension is imposed by the macrosemantics of HypoPL.

References to arrays can now be specified as follows:

```
operators

    (* Produce the L-value of the array with the given name,
       upper bounds, and element type. *)
    Array : NAME * VACTION * TACTION -> VACTION.

    (* Build a sequence of values from the two value actions *)
    ExprSeq : VACTION * VACTION -> VACTION.

    (* The null value action *)
    NullExpr : VACTION.

    (* Produce the L-value of the array element from the given
       array L-value and sequence of index values. *)
    Index : VACTION * VACTION -> VACTION.

semantic equations

    L [[ id "[" expr "]" ]] env =
       case lookup (id, env) of
          arrayM (arrayName, ub, _) =>
             let
                (* Elaborate the index expression action *)
                (t, vA) = E [[ expr ]] env.

                (* Build the array L-value action *)
                arrayAction =
                   Array (arrayName,
                          ExprSeq (Integer ub, NullExpr),
                          IntType).

                (* Build the array subscripting action *)
                subscriptAction = ExprSeq (vA, NullExpr)
             in
                ( int_type,
                  Index (arrayAction, subscriptAction) )
             end |

           _ => exprError [[ id ]] "Illegal array reference.".

    E [[ id "[" expr "]" ]] env =
       let (t, lA) = L [[ ... ]] env in
          (t, Rvalue (lA))
       end.
```

As with `DeclArrayVar`, the microsemantic operators `Array` and `Index` handle multidimensional arrays. Thus, sequences of value actions must be constructed via the `ExprSeq` operator in order to index an array. Interpretations for these new operators can be added to the microsemantics by adding denotations for value sequences and arrays:

```
DEN = union noValue |
            intValue of INT |
            boolValue of BOOL |
            seqValue of DEN list |
            arrayValue of ARRAY.

ARRAY = INT -> EV.

EV = union lvalue of LVALUE | rvalue of DEN.

LVALUE = union simple of NAME | index of NAME * INT.
```

The new denotation, `arrayValue`, models arrays as mappings from integers to expressible values. Also, the structure of L-values is augmented by an array index, modeled by a pair consisting of an array name and the index value. The operators are defined as follows:

```
NullExpr : VACTION is
NullExpr econt = econt (rval (seqValue nil)).

ExprSeq : VACTION * VACTION -> VACTION is
ExprSeq (vA, vAs) = fn econt.
   vA { fn (rval value).
      vAs { fn (seqValue values).
         econt (rval (seqValue (value :: values))) } }.

DeclArrayVar : NAME * INT list * TACTION -> DACTION is
DeclArrayVar (name, _, _) = fn dcont. { fn denv.
   dcont ([name => arrayValue (fn i. noValue)] denv) }.

Array : NAME * VACTION * TACTION -> VACTION is
Array (name, _, _) = fn econt. econt (lval (simple name)).

Index : VACTION * VACTION -> VACTION is
Index (arrayA, idxAs) = fn econt.
   arrayA { fn (lval (simple name)).
      vAs { fn (rval (seqValue (intValue idx :: _))).
         econt (lval (index (name, idx))) } }.
```

The `DeclArrayVar` operator binds the name to an array denotation with all array elements initialized to `noValue`. Notice that in both `DeclArrayVar` and `Array` the upperbound is ignored since there is no real allocation of storage—arrays are modeled by functions. In the definition of the `Index` operator, we can see the construction of the indexing L-value.

Since the structure of L-values has changed, all operators dealing with L-values must be modified.

```
Var : NAME * TACTION -> VACTION is
Var (name, _) = fn econt.
   { fn denv. econt (lval (simple name)) }.

Rvalue : VACTION -> VACTION is
Rvalue (lA) = fn econt. { fn denv.
   lA { fn lval.
      case lval of
         simple (name) =>
            econt (rval (denv name)) denv |
         index (name, idx) =>
            let arrayValue (array) = denv name in
               econt (rval (array idx)) denv
            end } }.

Assign : VACTION * VACTION -> IACTION is
Assign (lA, rA) = fn cont. { fn denv.
   lA { lval.
      rA { fn (rval v).
         case lval of
            simple (name) =>
               cont ([name => v] denv) |
            index (name, idx) =>
               let arrayValue (array) = denv name.
                  newArray = arrayValue ([idx => v] array)
               in
                  cont ([name => newArray] denv)
               end } } }.
```

As was the case with adding loop escapes, those portions of the macrosemantics and microsemantics requiring modification due to the addition of arrays are easy to find.

Adding procedures

As a last extension, recursive procedures with a single integer value parameter will be added to HypoPL. First of all, a new mode for procedures has to be added to the macrosemantics. This, along with some restructuring of the modes for variables and arrays, is reflected in the following domain definitions:

```
semantic domains

   MODE = union noneM |
                constM of CONST |
                varM of VAR |
                procM of (NAME * NAME) |
                paramM of PARAM.

   CONST = INT.
   VAR = NAME * TYPE.

   TYPE = union simpleT of SIMPLE_TYPE |
                arrayT of UPPERBOUND.

   SIMPLE_TYPE = union int_type | bool_type.

   UPPERBOUND = INT.

   PARAM = VAR.
```

Procedure modes contain the semantic names assigned to the procedure and its formal parameter (which is restricted to be an integer value parameter). Separate modes are specified for variables (varM) and formal parameters (paramM). This serves to preserve the distinction between these two kinds of variables.

   Procedures also introduce local scopes, and so the structure of environments must be changed to reflect this.

```
   ENV = ASSOC * LEVEL * INLOOP.

   ASSOC = ID -> (MODE * LEVEL).

   LEVEL = union global_L | local_L.
```

Environments now carry a value indicating the current scope level. (For the sake of simplicity, I have assumed two-level scoping, as in the C language.) In addition, a level indication is attached to each identifier in order to disambiguate between local and global versions of the same identifier.

The change to the environment means that some of the auxiliary functions need to be modified, as follows:

```
val emptyAssoc: ASSOC = fn id. (noneM, global_L).

val emptyEnv: ENV = (emptyAssoc, global_L, false).

lookup (id: ID, (assoc, currentlevel, _): ENV): MODE =
    let (mode, declLevel) = assoc id in
        if (declLevel = currentLevel) orelse
           (declLevel = global_L)
        then mode
        else noneM
    end.

notDeclared (id: ID, (assoc, currentLevel, _): ENV): BOOL =
    let (mode, declLevel) = assoc id in
        (mode = noneM) orelse (currentLevel <> declLevel)
    end.

addAssoc (id: ID, mode: MODE,
          (assoc, level, inloop): ENV): ENV =
    ([id => (mode, level)] assoc, level, inloop).

enterProc ((assoc, _, inloop): ENV): ENV =
    (assoc, local_L, inloop).
```

Finally, the macrosemantics of procedures can be given.

```
operators

    (* Retrieve the next procedure argument value and
     * bind it to the name *)
    BindValParam : NAME * TACTION -> DACTION.

    (* Bind the name to the procedure action *)
    BindProc : NAME * IACTION -> DACTION.

    (* Perform the parameter binding action, and then
     * the procedure body action. *)
    Proc : DACTION * IACTION -> IACTION.

    (* Call the named procedure with the given arguments. *)
    Call : NAME * VACTION -> IACTION.
```

```
    semantic equations

        D [[ "procedure" id1 "(" id2 ")" "is" block ]] env =
            if notDeclared (id1, env) then
                let
                    procName = name (id1).
                    paramName = alphaName (id2).

                    (* Build the action for the parameter *)
                    paramAction = BindValParam (paramName, IntType).

                    (* Build the environment for the body.
                     *
                     * The existing environment is extended with
                     * - the binding for the procedure identifier, and
                     * - the binding for the parameter identifier.
                     *
                     * Since the binding for the procedure identifier
                     * is visible inside the body, the procedure may
                     * be called recursively. *)
                    procMode = procM (procName, paramName).
                    paramMode = paramM (paramName, simpleT (int_type)).

                    procEnv = addAssoc (id1, procMode, env).
                    bodyEnv = addAssoc (id2, paramMode,
                                        (enterProc procEnv)).

                    (* Process the body *)
                    bodyAction = BR [[ block ]] bodyEnv
                in
                    ( procEnv,
                      BindProc (procName,
                                Proc (paramAction, bodyAction)) )
                end
            else
                declError env [[ id1 ]] "Procedure already declared.".
```

Procedure names are bound by a `BindProc` operation to an imperative action (produced by `Proc`) that binds the formal parameter to the actual argument value and then executes the body.

Identifiers declared in different procedures and scope levels must be mapped to distinct semantic names. A mapping of this nature is essentially an α-conversion which, in principle, can be accomplished by applying a function similar to Lisp's `gensym` function. Instead of `gensym`, the predefined function `alphaName` is used.

This function is thus similar to the name function described earlier, except that it guarantees the uniqueness of the generated name. The identifier argument allows semantic names to keep a close resemblance to the original syntactic identifiers; this is useful during experimentation and for instructional purposes.

In the semantic equation given above, alphaName is used to generate a unique semantic name for the formal parameter. Interestingly, the α-conversion of identifiers achieves lexical scoping in HypoPL. This is because identical syntactic identifiers declared in different blocks become bound to distinct semantic names in the environment. By merely changing the call to alphaName to a call to name, the name distinction between blocks is lost, thus resulting in dynamic scoping.

HypoPL is lexically scoped, and hence the semantic equations for the other kinds of declarations must be adjusted to carry out the α-conversions:

```
auxiliary functions

    declareVar (id: ID, t: TYPE, env: ENV, ast: AST)
              : (ENV * DACTION) =
      if notDeclared (id, env) then
        let name = alphaName (id).
            mode = varM (name, t).
            newEnv = addAssoc (id, mode, env)
        in
          case t of
            simpleT (st) =>
                (newEnv,
                 DeclSimpleVar (name, typeAction (st))) |
            arrayT (ub) =>
                (newEnv,
                 DeclArrayVar (name, [ub], IntType))
          end
      else declError env ast "Identifier already declared.".

semantic equations

    D [[ "int" id ]] env =
       declareVar (id, simpleT (int_type), env, [[ id ]]).

    D [[ "bool" id ]] env =
       declareVar (id, simpleT (bool_type), env, [[ id ]]).

    D [[ "array" id "[" int "]" ]] env =
       declareVar (id, arrayT (int), env, [[ id ]]).
```

Finally, an equation for procedure call completes the macrosemantics.

```
S [[ id "(" expr ")" ]] env =
    case lookup (id, env) of
        procM (name, _) =>
            let (t, vA) = E [[ expr ]] env in
                case t of
                    simpleT (int_type) =>
                        Call (name, ExprSeq (vA, NullExpr)) |
                    _ =>
                        stmtError [[ expr ]]
                                    "Argument must be Integer."
                end |
        _ =>
            stmtError [[ id ]] "Unknown procedure.".
```

The semantic name associated with the procedure is extracted from the environment and supplied to the microsemantic `Call` operator.

Modeling the new operators in the continuation-style microsemantics requires a extending the dynamic environment to account for the possibility of parameter passing and local variables.

```
semantic domains

    DENV = DENS * ARGS * INPUTFILE * ANSWER.

    DENS = STORE * ACTIVES.

    STORE = NAME -> DEN list.

    ARGS = DEN list.                (* Argument values *)

    DEN = union noValue |
                intValue of INT |
                boolValue of BOOL |
                seqValue of DEN list |
                arrayValue of ARRAY |
                procValue of PROC.

    PROC = IACTION.                 (* Procedure denotations *)

    ACTIVES = NAME list list.       (* Active names *)
```

Dynamic environments are extended in two ways. First, instead of a simple store, a structure consisting of a store and an active-name stack is maintained.

Names can now have multiple bindings since procedures may recurse, thereby creating new incarnations of the same name bindings. The store keeps track of all of the current bindings for each name. The "actives" stack keeps track of the currently active names. The top of the stack contains a list of the names allocated in the currently active procedure. When a procedure is entered, any names that are given new bindings are collected together in a list, which is then pushed onto the actives stack. When a return is executed, the bindings for the names on top of the stack are removed from the store, and then the stack is popped.

With these extensions, the operators can be defined as follows:

```
auxiliary functions

    bind (name:NAME, den:DEN) : DACTION =
        fn dcont.
            { fn ((store, active::prevActives), args, i, a):DENV.
                let denv = (* Add the binding for the name... *)
                        ( ( [name => den::(store name)]store,
                            (* ...and record the name as active *)
                            (name::active)::prevActives ),
                          args, i, a )
                in
                    dcont (denv:DENV)
                end }.

    unbind (names:NAME list, store:STORE) : STORE =
        case names of
            nil => store |
            name::rest =>
                unbind (rest, [name => tl (store name)]store).

    enterProc (cont:CONT) : CONT =
        fn ((store, actives), args, i, a):DENV.
            let procDenv = ((store, []::actives), args, i, a) in
                cont procDenv
            end.

    exitProc (cont:CONT) : CONT =
        fn ((store, active::prevActives), args, i, a):DENV.
            let prevDenv = ((unbind (active, store), prevActives),
                            args, i, a)
            in
                cont prevDenv
            end.
```

```
operators

    BindValParam : NAME * TACTION -> DACTION is
    BindValParam (name, _) = fn dcont.
        { fn (dens, argVal::restArgs, i, a):DENV.
            let denv = (dens, restArgs, i, a) in
                bind (name, argVal) dcont denv
            end }.

    BindProc : NAME * IACTION -> DACTION is
    BindProc (name, bodyA) = bind (name, procValue bodyA).

    Proc : DACTION * IACTION -> IACTION is
    Proc (paramA, bodyA) = fn lenv. fn cont.
        enterProc; paramA ; bodyA lenv; exitProc ; cont.

    Call : NAME * VACTION -> IACTION is
    Call (pname, argA) = fn lenv. fn cont.
        argA { fn (rval (seqValue args)).
            { fn (dens as (store, _), _, i, a):DENV.
                let procValue (procA) = hd (store pname).
                    denv = (dens, args, i, a)
                in
                    procA lenv cont denv
                end } }.
```

During a procedure call, a sequence of argument values is placed into the dynamic environment. The `BindValParam` action component of the procedure then retrieves the values and binds them to the formal parameters. Like the array operators, `Call` and `BindValParam` handle procedures with multiple arguments. The restriction to a single parameter is enforced by the macrosemantics (actually, the syntax) of HypoPL.

Since the structure of dynamic environments has changed, all operators that depend on this structure must be modified. In this example, the modifications are mainly confined to the auxiliary functions, as follows:

```
auxiliary functions

    val finalCont : CONT =
        fn (_, _, _, answer):DENV. close_output answer.
```

```
val initialDenv : DENV =
  ( ((fn name. [noValue]), [[]]),
    nil:ARGS,
    bottom:INPUTFILE,
    bottom:OUTPUTFILE ).

update (lv:LVALUE, rv:DEN,
        denv as ((store, actives), args, i, a):DENV): DENV =
  case lv of
    simple (name) =>
      ( ([name => rv::(tl (store name))]store, actives),
          args, i, a ) |
    arrayElt (name, idx) =>
      let arrayValue (array) = getDen (name, denv).
          newArray = arrayValue ([idx => rv] array)
      in
        ( ( [name => newArray::(tl (store name))]store,
            actives ),
          args, i, a )
      end.

operators

  Prog : STRING * STRING * IACTION -> IACTION is
  Prog (inFile, outFile, programA) = fn cont.
    { fn (initDens, _, _, _):DENV.
      let denv = (initDens,
                  [],
                  open_input inFile,
                  open_output outFile)
      in
        programA (cont:CONT) (denv:DENV)
      end }.

  DeclSimpleVar : NAME * TACTION -> DACTION is
  DeclSimpleVar (name, _) = bind (name, noValue).

  DeclArrayVar : NAME * INT list * TACTION -> DACTION is
  DeclArrayVar (name, _, _) =
    bind (name, arrayValue (fn i. noValue)).
```

Again, as was the case with arrays, those portions of the microsemantics requiring modification are easy to identify.

5.5 Summary

The high-level approach to semantic description overcomes the fundamental problems of traditional denotational semantics described in the previous chapter. In particular, high-level specifications preserve separability and can be easily extended.

The suitability of the high-level technique for realistic compiler specification is demonstrated by the MESS system, described in the next chapter.

6 The MESS System

The MESS[1] system generates compilers from high-level semantic descriptions. Figure 6.1 shows schematically how the system is structured. There are two major components, the front-end generator and the semantics analyzer. From a specification of the concrete syntax augmented with tree building rules (FE spec.), the front-end generator produces a compiler front-end (FE) that parses and builds abstract syntax trees for programs. In addition, a specification of the abstract syntax (AS spec.) is generated. This is used by the semantics analyzer to check the consistency of the abstract syntax expressions appearing in the front-end with those appearing in the macrosemantic specifications. The generated front-ends and the front-end generator itself are written in Pascal, using the Turbo Pascal implementation [Borland 85].

The semantics analyzer processes both the macrosemantic and microsemantic specifications. From a microsemantic specification, a Scheme program is generated which implements the semantic algebra, much in the same manner as the abstract machine shown on page 90. This program is called the microsemantics implementation (λ). A by-product of microsemantics analysis is the generation of a *microsemantics interface file* (Mi int.) which contains the names of the action domains and the names and functionalities of the operators, that is, a specification of the signature of the semantic algebra. A macrosemantic specification, along with a microsemantics interface file, is processed by the semantics analyzer in order to generate a compiler core (CC). The compiler core, which is also written in Scheme, translates abstract syntax trees into prefix-form operator terms (POTs). The semantics analyzer is itself written in Scheme, using the TI PC Scheme implementation [TI 85].

The combination of a front end and a compiler core constitutes a compiler that translates source programs into POTs. The POTs are written as Scheme s-expressions. Hence, they may be directly executed by the microsemantics implementation generated by the semantics analyzer. Alternatively, an abstract machine (AM), which can be conveniently written in Scheme, may be used. Finally, POTs may be processed by a code generator (CG) in order to obtain machine code. A number of techniques for the generation of code generators from formal specifications [Glanville & Graham 78, Ganapathi 80] may be used since the POTs are in a prefix format.

---

[1] The name, MESS, comes from the fact that high-level specifications are Modular, Extensible, and Separated Semantic specifications. Contrary to popular belief, the name has nothing to do with the current state of its implementation.

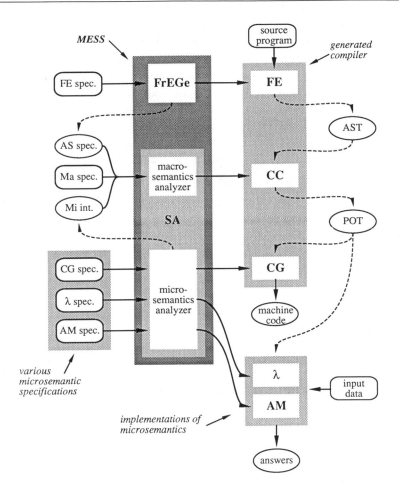

This schematic representation of MESS shows the various phases of compiler generation. The semantics analyzer (SA) processes the semantic specifications and from this generates the compiler core (CC). In addition, it produces an implementation of the microsemantic operators in a form corresponding to the type of microsemantics specified. If a code generator is produced, the combination of FE+CC+CG constitutes a realistic compiler.

Figure 6.1
The Big MESS

6.1   Comparison with Paulson's Semantics Processor

In order to make a direct performance comparison with another semantics-directed compiler generator, a continuation-style denotational specification was written in the form of a semantic grammar [Paulson 81], from which Paulson's Semantics Processor (PSP) [Paulson 82] could generate a compiler. The MESS system was likewise given the macrosemantic specification for HypoPL (shown in Appendix B) along with the continuation-style microsemantics (given in Appendix C). Figure 6.2 shows the results of the comparison, which are also discussed in [Lee & Pleban 87].

All timings are given in seconds, and were recorded on an IBM PC with an 8 MHz iAPX80286 processor, 640 kilobytes of random-access memory, and a hard disk with an average access time of approximately 65 milliseconds. Combined, the macrosemantic and microsemantic specifications processed by MESS are about 900 (well-commented) lines long, requiring approximately six man-hours to write and debug. The PSP specification is about 1100 lines long.

As the figure shows, MESS takes considerably longer to generate a HypoPL compiler than does PSP. The semantics analyzer for MESS executes in an implementation of Scheme that compiles to interpreted byte codes. Thus, MESS runs at least a factor of three slower than it might if it were compiled to native code. Still, the MESS-generated compiler is nearly 25 times faster than the PSP-generated compiler in compiling the HypoPL bubble-sort program shown in Appendix E.

For both the MESS-generated and PSP-generated compiler timings, some unnecessary I/O overhead time has been discounted. In particular, for the PSP-generated compiler, the time required for the universal translator to read the language description file was not counted. Of its 105 seconds of compile time, the PSP-generated compiler spends more than 66 seconds performing β-reductions. The MESS-generated compiler passes abstract syntax trees via disk files rather than in-memory structures. This is because there is currently no provision for direct data communication between Turbo Pascal and TI PC Scheme programs. The time required for the MESS-generated compiler core to read in the abstract syntax tree was not counted in its timing.

An exact comparison of the sizes of the target programs produced by the two compilers is difficult to make. The MESS-generated HypoPL compiler produces POTs, whereas the PSP-generated compiler produces SECD instructions. The third graph in Figure 6.2 compares the number of POT nodes with the number of SECD

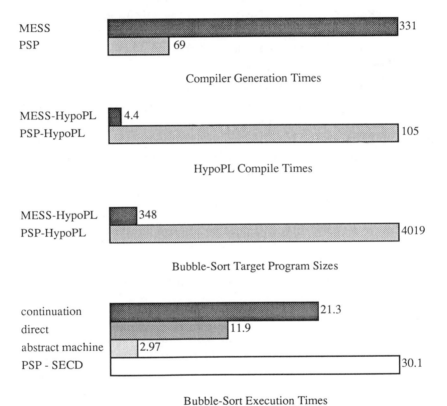

Figure 6.2
Performance Comparison Between MESS and PSP

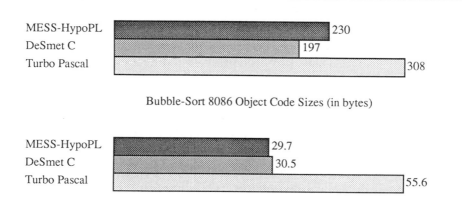

Figure 6.3
Performance Comparison Between MESS and Commercial Compilers

instructions generated for the bubble-sort program.

Finally, the last graph in Figure 6.2 compares execution times for the bubble-sort program. For these timings, the input value supplied to the program was 10. The graph shows that the implementation of the microsemantics compares well against the LISP SECD machine, both of which are executing similar, continuation-style specifications. The direct-style and abstract machine microsemantic implementations show correspondingly better timings.

The code generator specified at the end of Appendix C is able to translate the POTs produced by the MESS-generated HypoPL compiler into machine code for the Intel iAPX8086 processor (the central processing unit of the IBM PC). Figure 6.3 shows the comparison of the sizes and speeds of the object programs produced by the MESS-generated HypoPL compiler and two commercially available C and Pascal compilers. The C compiler is from DeSmet [DeSmet83], and the "Turbo" Pascal Compiler by Borland International [Borland 85]. The quality of the object code produced by the MESS-generated compiler compares well with the object codes produced by the commercial compilers.

6.2   Generating the Compiler

There are three basic steps in generating a compiler with the MESS system: specification of the microsyntax, syntax, and tree-building rules; specification of the
macrosemantics; and specification of the semantic algebra on which the macrosemantics is based.   These steps may be performed in any order, although one
normally starts by specifying the front end.   Besides a compiler front end, the
front-end generator produces a specification of the abstract syntax, which is necessary for macrosemantics processing.

In addition to the abstract syntax specification, MESS requires a microsemantics
interface file in order to process the macrosemantics. The file specifies the signature of the semantic algebra. MESS automatically generates this interface file
whenever it processes a microsemantic specification.   Alternatively, a microsemantics "stub" may be given. In such a stub, only the signature of the semantic
algebra is given, from which MESS can generate the microsemantics interface file,
but no implementation.

Once the microsemantics interface file is obtained, the macrosemantics can be
analyzed by MESS. This results in a compiler core written in Scheme. Excerpts
of the compiler core generated from the HypoPL macrosemantics are shown in
Appendix D. The fragment of the compiler that handles statement sequencing
is the following:

```
(|`STMT1 ";" STMT2|
  (APPLY
    (LAMBDA (!STMT1 !STMT2)
      (LAMBDA (!ENV)
        ((LAMBDA (!ENV)
           (LIST '!STMTSEQ
                 ((!S !STMT1) !ENV)
                 ((!S !STMT2) !ENV)))
         !ENV)))
    ARGS))
```

The name of the microsemantic operator, in this case !STMTSEQ (written before
as StmtSeq), is quoted—it is this quoting that prevents the evaluation of the
microsemantic operators at compile time, thereby making partial evaluation unnecessary.

6.3   Compiling Programs

Compilation of the HypoPL statement,

```
x(2) := 5;
```

proceeds as follows. First, the statement is translated into an abstract syntax tree by the front end. The trees are written as Scheme s-expressions:

```
(|LVAR ":=" EXPR|
  (|ID "[" EXPR "]"| (|ID| x) (|int| 2))
  (|int| 5))
```

This is then translated by the compiler core into the following POT:

```
(!ASSIGN
  (!INDEX (!ARRAY x
                  (!EXPRSEQ (!INTEGER 10) !NULLEXPR)
                  (!INTEGERTYPE)))
          (!EXPRSEQ (!INTEGER 2) !NULLEXPR))
  (!INTEGER 5))
```

where x is the semantic name given for the syntactic identifier x, and the upper-bound of the array is 10. The complete POT for the sort procedure in the HypoPL bubble-sort program is shown in Appendix E.

6.4   Executing the Compiled Programs

POTs can be executed in a number of ways. First, the Scheme implementation of the microsemantics generated by the MESS system can be used. Excerpts of the implementation derived from the continuation-style microsemantics are shown in the second half of Appendix D. The StmtSeq operator, for example, is translated by MESS into the following Scheme code:

```
(DEFINE !STMTSEQ
  (REC !STMTSEQ
    (LAMBDA (|v80| |v81|)
      (LET ((|v78| (LIST |v80| |v81|)))
        ((LAMBDA (|v79|)
          (LET ((!IA1 (CAR |v79|))
                (!IA2 (CADR |v79|)))
```

```
(LAMBDA (!CONT)
    (!IA1 (!IA2 !CONT)))))
|v78|))))))
```

Alternatively, one can write a program by hand that interprets the POTs, as I have done in the abstract machine program given in Appendix C. My handwritten version of the StmtSeq operator, written in Scheme, is as follows:

```
(macro !stmtseq
  (lambda (e)
    (let ((stmt1 (cadr e))
          (stmt2 (caddr e)))
      '(begin ,stmt1 ,stmt2))))
```

Finally, since the POTs are prefix-form expressions comprised solely of applications of operators, a formally specified code generator can be used to obtain machine code. The sample code generator specification shown in Appendix C translates the pot given above into the following iAPX8086 machine code. (Assume that subscript checking has been disabled, and that $x0$ defines the base address of the array.):

```
mov    ax, 2
shl    ax, 1
lea    bx, OFFSET x0
add    bx, ax
mov    WORD [bx], 5
```

Appendix E shows the iAPX8086 assembly code generated for the sort procedure in the HypoPL bubble-sort program.

7 | A SOL/C Compiler

As a nontrivial test of the MESS system, a high-level semantics for the programming language SOL/C was written and a compiler generated [Pleban & Lee 88]. SOL/C is a strongly typed, imperative language "sort of like C." It features two-level binding, recursive procedures with value and reference parameters, multidimensional arrays, integer, boolean, and character data types, arithmetic, relational, and boolean expressions, simple input and output, and the usual complement of control structures, including **goto**. Reference array parameters may be conformant, or "flexible."

Appendix G shows four sample Sol/C programs used for benchmarks.

The complete specification of SOL/C consists of a grammar, a macrosemantics, and a microsemantics. The grammar specifies the concrete syntax and abstract syntax tree-building rules, and is processed into a compiler front end (parser and tree builder). The grammar specification is approximately 600 lines long, 200 of which are either commentary or blank.

The complete macrosemantic specification for SOL/C is given in Appendix F. Fragments of the code generator specification of the microsemantics are given at the end of Appendix C. The macrosemantics is about 1,200 well-commented lines long. The code generator specification is by far the most involved microsemantics, as it describes the generation of machine code for the iAPX8086 processor. The other interpretations, such as the continuation-style microsemantics, are much simpler. In its entirety, the specification for the microsemantics consists of almost 300 functions, and is roughly 3,500 well-commented lines long (about 2,100 lines without comments). Almost 500 of the 3,500 lines deal with the vagaries of assembly code output.

7.1 The Generation of a Compiler for Sol/C

The front-end generator converts the Sol/C grammar into Pascal tables which are incorporated into a skeletal parser and tree builder. Front-end generation takes approximately 49 seconds. As before, all timings are given in seconds, and were taken on an IBM PC running with an 8 MHz iAPX80286 processor, 640 kilobytes of main memory, and a hard disk with an average access time of 65 milliseconds.

The MESS semantics analyzer takes 5 minutes and 45 seconds to produce a compiler core from the SOL/C macrosemantics. This includes roughly 53 seconds for parsing the specification and writing its syntax tree to a file. The microsemantics is converted into a code generator for the 8086 in roughly 16 minutes. This time includes about 2 minutes and 45 seconds for parsing the specification and writing its abstract syntax tree to a file.

7.2 Compilation of SOL/C Programs

The compiler core takes as input an abstract syntax tree generated by the front end, performs type checking, and converts it to a POT. (Recall from the previous chapter that the front end and the compiler core must communicate via a disk file because the front end (written in Pascal) does not have access to the Scheme heap.) The code generator then produces 8086 assembly code from the POT.

7.3 Performance Evaluation of the Compiler

For the performance evaluation, three compilers were compared on the following four benchmark programs:

fib:	compute the 22nd Fibonacci number 50 times
sort:	bubble sort 1000 numbers
sieve:	30 iterations of the sieve of Eratosthenes
matMult:	100 iterations of multiplying two 20x20 matrices

Listings of the SOL/C versions of these programs are given in Appendix G. As before, the two other compilers in the comparison are commercially available C and Pascal compilers from DeSmet [DeSmet83] and Borland International [Borland 85], respectively.

For the matrix multiplication program, the generated SOL/C compiler exhibits the following compile times:

parsing and tree building	0.95 secs
translation to POT	3.80 secs
code generation	11.95 secs
TOTAL	16.70 secs

The above times do not include the I/O overhead due to writing and reading the syntax tree. Recall that programs are compiled to interpreted byte codes by the Scheme system, which slows down the SOL/C compiler by at least a factor of three.

Figure 7.1 shows the object code sizes for the programs, as generated by the three compilers. Figure 7.2 compares the execution times.

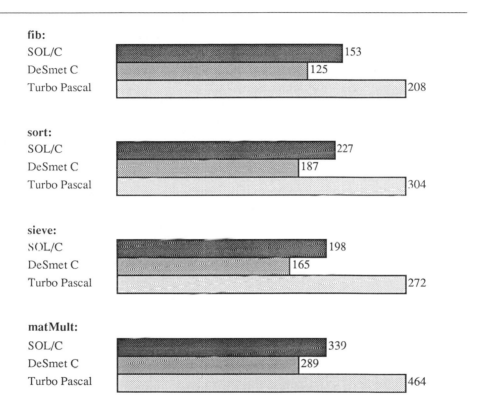

Figure 7.1
Object Code Sizes for the SOL/C Benchmark Programs

7.4 Correctness Concerns

The figures show that the performance characteristics of the SOL/C compiler compare quite favorably with those exhibited by the commercially available compilers. But is it provably correct with respect to the standard denotational semantics of SOL/C? Unfortunately, only the compiler core is. The correctness of the code generator would have to be established by a tedious congruence proof involving the microsemantics which defines the operators as higher order functions in the denotational style.

To do this, the code generator specification needs to be broken up into several passes, each of which implements a small set of transformations on the POT. For example, in a first pass, terms involving high level operators such as the `While` operator can be transformed into lower level terms involving labels and jumps. Such transformations are easy to validate with respect to a denotational interpretation of the `While` operator, as has been done in [Stoy 77], for example. A second pass could process the declaration operators and perform storage allocation. It should not be very difficult to validate this pass with respect to a denotational model which reflects certain characteristics of an "abstract target machine." Finally, instruction selection and register allocation should occur in the last pass. Proving their correctness would be the most involved task. On the whole, however, the indicated separation of the code generator specification into several modules would vastly simplify a proof that the resulting code generator, and therefore the entire compiler, is correct.

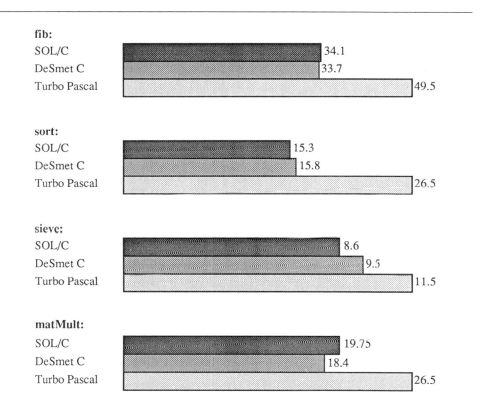

Figure 7.2
Execution Times for the SOL/C Benchmark Programs

8 Conclusions

This research was motivated by Pleban's development of normal form semantics [Pleban 84]. His work was directly inspired by Wand's research on deriving postfix code from continuation semantics [Wand 82], and research in the area of code generator specification languages [Glanville & Graham 78, Ganapathi 80, Bird 82]. The study of Mosses' abstract semantic algebras [Mosses 82] precipitated the principle of separability and the concepts of macrosemantics and microsemantics. Watt's work on executable semantic descriptions [Watt 84] indicated that the implementation of high-level semantics was feasible. Choosing ML as the basis for my semantic metalanguage avoided the invention of new square wheels. Looking back, this decision was most fortuitous. After settling the implementation problems connected with MESS, I concentrated on properly formulating high-level semantic definitions, with particular emphasis on the choice of semantic operators.

I know of three semantics-based compiler generators that are similar in spirit to MESS. The CERES system of Jones and Christiansen [Jones & Christiansen 82] accepts semantic specifications expressed in terms of a small number of action-oriented operators inspired by those of Mosses. Sethi's system [Sethi 81] generates efficient compilers by treating fundamental "runtime" operators in the semantic specification as uninterpreted symbols. His work was also motivated by that of Mosses, but still refers to microsemantic concepts such as continuations and stores. Both systems have only been used for generating compilers for languages with control structures for sequencing, looping and decision making, and simple expressions. Also, the intermediate code produced by the generated compilers must be translated by a code generator in an *ad hoc* manner. A third system by Gaudel, called Perluette, allows the semanticist to design the semantic algebra, as in a high-level semantics [Gaudel 81]. Unfortunately, I know very little about this system, and there are few published descriptions of its semantic foundations.

The possibility of providing alternative implementations for the operators of a semantic algebra was mentioned by Watt during his experimentation with ML as a semantic metalanguage [Watt 84]. However, MESS is the first implementation generator that *enforces* the separation of the microsemantics from the macrosemantics.

Nielson and Nielson have described an approach to semantics-directed compiler generation using a two-level metalanguage that enforces the distinction between compile-time and runtime domains [Nielson & Nielson 86]. The composition of the two portions of a two-level specification corresponds directly to the composition of macrosemantic and microsemantic definitions.

Finally, the work of Mosses and Watt on *action semantics* [Mosses & Watt 86] bears some strong similarities with high-level semantics. In particular, the choice of operators in both approaches is surprisingly similar. There are three principle differences between high-level semantics and action semantics: (1) operators in action semantics are defined by means of fundamental, or "basic," operators; (2) compile time and runtime aspects are not distinguished in action semantics; (3) in action semantics, transformations on the static environment are also formulated via semantic operators rather than by means of λ-abstractions.

8.1   Extensions to MESS

I have found the MESS system to be a useful tool for semantics-directed compiler generation. In particular, the strong polymorphic type checking and pattern matching features of the ML-like semantic metalanguage make the process of writing semantic descriptions much easier than with previous systems. In addition, the system and the generated compilers run acceptably fast on a personal computer. However, several extensions to MESS are planned that should improve its usefulness.

- *Specification of multipass compiler cores.* The comprehensibility of high-level semantic descriptions could be improved by allowing the static and dynamic semantics of a language to be described in separate macrosemantic specifications. Each specification would in essence specify a separate pass of the compiler core.

- *Modular semantic specifications.* Splitting a macrosemantics into piesces according to static and dynamic semantics improves the modularity of the semantic specifications. Modularity can also be obtained by grouping the semantic equations, domain definitions, and operator definitions into separate modules according to the language features they provide. These modules might then be reused as a part of other language descriptions.

- *Specification of abstract machines in* MESS. The MESS semantic metalanguage is purely applicative—it does not support ML assignments (**ref**) or arrays. Adding these features to the metalanguage would allow efficient abstract machines to be specified in the MESS system, rather than having to write untyped Scheme code.

8.2 A Language Designer's Workbench

I am encouraged by the success of the MESS system and the apparent suitability of the high-level semantics approach as a means of formally defining programming languages *and* specifying realistic compiler implementations. However, I believe that there are still a considerable number of possibilites for further research. In fact, I view MESS as only the first step toward the realization of a *Language Designer's Workbench*. The concept and its name are due to Pleban [Pleban 84].

The purpose of the *Workbench* is to drastically improve the language design process by appropriately supporting the development and direct implementation of formal specifications of all aspects of programming languages. This is based on three central ideas:

1. Formal specifications of the various aspects of a programming language (syntax, static semantics, dynamic semantics, runtime model) should be developed to serve as an *unambiguous standard of reference*, and as a foundation for informal expositions of the language.

2. It should be possible to test the specifications and check the consistency of the design without too much effort by *directly implementing* the formal definitions, thus quickly obtaining prototype interpreters or compilers for the language. The prototypes should be efficient enough to allow the necessary experimentation with the language design.

3. It should be possible to generate realistic, "non pessimizing" compilers by changing only model-dependent or other details, but leaving the actual language semantics intact.

In addition to these points, there should be a high level of support for the engineering of language definitions. This includes mechanisms to enhance the readability, maintainability, and modularity of specifications. Debugging and testing of specifications requires special support. Any set of semantic equations defines the semantics of some language—in this sense semantic descriptions are always "correct." However, it may happen that a specification does not reflect the intentions of the designer. I call this the problem of *semantic intention vs. semantic reality*. The *Workbench* should aid in the discovery and repair of such "bugs."

I envision that the implementation of such a system will have the following features:

- *Support for language definition modules.* A high degree of modularization will be possible. In addition to the modularity provided by the separation of the microsemantic details from the semantics, high-level semantic descriptions may exhibit two other kinds of modularity. First, the static semantics may be separated from the dynamic semantics. Second, any (macro- or micro-)semantic specification may be written as a collection of semantic modules, whose interfaces are subject to consistency checking. For example, there may be a module for the semantics of imperative constructs, one for expressions, and one for declarations. This will allow for the incremental development of semantic definitions. As an additional benefit, microsemantic modules may be reused as parts of "semantic libraries."

- *A database for language definition modules.* Language definition modules will be highly interchangeable, and it will be possible to store the modules in a database for later use in other designs.

- *Possibility of generating conventional machine code.* For Algol-like languages, the generated compilers will be able to compile code into an ordinary intermediate representation, so that further processing by a (possibly automatically generated) code generator will be possible. For other types of languages with less conventional features, for example backtracking or higher-order functions, the full generality of denotational semantics would be available at the expense of efficient implementation.

- *Accessibility with minimal knowledge of the underlying theory.* It should not be necessary to be an expert in the idiosyncrasies of standard denotational semantics, for instance continuations. Instead, one will be able to rely on a knowledge of standard programming language concepts in order to write the semantics.

- *Support for interactive and incremental development and testing of the specifications.* The system will be "intelligent" about fundamental concepts of programming languages, perhaps using a knowledge base in order to allow the designer to think in terms of fundamental language concepts. The system, and not the designer, will worry about many of the technical aspects of the formal descriptions and implementations.

- *Complete "realism" in the generated compilers.* The compilers generated by the *Workbench* will be realistic in every respect. For example, high-quality syntactic and semantic error recovery, common data types, and listing control will all be supported.

I believe that high-level semantics and the MESS system make an excellent start towards the realization of a Language Designer's Workbench.

Bless
this
MESS

A | A Traditional Denotational Semantics for HypoPL

This appendix gives a traditional denotational semantics for the HypoPL language. Like the ToyPL semantics presented in Chapter 3, this specification is based on Gordon's denotational description of SMALL [Gordon 79]. Some notable differences between this semantics and the ToyPL semantics:

- HypoPL has zero-based, one-dimensional, integer arrays. These are modeled by tuples consisting of the index upper bound and a function mapping array indices to storage locations.

- Recursive procedures with one integer value parameter are supported by HypoPL. Procedures are elements of the domain

$$PROC = CONT \rightarrow EV \rightarrow CONT = CONT \rightarrow ECONT$$

which can be thought of as containing functions that, when given a "return continuation" and actual parameter value, will produce a new continuation.

- Unlike in ToyPL, the domains of expressible and denotable values in HypoPL are not identical. This is because procedures and arrays are denotable, but not expressible.

- L-values have been added to the domain of expressible values in order to model assignments to elements of arrays. Array-indexing expressions result in L-values, and are then coerced into R-values by the valuation function R when necessary.

- HypoPL programs can declare boolean variables in addition to integer variables. However, as is customary in traditional denotational semantics, this declaration information is not used for any type checking purposes. Type compatibility errors are "caught" when a HypoPL arithmetic or boolean operation is "evaluated."

- Although not strictly necessary, this semantics has been written in the continuation style.

```
abstract syntax

   prog -> block

   decl -> "int" id |
           "bool" id |
           "const" id "=" int |
           "array" id "[" int "]" |
           "procedure" id1 "(" id2 ")" block |
           decl1 ";" decl2.

   block -> decl "begin" stmt "end" |
            "begin" stmt "end".

   stmt -> expr1 ":=" expr2 |
           "write" expr |
           "read" expr |
           "if" expr "then" stmt1 "else" stmt2 |
           "while" expr "do" stmt |
           id "(" expr ")" |
           stmt1 ";" stmt2 |
           "skip".

   expr -> "true" | "false" | num | id |
           id "[" expr "]" |
           expr1 "+" expr2 |
           expr1 "-" expr2 |
           expr1 "<" expr2 |
           expr1 "=" expr2 |
           "not" expr |
           expr1 "and" expr2.


semantic domains

   DV = union unbound |                      (* Denotable values *)
               variable of LOC |
               constant of RV |
               array of ARRAY |
               procedure of PROC.
   LOC   = INT.
   RV    = SV.
   ARRAY = INT * (INT -> LOC).
   PROC  = CONT -> ECONT.

   SV = union uninit |                       (* Storable values *)
               integer of INT |
               boolean of BOOL.

   EV = union rvalue of RV |                 (* Expressible values *)
               lvalue of LOC.

   ENV = ID -> DV.                           (* Environments *)
```

```
STORE   = MEMORY * FREELOC * INPUTFILE.  (* Stores *)
MEMORY  = LOC -> SV.
FREELOC = LOC.

CONT  = STORE -> ANSWER.        (* Command continuations *)
ECONT = EV -> CONT.             (* Expression continuations *)
DCONT = ENV -> CONT.            (* Declaration continuations *)

ANSWER = union halt |           (* Final answers *)
                error |
                output of RV * ANSWER.
```

auxiliary functions

```
    (* err : CONT.  The error continuation. *)
    err = { fn store. error }.

    (* quit : CONT.  The final continuation. *)
    quit = { fn store. halt }.

    (* initStore : INPUTFILE -> STORE
     * Given an input file, create an initial store. *)
    initStore input = ( (fn loc. uninit), 0, input ).

    (* initEnv : ENV
     * Create an empty environment. *)
    initEnv = fn id. unbound.

    (* bind : Ide -> DV -> ENV
     * Create an environment with the given id bound to the given value. *)
    bind id value = fn i. if i = id then value else unbound.

    (* combine : ENV -> ENV -> ENV
     * Update the first environment with the bindings of the second. *)
    combine env1 env2 = fn id.
        let dv1 = env2 id in
            if dv1 = unbound then env1 id else dv1
        end.

    (* isLoc : ECONT -> ECONT (= ECONT -> EV -> CONT)
     * Check for an L-value, and pass it to the continuation. *)
    isLoc econt =
        { fn val. case val of
            lvalue (_) => econt val |
            _          => err }.

    (* isRvalue : ECONT -> ECONT (= ECONT -> EV -> CONT)
     * Check for an R-value, and pass it to the continuation. *)
    isRvalue econt =
        { fn val. case val of
            rvalue (_) => econt val |
            _          => err }.
```

```
(* contents : ECONT -> ECONT (= ECONT -> EV -> ECONT)
 * Check for an L-value, and then retrieve its contents from
 * the store and pass the result to the continuation. *)
contents econt =
    { fn val. { fn store.
        case val of
            lvalue (loc) =>
                let (mem, _, _) = store in
                    ( case mem loc of
                        uninit => error |
                        value  => econt value store )
                    end |
            _ => error } }.

(* update : LOC -> CONT -> ECONT (= LOC -> CONT -> EV -> CONT)
 * Store the value into the given location, and pass the
 * resulting store on to the continuation. *)
update loc cont =
    { fn val. { fn store.
        let (mem, freeLoc, input) = store in
            case val of
                rvalue (val) =>
                    cont ( ([loc => val] mem), freeLoc, input ) |
                _ => error
            end } }.

(* read : LOC -> CONT -> CONT
 * Read the next input value, and store it into the given location.
read loc cont =
    { fn store.
        let (mem, freeLoc, input) = store.
            (nextInput, rest) = read input
        in
            case nextInput of
                i_input (v) =>
                    cont (([loc => nextInput] mem), freeLoc, rest) |
                _ => error
            end }.

(* ref : ECONT -> ECONT (= ECONT -> EV -> CONT)
 * Allocate a store location, initialize it with the given
 * value and pass it and the new store on to the continuation. *)
ref econt =
    { fn val. { fn store.
        let (mem, freeLoc, input) = store.
            newVar = lvalue freeLoc.
            newStore = (mem, freeLoc + 1, input)
        in
            update freeLoc (econt newVar) val newStore
        end } }.

(* deref : ECONT -> ECONT (= ECONT -> EV -> CONT)
 * Check for an lvalue, and then dereference it and pass the
```

```
      * result to the continuation.  Otherwise, pass the value itself. *)
      deref econt =
         { fn val. { fn store.
            case val of
               lvalue (_) => contents econt val store |
               _          => econt val store } }.

      (* newArray : INT -> STORE -> (ARRAY * STORE)
       * Return a pair consisting of:
       *  (1) an array mapping 0...n to consecutive new store locations
       *  (2) a new store with those locations allocated. *)
      newArray n store =
         let (mem, freeLoc, input) = store in
            let fun makeArray index =
               (* Helper function to build a new array. *)
               if index = n then (fn i. (bottom:int))
               else [index => index + freeLoc] (makeArray (index + 1))
            in
               ( (n, (makeArray 0)), (mem, freeLoc + n, input) )
            end
         end.

      (* subscript : ARRAY -> ECONT -> ECONT
       * Check the subscript and if it is OK, then index the array
       * and pass the L-value on to the continuation. *)
      subscript a econt val =
         { case val of
            rvalue (integer (i)) ->
               let (upperbound, arrayFun) = a in
                  if i < upperbound then econt (lvalue (arrayFun i)) else err
               end
            _ => err }.


   semantic functions

      P : prog -> INPUTFILE -> ANSWER.      (* Program meanings *)
      D : decl -> ENV -> DCONT -> CONT.     (* Declaration meanings *)
      B : block -> ENV -> CONT -> CONT.     (* Scope block meanings *)
      C : stmt -> ENV -> CONT -> CONT.      (* Command meanings *)
      R : expr -> ENV -> ECONT -> CONT.     (* R-value meanings *)
      E : expr -> ENV -> ECONT -> CONT.     (* Expression meanings *)


   semantic equations

      P [[ block ]] input = B [[block]] initEnv quit (initStore input).

      (* Declarations *)

      D [[ "int" id ]] env dcont =
         { ref { fn (lvalue loc).
            dcont (bind id (variable loc)) } (rvalue uninit) }.
```

```
D [[ "bool" id ]] env dcont =
   { ref { fn (lvalue loc).
      dcont (bind id (variable loc)) } (rvalue uninit) }.

D [[ "const" id "=" int ]] env dcont =
   R [[int]] { fn (rvalue val). dcont (bind id (constant val)) }.

D [[ "array" id "[" int "]" ]] env dcont =
   { fn store.
      R [[int]] { fn (rvalue (integer n)).
         let (arrayVal, newStore) = newArray n store in
            dcont (bind id (array arrayVal)) newStore
         end } }.

D [[ "procedure" id1 "(" id2 ")" block ]] env dcont =
   let proc =
         fn returnCont.
            { deref { ref { fn (lvalue loc).
               { B [[block]]
                  (combine env (bind id2 (variable loc)))
                  returnCont } } } }
   in
      dcont (bind id1 (procedure proc))
   end.

D [[ decl1 ";" decl2 ]] env dcont =
   D [[decl1]] env { fn env1.
      D [[decl2]] (combine env env1) { fn env2.
         dcont (combine env (combine env1 env2)) } }.

(* Blocks *)

B [[ decl "begin" stmt "end" ]] env cont =
   D [[decl]] env { fn localEnv.
      C [[stmt]] (combine env localEnv) cont }.

B [[ "begin" stmt "end" ]] env cont = C [[stmt]] env ; cont.

(* Commands *)

C [[ expr1 ":=" expr2 ]] env cont =
   E [[expr1]] env ; isLoc { fn (lvalue loc).
      R [[expr2]] env ; update loc ; cont }.

C [[ "write" expr ]] env cont =
   R [[expr]] env ; isRvalue { fn (rvalue val).
      { fn store. output (val, cont store) } }.

C [[ "read" expr ]] env cont =
   E [[expr]] env ; isLoc { fn (lvalue loc). read loc cont }.

C [[ "if" expr "then" stmt1 "else" stmt2 ]] env cont =
   R [[expr]] env ; isRvalue { fn (rvalue (boolean v)).
      if v then C [[stmt1]] env cont else C [[stmt2]] env cont }.
```

```
C [[ "while" expr "do" stmt ]] env cont =
   R [[expr]] env ; isRvalue { fn (rvalue (boolean v)).
      if v then C [[stmt]] env { C [["while" expr "do" stmt]] env cont }
      else cont }.

C [[ id "(" expr ")" ]] env cont =
   { case (env id) of
      procedure (proc) => E [[expr]] env ; proc ; cont
      _                => err }.

C [[ stmt1 ";" stmt2 ]] env cont =
   C [[stmt1]] env ; C [[stmt2]] env ; cont.

C [[ "skip" ]] env cont = cont.

(* R-values *)

R [[ expr ]] env econt - E [[expr]] env ; deref ; isRvalue ; econt.

(* Expressions *)

E [[ "true" ]] env econt = econt (rvalue (boolean true)).

E [[ "false" ]] env econt = econt (rvalue (boolean false)).

E [[ int ]] env econt = econt (rvalue (integer int)).

E [[ id ]] env econt =
   { case (env id) of
      variable (loc) => econt (lvalue loc) |
      constant (val) -> econt (rvalue val) |
      _              -> err }.

E [[ id "[" expr "]" ]] env econt
   { case (env id) of
      array (a) =>
         R [[expr]] env { fn index. subscript a econt index } |
      _ => err }.

E [[ expr1 "+" expr2 ]] env econt =
   R [[expr1]] env { fn (rvalue (integer v1)).
      R [[expr2]] env { fn (rvalue (integer v2)).
         econt (rvalue (integer (v1 + v2))) } }.

E [[ expr1 "-" expr2 ]] env econt =
   R [[expr1]] env { fn (rvalue (integer v1)).
      R [[expr2]] env { fn (rvalue (integer v2)).
         econt (rvalue (integer (v1 - v2))) } }.

E [[ expr1 "<" expr2 ]] env econt =
   R [[expr1]] env { fn (rvalue (integer v1)).
      R [[expr2]] env { fn (rvalue (integer v2)).
         econt (rvalue (boolean (v1 < v2))) } }.
```

```
E [[ expr1 "=" expr2 ]] env econt =
  R [[expr1]] env { fn val1.
    R [[expr2]] env { fn val2.
      econt (rvalue (boolean (val1 = val2))) } }.

E [[ "not" expr ]] env econt =
  R [[expr]] env { fn (rvalue (boolean v)).
    econt (rvalue (boolean (not v))) }.

E [[ expr1 "and" expr2 ]] env econt =
  R [[expr1]] env { fn (rvalue (boolean v1)).
    R [[expr2]] env { fn (rvalue (boolean v2)).
      econt (rvalue (boolean (v1 andalso v2))) } }.

end
```

B A Macrosemantics for HypoPL

This appendix presents a macrosemantics for HypoPL. The abstract syntax is the same as that given in Appendix A. However, the language defined here is slightly different. The differences are as follows:

- Procedure declarations are not allowed to be nested. Hence, only two level scoping, as in the C language, is supported.

- Programs begin with a header declaration:

```
prog -> "program" id "(" string1 "," string2 ")" "is" block
```

  The two strings specify the name of the input and output files for the program.

This macrosemantic specification was actually processed by the MESS system. Hence, it differs in several ways from the excerpts discussed in Chapter 5. The following list describes the differences.

- The `abstract syntax`, `action domains`, and `operators` sections are not given in a MESS macrosemantics. Instead, `interface` and `microsemantics` declarations are used to specify disk files that contain the abstract syntax and microsemantic signature, respectively.

- MESS does not distinguish between the various syntactic categories such as `expr`, `stmt`, and so on, but rather groups all abstract syntax trees into the single domain, `AST`.

- Static semantic errors are handled by the predefined function, `error`, which has functionality:

$$\texttt{error} : \quad 'a \to \texttt{AST} \to \texttt{STRING} \to 'a$$

  This function marks the source text corresponding to the given abstract syntax tree with the given diagnostic message. It then returns its first argument as its result.

- The microsemantic operators `Initialize` and `Finalize` are used to perform initialization and "wrap up" actions for program bodies.

Several examples of microsemantic specifications for the algebras used in this macrosemantics are given in Appendix C. The characteristics of the HypoPL compiler generated from this specification are described in Chapter 6.

```
(* FILE:         hypopl.mes
 * CONTENTS:      MESS macrosemantics for HypoPL
 *
 * Naming conventions:
 *
 * - Domain names are in uppercase, e.g. MODE.
 * - Microsemantic operators start with an uppercase character.
 *)

semantics HypoPL

interface       "HypoPL"
microsemantics "SC86"

semantic domains

    (* Static environments keep track of the statically-determined
     * information (the MODE) for each declared identifier.  In
     * addition to mapping identifiers to modes, the current scope
     * level is maintained here. *)
    ENV   = ASSOC * LEVEL.
    ASSOC = ID -> (MODE * LEVEL).
    LEVEL = union global_L | local_L.

    (* MODE: Identifier modes.
     * The denotations for identifiers in the static environment
     * are as follows:
     *     noneM:       undeclared
     *     constM:      constants
     *     varM:        scalar variables
     *     procM:       procedures
     *     paramM:      formal parameters *)
    MODE = union noneM |
                 constM of CONST |
                 varM of VAR |
                 procM of (NAME * NAME) |
                 paramM of PARAM.

    CONST = INT.

    VAR = NAME * TYPE.

    TYPE = union simpleT of SIMPLE_TYPE | arrayT of UPPERBOUND.

    SIMPLE_TYPE = union int_type | bool_type.

    UPPERBOUND = INT.

    PARAM = VAR.
```

```
auxiliary functions

   (**** Name handling ****)

   mkAlphaName (id: ID) : NAME = alphaName ("", id, "").

   (**** Error handling ****)

   declError env id msg = error (env, NullDecl) id msg.
   exprError exp msg = error (simpleT (int_type), NullExpr) exp msg.
   stmtError ast msg = error (NullStmt) ast msg.

   (**** Type Handling ****)

   (* Return the type-producing microsemantic operation
    * corresponding to the given simple type. *)
   runtimeType (st: SIMPLE_TYPE) : TACTION =
      case st of
         int_type  => IntType |
         bool_type => BoolType.

   (* integerType: TACTION. *)
   val integerType = runtimeType (int_type).

   (**** Environment Handling ****)

   (* The initial environment. *)

   val emptyAssoc: ASSOC = fn id. (noneM, global_L).
   val emptyEnv: ENV = (emptyAssoc, global_L).

   (* Retrieve the mode of the given identifier from the
    * given environment. *)
   lookup (id: ID, (assoc, currentlevel): ENV): MODE =
      let (mode, declLevel) = assoc id in
         if (declLevel = currentLevel) orelse (declLevel = global_L)
         then mode
         else noneM
      end.

   (* Check that an identifier is not yet declared in the
    * current block. *)
   notDeclared (id: ID, (assoc, currentLevel): ENV): BOOL =
      let (mode, declLevel) = assoc id in
         (mode = noneM) orelse not (currentLevel = declLevel)
      end.

   (* Add a new association pair to the environment. *)
   addAssoc (id: ID, mode: MODE, (assoc, level): ENV): ENV =
      ([id => (mode, level)] assoc, level).

   (* Declare the variable. *)
   declareVar (id: ID, t: TYPE, env as (assoc, level): ENV, ast: AST)
            : (ENV * DACTION) =
```

```
        if notDeclared (id, env) then
           let name = mkAlphaName (id).
               mode = varM (name, t).
               newEnv = addAssoc (id, mode, env)
           in
              case t of
                 simpleT (st) =>
                    (newEnv, DeclSimpleVar (name, runtimeType (st))) |
                 arrayT (ub) =>
                    (newEnv, DeclArrayVar (name, [ub], integerType))
              end
           else declError env ast "Identifier already declared.".

   (* Retrieve the current level indication. *)
   currentLevel ((_, level): ENV): LEVEL = level.

   (* Reflect that we are now in a local scope. *)
   enterProc ((assoc, _): ENV): ENV = (assoc, local_L).

(* ---------------------------------------------------------------- *)

semantic functions

   M:  AST -> OUTPUTFILE.                    (* program meanings *)
   D:  AST -> ENV -> (ENV * DACTION).        (* declarations *)
   BP: AST -> ENV -> IACTION.                (* program blocks *)
   BR: AST -> ENV -> IACTION.                (* routine blocks *)
   S:  AST -> ENV -> IACTION.                (* statements *)
   L:  AST -> ENV -> (TYPE * VACTION).       (* l-value expressions *)
   E:  AST -> ENV -> (TYPE * VACTION).       (* expressions *)


semantic equations

(* ---------------------------------------------------------------- *)
(* ---                        programs                        --- *)
(* ---------------------------------------------------------------- *)

M [[ "program" id "(" string1 "," string2 ")" "is" block ]] =
   (* The program identifier is ignored.
    * string1, string2 are the names of the input and output files *)
   let programBody = BP [[ block ]] emptyEnv in
      execute (
         Prog (string1, string2, programBody ) )
   end.


(* ---------------------------------------------------------------- *)
(* ---                     program blocks                     --- *)
(* ---------------------------------------------------------------- *)

(* The semantics of program blocks differs from that of routine
 * blocks in that the Initialize and Finalize actions surround the
 * actions for program blocks. *)
```

```
BP [[ decl "begin" stmt "end" ]] env =
    let (env', dAs) = D [[ decl ]] env in
        Block (dAs,
            StmtSeq (Initialize,
                StmtSeq (S [[ stmt ]] env',
                    Finalize)))
    end.
```

```
(* ----------------------------------------------------------------- *)
(* ---                    routine blocks                        --- *)
(* ----------------------------------------------------------------- *)
```

```
BR [[ decl "begin" stmt "end" ]] env =
    let (env', dAs) = D [[ decl ]] env in
        Block (dAs, S [[ stmt ]] env')
    end.
```

```
(* ----------------------------------------------------------------- *)
(* ---                    declarations                          --- *)
(* ----------------------------------------------------------------- *)
```

```
D [[ decl1 ";" decl2 ]] env =
    let (env1, dA1) = D [[ decl1 ]] env in
        let (env2, dA2) = D [[ decl2 ]] env1 in
            (env2, DeclSeq (dA1, dA2))
        end
    end.
```

```
D [[ ]] env = (env, NullDecl).
```

```
D [[ "int" id ]] env = declareVar (id, simpleT (int_type), env, [[ id ]]).
```

```
D [[ "bool" id ]] env =
    declareVar (id, simpleT (bool_type), env, [[ id ]]).
```

```
D [[ "array" id "[" int "]" ]] env =
    declareVar (id, arrayT (int), env, [[ id ]]).
```

```
D [[ "const" id "=" int ]] env =
    if notDeclared (id, env) then
        let level = currentLevel (env).
            mode = constM (int)
        in
            ( addAssoc (id, mode, env), NullDecl )
        end
    else declError env [[id]] "Identifier already declared.".
```

```
D [[ "procedure" id1 "(" id2 ")" "is" block ]] env =
    if notDeclared (id1, env) then
        let
        (* For procedure names it does'nt matter whether alphaName
         * or name is used, since procedures can't be nested. *)
            procName = name (id1).
            paramName = mkAlphaName (id2).
```

```
        (* Build the action for the parameter *)
           paramAction = BindValParam (paramName, integerType).

        (* Build the environment in which to process the body.
         *
         * The existing environment is extended with
         * - the binding for the procedure identifier, and
         * - the binding for the parameter identifier.
         *
         * Since the binding for the procedure identifier id is
         * visible in the body, the procedure may be recursive. *)
           procMode = procM (procName, paramName).
           paramMode = paramM (paramName, simpleT (int_type)).

           procEnv = addAssoc (id1, procMode, env).
           bodyEnv = addAssoc (id2, paramMode, (enterProc procEnv)).

        (* Process the body *)
           bodyAction = BR [[ block ]] bodyEnv
        in
           ( procEnv,
             BindProc (procName, Proc (paramAction, bodyAction)) )
        end
     else
        declError env [[ id1 ]] "Procedure already declared.".

(* ------------------------------------------------------------ *)
(* ---                       statements                    --- *)
(* ------------------------------------------------------------ *)

S [[ stmt1 ";" stmt2 ]] env =
   StmtSeq (S [[ stmt1 ]] env, S [[ stmt2 ]] env).

S [[ ]] env = NullStmt.

S [[ lvar ":=" expr ]] env =
   let (ltype, lA) = L [[ lvar ]] env
   and (rtype, rA) = E [[ expr ]] env in
      if ltype = rtype then
         Assign (lA, rA)
      else
         stmtError [[ lvar ]] "Type mismatch in assignment."
   end.

S [[ "if" expr "then" stmt1 "else" stmt2 ]] env =
   let (t, vA) = E [[ expr ]] env in
      case t of
         simpleT (bool type) =>
            Test (vA, S [[ stmt1 ]] env, S [[ stmt2 ]] env) |
         _ =>
            stmtError [[ expr ]] "IF expression must be Boolean."
   end.
```

```
S [[ "while" expr "do" stmt ]] env =
   let (t, vA) = E [[ expr ]] env in
      case t of
         simpleT (bool_type) => While (vA, S [[ stmt ]] env) |
         _ => stmtError [[ expr ]] "WHILE expression must be Boolean."
   end.

S [[ id "(" expr ")" ]] env =
   case lookup (id, env) of
      procM (name, _) =>
         let (t, vA) = E [[ expr ]] env in
            case t of
               simpleT (int_type) =>
                  Call (name, ExprSeq (vA, NullExpr)) |
               _ =>
                  stmtError [[ expr ]] "Procedure argument must be Integer."
         end |
      _ =>
         stmtError [[ id ]] "Unknown procedure.".

S [[ "read" lvar ]] env =
   let (t, lA) = L [[ lvar ]] env in
      case t of
         simpleT (int_type)  => ReadInt (lA) |
         _ => stmtError [[ lvar ]] "READ argument must be of Integer."
   end.

S [[ "write" expr]] env =
   let (t, vA) = E [[ expr ]] env in
      case t of
         simpleT (int_type)  => WriteInt (vA) |
         _ => stmtError [[ expr ]] "WRITE argument must be Integer."
   end.

S [[ "skip" ]] env = NullStmt.

(* ---------------------------------------------------------------- *)
(* ---                       L-values                         --- *)
(* ---------------------------------------------------------------- *)

L [[ id ]] env =
   case lookup (id, env) of
      noneM =>
         exprError [[ id ]] "Variable not declared." |

      varM (name, t as simpleT (st)) =>
         ( t, Var (name, runtimeType (st)) ) |

      paramM (name, t) =>
         ( t, ValParam (name, integerType) ) |

      _ =>
         exprError [[ id ]] "Object cannot be assigned.".
```

```
L [[ id "[" expr "]" ]] env =
   case lookup (id, env) of
      varM (name, arrayT (ub)) =>
         let (t, vA) = E [[ expr ]] env.
            arrayAction = Array (name, ExprSeq (Integer (ub), NullExpr),
                                 integerType).
            subscriptAction = ExprSeq (vA, NullExpr)
         in
            ( simpleT (int_type),
              Index (arrayAction, subscriptAction) )
         end |
      _ =>
         exprError [[ id ]] "Illegal array reference.".

L [[ _ ]] env = exprError [[ ... ]] "Expression has no Lvalue.".

(* ------------------------------------------------------------- *)
(* ---                     expressions                     --- *)
(* ------------------------------------------------------------- *)

E [[ expr1 "+" expr2 ]] env =
   let (t1, vA1) = E [[ expr1 ]] env
   and (t2, vA2) = E [[ expr2 ]] env
   in
      if (t1 = simpleT (int_type)) andalso (t1 = t2) then
         (simpleT (int_type), Add (vA1, vA2))
      else
         exprError [[ ... ]] "Can only add integers."
   end.

E [[ expr1 "-" expr2 ]] env =
   let (t1, vA1) = E [[ expr1 ]] env
   and (t2, vA2) = E [[ expr2 ]] env
   in
      if (t1 = simpleT (int_type)) andalso (t1 = t2) then
         (simpleT (int_type), Sub (vA1, vA2))
      else
         exprError [[ ... ]] "Can only subtract integers."
   end.

E [[ expr1 "=" expr2 ]] env =
   let (t1, vA1) = E [[ expr1 ]] env
   and (t2, vA2) = E [[ expr2 ]] env
   in
      if (t1 = t2) then (simpleT (bool_type), Equal (vA1, vA2))
      else exprError [[ ... ]] "Mismatched types in equality test."
   end.

E [[ expr1 "<" expr2 ]] env =
   let (t1, vA1) = E [[ expr1 ]] env
   and (t2, vA2) = E [[ expr2 ]] env
   in
      if (t1 = simpleT (int_type)) andalso (t1 = t2) then
         (simpleT (bool_type), Less (vA1, vA2))
```

```
            else
                exprError [[ ... ]] "Mismatched types in inequality test."
        end.

E [[ expr1 "and" expr2 ]] env =
    let (t1, vA1) = E [[ expr1 ]] env
    and (t2, vA2) = E [[ expr2 ]] env
    in
        if (t1 = simpleT (bool_type)) andalso (t1 = t2) then
            (simpleT (bool_type), BoolAnd (vA1, vA2))
        else
            exprError [[ ... ]] "Mismatched types in inequality test."
    end.

E [[ "not" expr ]] env =
    let (t, vA) = E [[ expr ]] env in
        case t of
            simpleT (bool_type) => (t, BoolNot (vA)) |
            _ => exprError [[ expr ]] "Can't apply NOT to a non-Boolean."
    end.

E [[ id ]] env =
    case lookup (id, env) of
        constM (n) => (simpleT (int_type), Integer (n)) |
        _ => let (t, lA) = L [[ ... ]] env in
                (t, Rvalue (lA))
            end.

E [[ id "[" expr "]" ]] env =
    let (t, lA) = L [[ ... ]] env in
        (L, Rvalue (lA))
    end.

E [[ bool ]] env = (simpleT (bool_type), Boolean (bool)).

E [[ int ]] env = (simpleT (int_type), Integer (int)).

end semantics
```

C | Four Microsemantic Specifications for HypoPL

This appendix presents four "plug-compatible" specifications of microsemantics for the semantic algebra used in the HypoPL macrosemantics given in Appendix B. All four specifications define same microsemantic signature, but are based on different models of interpretation. The first two use denotational models, using both continuation-based and direct styles. In the third, an abstract machine written in Scheme is used to interpret the algebra. Finally, the fourth interpretation is given in the form of a code generator specification.

There are a few places in the specifications where MESS-specific features are used. They are as follows:

- Every microsemantic specification processed by MESS must define an auxiliary function called `execute`. As the name implies, this function, after being "compiled" by MESS, controls the execution of POTs produced by the generated compilers.

  Semantically, `execute` simply coerces a program's meaning, which is some kind of action, to its final answer.

- Input and output are accomplished in MESS via the `read` and `write` primitives.

  The `write` primitive has the type,

  ```
  OUTPUTFILE * 'a -> OUTPUTFILE
  ```

  where OUTPUTFILE is a primitive MESS type. The `write` function behaves something like cons, essentially appending a printing representation of a data object to the end of the output file.

  The `read` primitive has the type,

  ```
  INPUTFILE -> INPUT_VALUE * INPUTFILE
  ```

  where INPUTFILE is a primitive MESS type, and INPUT_VALUE is defined as follows:

  ```
  INPUT_VALUE = union eof |
                      i_input of int |
                      r_input of real |
                      s_input of string |
                      t_input of token.
  ```

Input values are essentially type-tagged data objects. A `read` operation retrieves a tagged data object from the given input file, and returns it along with a new input file with this object removed. Note that this is an applicative read—previous input files may be saved and read "again."

C.1   Continuation-Style Microsemantics

```
(* FILE:        cont.mes
 * CONTENTS:    HypoPL microsemantics in continuation style
 *)

microsemantics cont

semantic domains

(* Dynamic environments.
 * These have four components:
 *   1 - a structure giving denotations to names, consisting of:
 *      a. an idealized store mapping names to the values it denotes
 *      b. a stack of name lists giving the currently "active" names
 *   2 - a list of argument values being passed to a procedure
 *   3 - the program input file
 *   4 - the program output file *)
DENV = DENS * ARGS * INPUTFILE * ANSWER.

DENS = STORE * ACTIVES.                    (* Name denotations *)

STORE = NAME -> DEN list.                  (* Idealized store *)

DEN = union noValue |                      (* Denotations *)
            intValue of INT |
            boolValue of BOOL |
            seqValue of DEN list |
            arrayValue of ARRAY |
            procValue of PROC.

ARRAY = INT -> DEN.                         (* Array denotations *)

PROC = IACTION.                            (* Procedure denotations *)

ACTIVES = NAME list list.                  (* Active names *)

(* Values from value-producing actions *)
EV = union lval of LVALUE | rval of DEN.

(* L-values *)
LVALUE = union simple of NAME | arrayElt of NAME * INT.

(* Types from type-producing actions *)
TYPE = union intT | boolT.
```

```
(* Actual argument values lists *)
ARGS = DEN list.

(* Continuation domains *)
CONT  = DENV -> ANSWER.      (* Command continuations *)
DCONT = CONT.                (* Declaration continuations *)
ECONT = EV -> CONT.          (* Expression continuations *)

ANSWER = OUTPUTFILE.


action domains

IACTION = CONT -> CONT.      (* Imperative actions *)
DACTION = DCONT -> CONT.     (* Declarative actions *)
VACTION = ECONT -> CONT.     (* Value-producing actions *)
TACTION = unit -> TYPE.      (* Type-producing actions *)


auxiliary functions

(*
 * The mandatory "execute" function
 *)

(* First, define the final continuation and the initial environment *)
val finalCont    : CONT = fn (_, _, _, answer):DENV. close_output answer.

val initialDenv : DENV = ( ( ((fn name. [noValue]), [[]]),
                             nil:ARGS,
                             bottom:INPUTFILE,
                             bottom:OUTPUTFILE ).

execute (program:IACTION) : ANSWER =
   program finalCont initialDenv.

(*
 * Various auxiliary functions for handling dynamic environments
 *)

(* Bind the name to the denotation in the environment *)
bind (name:NAME, den:DEN) : DACTION =
   fn dcont. { fn ((store, active::prevActives), args, i, a):DENV.
      let denv =
               (* Add the binding for the name to the store... *)
            ( ( [name => den::(store name)]store,
                (* ...and record the name as currently active *)
                (name::active)::prevActives ),
              args, i, a )
      in
         dcont (denv:DENV)
      end }.
```

```
(* Unbind the names in the store *)
unbind (names:NAME list, store:STORE) : STORE =
   case names of
      nil         => store |
      name::rest => unbind (rest, [name => tl (store name)]store).

(* Get the denotation for the given name *)
getDen (name:NAME, ( (store, _), _, _, _):DENV) : DEN = hd (store name).

(* Update the L-value with the R-value *)
update (lv:LVALUE, rv:DEN,
        denv as ((store, actives), args, i, a):DENV) : DENV =
   case lv of
      simple (name) =>
         ( ([name => rv::(tl (store name))]store, actives), args, i, a ) |
      arrayElt (name, idx) =>
         let arrayValue (array) = getDen (name, denv).
            newArray = arrayValue ([idx => rv] array)
         in
            ( ([name => newArray::(tl (store name))]store, actives),
              args, i, a )
         end.

(* Set up for entry into a procedure *)
enterProc (cont:CONT) : CONT =
   fn ((store, actives), args, i, a):DENV.
      let procDenv = ((store, []::actives), args, i, a) in
         cont procDenv
      end.

(* Exit from a procedure *)
exitProc (cont:CONT) : CONT =
   fn ((store, active::prevActives), args, i, a):DENV.
      let prevDenv = ((unbind (active, store), prevActives), args, i, a)
      in
         cont prevDenv
      end.


operators

(*
 * The program operator
 *)

(* Open the input and output files, start program execution *)
Prog : STRING * STRING * TACTION -> IACTION is
Prog (inFile, outFile, programA) = fn cont.
   { fn (initDens, _, _, _):DENV.
      let denv = (initDens, [],
                  open_input inFile, open_output outFile)
      in
         programA (cont:CONT) (denv:DENV)
      end }.
```

```
(*
 * Type-producing operators
 *)

IntType : TACTION is
IntType () = intT.

BoolType : TACTION is
BoolType () = boolT.

(*
 * Declarative actions
 *)

(* Perform the declaration actions in sequence *)
DeclSeq : DACTION * DACTION -> DACTION is
DeclSeq (dA1, dA2) = fn dcont. { fn denv.
   dA1 { fn denv1.
      dA2 { fn denv2.
         dcont denv2 } denv1 } denv }.

(* The null declaration action *)
NullDecl : DACTION is
NullDecl dcont = dcont.

(* Bind the name to a procedure denotation *)
BindProc : NAME * IACTION -> DACTION is
BindProc (name, bodyA) = bind (name, procValue bodyA).

(* Bind the name to a value parameter denotation *)
BindValParam : NAME * TACTION -> DACTION is
BindValParam (name, _) = fn dcont.
   { fn (dens, argVal::restArgs, i, a):DENV.
      let denv = (dens, restArgs, i, a) in
         bind (name, argVal) dcont denv
      end }.

(* Declare the simple variable. *)
DeclSimpleVar : NAME * TACTION -> DACTION is
DeclSimpleVar (name, _) = bind (name, noValue).

(* Declare the array variable *)
DeclArrayVar : NAME * INT list * TACTION -> DACTION is
DeclArrayVar (name, _, _) = bind (name, arrayValue (fn i. noValue)).

(*
 * Imperative actions
 *)

(* Perform the actions in sequence *)
StmtSeq : IACTION * IACTION -> IACTION is
StmtSeq (iA1, iA2) =
   fn cont. iA1 ; iA2 ; cont.
```

```
(* Do nothing *)
NullStmt : IACTION is
NullStmt cont = cont.

(* Elaborate the declarations, perform the imperative action. *)
Block : DACTION * IACTION -> IACTION is
Block (declA, bodyA) = fn cont. declA { fn denv. bodyA cont denv }.

(* Elaborate the parameter binding, then perform the body action *)
Proc : DACTION * IACTION -> IACTION is
Proc (paramA, bodyA) =
    fn cont. enterProc; paramA ; bodyA; exitProc ; cont.

(* Perform program initialization actions *)
Initialize : IACTION is
Initialize cont = cont.

(* Perform program termination actions *)
Finalize : IACTION is
Finalize cont = cont.

(* Assign the R-value to the L-value. *)
Assign : VACTION * VACTION -> IACTION is
Assign (lA, rA) = fn cont.
   lA { fn (lval lv).
      rA { fn (rval rv).
        { fn denv. cont (update (lv, rv, denv)) } } }.

(* Conditionally perform one of the given imperative actions *)
Test : VACTION * IACTION * IACTION -> IACTION is
Test (ifA, thenA, elseA) = fn cont.
   ifA { fn (rval (boolValue testVal)).
      if testVal then thenA cont
                else elseA cont }.

(* Perform the given imperative action in a loop as long as the
 * value action produces a true value *)
While : VACTION * IACTION -> IACTION is
While (testA, bodyA) = fn cont.
   testA { fn (rval (boolValue testVal)).
      if testVal then bodyA { While (testA, bodyA) cont }
                else cont }.

(* Call the procedure, passing the given argument value *)
Call : NAME * VACTION -> IACTION is
Call (pname, argA) = fn cont.
   argA { fn (rval (seqValue args)).
      { fn (dens as (store, _), _, i, a):DENV.
         let procValue (procA) = hd (store pname).
            denv = (dens, args, i, a)
         in
            procA cont denv
         end } }.
```

```
(* Read an integer from the input file into the given L-value *)
ReadInt : VACTION -> IACTION is
ReadInt (lA) = fn cont.
   lA { fn (lval lv).
      { fn (dens, args, i, a):DENV.
         let (i_input (n), newI) = read i.
            denv' = (dens, args, newI, a)
         in
            cont (update (lv, intValue n, denv'))
         end } }.

(* Write the integer value to the output file. *)
WriteInt : VACTION -> IACTION is
WriteInt (vA) = fn cont.
   vA { fn (rval (intValue n)).
      { fn (dens, args, i, a):DENV.
         let denv = (dens, args, i, write (a, n)) in
            cont (denv:DENV)
         end } }.

(*
 * Value-producing actions
 *)

(* Combine the expression sequences *)
ExprSeq : VACTION * VACTION -> VACTION is
ExprSeq (vA, vAs) = fn econt.
   vA { fn (rval value).
      vAs { fn (rval (seqValue values)).
         econt (rval (seqValue (value :: values))) } }.

(* The null expression sequence *)
NullExpr : VACTION is
NullExpr econt = econt (rval (seqValue nil)).

(* Coerce the L-value into an R-value *)
Rvalue : VACTION -> VACTION is
Rvalue vA = fn econt.
   vA { fn (lval lv).
      { fn denv.
         case lv of
            simple (name) =>
               econt (rval (getDen (name, denv))) denv |
            arrayElt (name, idx) =>
               let arrayValue (array) = getDen (name, denv) in
                  econt (rval (array idx)) denv
               end } }.

(* Generate a simple variable L-value *)
Var : NAME * TACTION -> VACTION is
Var (name, _) = fn econt. econt (lval (simple name)).
```

```
(* Generate a value parameter L-value *)
ValParam : NAME * TACTION -> VACTION is
ValParam (name, t) = Var (name, t).

(* Generate an L-value for the array with the given upperbounds.
   Note: The upperbounds actions are ignored since no checking is
   supported by this microsemantics *)
Array : NAME * VACTION * TACTION -> VACTION is
Array (name, _, _) = fn econt. econt (lval (simple name)).

(* Generate an L-value for an array element *)
Index : VACTION * VACTION -> VACTION is
Index (arrayA, idxA) = fn econt.
   arrayA { fn (lval (simple name)).
      idxA { fn (rval (seqValue (intValue (idx) :: _))).
         econt (lval (arrayElt (name, idx))) } }.

(*
 * Arithmetic and relational operations.
 *)

Add : VACTION * VACTION -> VACTION is
Add (vA1, vA2) = fn econt.
   vA1 { fn (rval (intValue v1)).
      vA2 { fn (rval (intValue v2)).
         econt (rval (intValue (v1 + v2))) } }.

Sub : VACTION * VACTION -> VACTION is
Sub (vA1, vA2) = fn econt.
   vA1 { fn (rval (intValue v1)).
      vA2 { fn (rval (intValue v2)).
         econt (rval (intValue (v1 - v2))) } }.

Mult : VACTION * VACTION -> VACTION is
Mult (vA1, vA2) = fn econt.
   vA1 { fn (rval (intValue v1)).
      vA2 { fn (rval (intValue v2)).
         econt (rval (intValue (v1 * v2))) } }.

Divi : VACTION * VACTION -> VACTION is
Divi (vA1, vA2) = fn econt.
   vA1 { fn (rval (intValue v1)).
      vA2 { fn (rval (intValue v2)).
         econt (rval (intValue (v1 div v2))) } }.

Equal : VACTION * VACTION -> VACTION is
Equal (vA1, vA2) = fn econt.
   vA1 { fn (rval (intValue v1)).
      vA2 { fn (rval (intValue v2)).
         econt (rval (boolValue (v1 = v2))) } }.

Less : VACTION * VACTION -> VACTION is
Less (vA1, vA2) = fn econt.
   vA1 { fn (rval (intValue v1)).
```

```
         vA2 { fn (rval (intValue v2)).
            econt (rval (boolValue (v1 < v2))) } }.

BoolAnd : VACTION * VACTION -> VACTION is
BoolAnd (vA1, vA2) = fn econt.
   vA1 { fn (rval (boolValue v1)).
      vA2 { fn (rval (boolValue v2)).
         econt (rval (boolValue (v1 andalso v2))) } }.

BoolNot : VACTION -> VACTION is
BoolNot (vA) = fn econt.
   vA { fn (rval (boolValue v)).
      econt (rval (boolValue (not v))) }.

Integer : INT -> VACTION is
Integer (n) = fn econt. econt (rval (intValue n)).

Boolean : BOOL -> VACTION is
Boolean (b) = fn econt. econt (rval (boolValue b)).

end microsemantics
```

C.2 Direct-Style Microsemantics

```
(* FILE:        direct.mes
 * CONTENTS:    HypoPL microsemantics in direct style
 *)

microsemantics direct

semantic domains

(* Program states.
 * These have four components:
 *    1 - a structure giving denotations to names, consisting of:
 *       a. an idealized store mapping names to the values it denotes
 *       b. a stack of name lists giving the currently "active" names
 *    2 - a list of argument values being passed to a procedure
 *    3 - the program input file
 *    4 - the program output file *)
STATE = DENS * ARGS * INPUTFILE * ANSWER.

DENS = STORE * ACTIVES.                         (* Name denotations *)

STORE = NAME -> DEN list.                        (* Idealized store *)

DEN = union noValue |                            (* Denotations *)
            intValue of INT |
            boolValue of BOOL |
            seqValue of DEN list |
            arrayValue of ARRAY |
            procValue of PROC.

ARRAY = INT -> DEN.                              (* Array denotations *)

PROC = IACTION.                                  (* Procedure denotations *)

ACTIVES = NAME list list.                        (* Active names *)

(* Values from value-producing actions *)
EV = union lval of LVALUE | rval of DEN.

(* L-values *)
LVALUE = union simple of NAME | arrayElt of NAME * INT.

(* Types from type-producing actions *)
TYPE = union intT | boolT.

(* Actual argument values lists *)
ARGS = DEN list.

ANSWER = OUTPUTFILE.


action domains
```

```
IACTION = STATE -> STATE.   (* Imperative actions *)
DACTION = STATE -> STATE.   (* Declarative actions *)
VACTION = STATE -> EV.      (* Value-producing actions *)
TACTION = unit -> TYPE.     (* Type-producing actions *)


auxiliary functions

(*
 * The mandatory "execute" function
 *)

(* First, define the initial program state *)
val initialState : STATE = ( ((fn name. [noValue]), [[]]),
                             nil:ARGS,
                             bottom:INPUTFILE,
                             bottom:OUTPUTFILE ).

execute (program:IACTION) : ANSWER =
   let (_, _, _, answer) = program initialState in
      answer
   end.

(*
 * Various auxiliary functions for handling dynamic environments
 *)

(* Bind the name to the denotation in the environment *)
bind (name:NAME, den:DEN) : DACTION = fn (state:STATE).
   let ((store, active::prevActives), args, i, a) = state in
           (* Add the binding for the name to the store... *)
      ( ( [name => den::(store name)]store,
           (* ...and record the name as currently active *)
           (name::active)::prevActives ),
         args, i, a )
   end.

(* Unbind the names in the store *)
unbind (names:NAME list, store:STORE) : STORE =
   case names of
      nil       => store |
      name::rest => unbind (rest, [name => tl (store name)]store).

(* Get the denotation for the given name *)
getDen (name:NAME, ( (store, _), _, _, _):STATE) : DEN =
   hd (store name).

(* Update the L-value with the R-value *)
update (lv:LVALUE, rv:DEN,
        state as ((store, actives), args, i, a):STATE) : STATE =
   case lv of
      simple (name) =>
         ( ([name => rv::(tl (store name))]store, actives), args, i, a ) |
```

```
        arrayElt (name, idx) =>
            let arrayValue (array) = getDen (name, state).
                newArray = arrayValue ([idx => rv] array)
            in
                ( ([name => newArray::(tl (store name))]store, actives),
                  args, i, a )
            end.
(* Set up for entry into a procedure *)
enterProc ( ((store, actives), args, i, a):STATE ) : STATE =
    ((store, []::actives), args, i, a).

(* Exit from a procedure *)
exitProc ( ((store, active::prevActives), args, i, a ):STATE) : STATE =
    ((unbind (active, store), prevActives), args, i, a).


operators

(*
 * The program operator
 *)

(* Open the input and output files, start program execution *)
Prog : STRING * STRING * IACTION -> IACTION is
Prog (inFile, outFile, programA) = fn (state:STATE).
    let (initDens, _, _, _) = state.
        state' = (initDens, [],
                    open_input inFile, open_output outFile)
    in
        programA (state':STATE)
    end.

(*
 * Type-producing operators
 *)

IntType : TACTION is
IntType () = intT.

BoolType : TACTION is
BoolType () = boolT.

(*
 * Declarative actions
 *)

(* Perform the declaration actions in sequence *)
DeclSeq : DACTION * DACTION -> DACTION is
DeclSeq (dA1, dA2) = fn state. dA2 (dA1 state).

(* The null declaration action *)
NullDecl : DACTION is
NullDecl state = state.
```

```
(* Bind the name to a procedure denotation *)
BindProc : NAME * IACTION -> DACTION is
BindProc (name, bodyA) = bind (name, procValue bodyA).

(* Bind the name to a value parameter denotation *)
BindValParam : NAME * TACTION -> DACTION is
BindValParam (name, _) = fn (state:STATE).
   let (dens, argVal::restArgs, i, a) = state.
       state' = (dens, restArgs, i, a)
   in
      bind (name, argVal) (state':STATE)
   end.

(* Declare the simple variable. *)
DeclSimpleVar : NAME * TACTION -> DACTION is
DeclSimpleVar (name, _) = bind (name, noValue).

(* Declare the array variable *)
DeclArrayVar : NAME * INT list * TACTION -> DACTION is
DeclArrayVar (name, _, _) = bind (name, arrayValue (fn i. noValue)).

(*
 * Imperative actions
 *)

(* Perform the actions in sequence *)
StmtSeq : IACTION * IACTION -> TACTION is
StmtSeq (iA1, iA2) = fn state. iA2 (iA1 state).

(* Do nothing *)
NullStmt : IACTION is
NullStmt state = state.

(* Elaborate the declarations, perform the imperative action. *)
Block : DACTION * IACTION -> IACTION is
Block (declA, bodyA) = fn state. bodyA (declA state).

(* Elaborate the parameter binding, then perform the body action *)
Proc : DACTION * IACTION -> IACTION is
Proc (paramA, bodyA) =
   fn state. exitProc (bodyA (paramA (enterProc state))).

(* Perform program initialization actions *)
Initialize : IACTION is
Initialize state = state.

(* Perform program termination actions *)
Finalize : IACTION is
Finalize state = state.

(* Assign the R-value to the L-value. *)
Assign : VACTION * VACTION -> IACTION is
Assign (lA, rA) = fn state.
```

```
        let lval lv = lA state
        and rval rv = rA state
        in
            update (lv, rv, state)
        end.

(* Conditionally perform one of the given imperative actions *)
Test : VACTION * IACTION * IACTION -> IACTION is
Test (ifA, thenA, elseA) = fn state.
    let rval (boolValue testVal) = ifA state in
        if testVal then thenA state
                   else elseA state
    end.

(* Perform the given imperative action in a loop as
 * long as the value action produces a true value *)
While : VACTION * IACTION -> IACTION is
While (testA, bodyA) = fn state.
    let rval (boolValue testVal) = testA state in
        if testVal then
            let state' = bodyA state in
                While (testA, bodyA) state'
            end
        else
            state
    end.

(* Call the procedure, passing the given argument value *)
Call : NAME * VACTION -> IACTION is
Call (pname, argA) = fn (state:STATE).
    let rval (seqValue args) = argA state.
        (dens as (store, _), _, i, a) = state.
        state' = (dens, args, i, a).
        procValue procA = hd (store pname)
    in
        procA (state':STATE)
    end.

(* Read an integer from the input file into the given L-value *)
ReadInt : VACTION -> IACTION is
ReadInt (lA) = fn (state:STATE).
    let lval lv = lA state.
        (dens, args, i, a) = state.
        (i_input (n), newI) = read i.
        state' = (dens, args, newI, a)
    in
        update (lv, intValue n, state')
    end.

(* Write the integer value to the output file. *)
WriteInt : VACTION -> IACTION is
WriteInt (vA) = fn (state:STATE).
    let rval (intValue n) = vA state
    and (dens, args, i, a) = state
```

```
      in
         (dens, args, i, write (a, n))
      end.

(*
 * Value-producing actions
 *)

(* Combine the expression sequences *)
ExprSeq : VACTION * VACTION -> VACTION is
ExprSeq (vA, vAs) = fn state.
   let rval value = vA state
   and rval (seqValue values) = vAs state
   in
      rval (seqValue (value :: values))
   end.

(* The null expression sequence *)
NullExpr : VACTION is
NullExpr state = rval (seqValue nil).

(* Coerce the L-value into an R-value *)
Rvalue : VACTION -> VACTION is
Rvalue vA = fn state.
   let lval lv = vA state in
      case lv of
         simple (name) =>
            rval (getDen (name, state)) |
         arrayElt (name, idx) =>
            let arrayValue (array) = getDen (name, state) in
               rval (array idx)
            end
   end.

(* Generate a simple variable L-value *)
Var : NAME * TACTION -> VACTION is
Var (name, _) = fn state. lval (simple name).

(* Generate a value parameter L-value *)
ValParam : NAME * TACTION -> VACTION is
ValParam (name, t) =·Var (name, t).

(* Generate an L-value for the array with the given upperbounds.
   Note: The upperbounds actions are ignored since no checking is
   supported by this microsemantics *)
Array : NAME * VACTION * TACTION -> VACTION is
Array (name, _, _) = fn state. lval (simple name).

(* Generate an L-value for an array element *)
Index : VACTION * VACTION -> VACTION is
Index (arrayA, idxA) = fn state.
   let lval (simple name) = arrayA state
   and rval (seqValue (intValue (idx) :: _)) = idxA state
   in
```

```
            lval (arrayElt (name, idx))
         end.

(*
 * Arithmetic and relational operations.
 *)

Add : VACTION * VACTION -> VACTION is
Add (vA1, vA2) = fn state.
   let rval (intValue v1) = vA1 state
   and rval (intValue v2) = vA2 state
   in
      rval (intValue (v1 + v2))
   end.

Sub : VACTION * VACTION -> VACTION is
Sub (vA1, vA2) = fn state.
   let rval (intValue v1) = vA1 state
   and rval (intValue v2) = vA2 state
   in
      rval (intValue (v1 - v2))
   end.

Mult : VACTION * VACTION -> VACTION is
Mult (vA1, vA2) = fn state.
   let rval (intValue v1) = vA1 state
   and rval (intValue v2) = vA2 state
   in
      rval (intValue (v1 * v2))
   end.

Divi : VACTION * VACTION -> VACTION is
Divi (vA1, vA2) = fn state.
   let rval (intValue v1) = vA1 state
   and rval (intValue v2) = vA2 state
   in
      rval (intValue (v1 div v2))
   end.

Equal : VACTION * VACTION -> VACTION is
Equal (vA1, vA2) = fn state.
   let rval (intValue v1) = vA1 state
   and rval (intValue v2) = vA2 state
   in
      rval (boolValue (v1 = v2))
   end.

Less : VACTION * VACTION -> VACTION is
Less (vA1, vA2) = fn state.
   let rval (intValue v1) = vA1 state
   and rval (intValue v2) = vA2 state
   in
      rval (boolValue (v1 < v2))
   end.
```

```
BoolAnd : VACTION * VACTION -> VACTION is
BoolAnd (vA1, vA2) = fn state.
   let rval (boolValue v1) = vA1 state
   and rval (boolValue v2) = vA2 state
   in
      rval (boolValue (v1 andalso v2))
   end.

BoolNot : VACTION -> VACTION is
BoolNot (vA) = fn state.
   let rval (boolValue v) = vA state in
      rval (boolValue (not v))
   end.

Integer : INT -> VACTION is
Integer (n) = fn state. rval (intValue n).

Boolean : BOOL -> VACTION is
Boolean (b) = fn state. rval (boolValue b).

end microsemantics
```

C.3   Abstract-Machine Microsemantics

```
; FILE:         am.s
; CONTENTS:     Abstract machine definition of the HypoPL microsemantics

(define *memory*       ; The store
  (make-vector 3000 nil))
(define *next-free*)   ; Next free location to allocate
(define *input*)       ; Input file
(define *output*)      ; Output file
(define *in-scope*)    ; Currently allocated variables
(define *procs*)       ; A-list of procedure bindings
(define *args*)        ; Procedure argument list

(define-integrable (!execute a) nil)

(load "\\mess\\messrun.fsl")     ; Standard MESS runtime utilities

; Open the input and output files, start program execution.
(macro !prog
  (lambda (e)
    (let ((inFile (cadr e))
          (outFile (caddr e))
          (program (cadddr e)))
      `(begin
        ; Open the input file
        (set! *input*
          (if (string-ci=? ,inFile "stdin")
              standard-input
              (open-input-file ,inFile)))

        ; Open the output file
        (set! *output*
          (if (string-ci=? ,outFile "stdout")
              standard-output
              (open-input-file ,outFile)))

        ; Start allocating storage at address 0
        (set! *next-free* 0)

        ; No procedures or arguments yet
        (set! *procs* nil)
        (set! *args* nil)
        (set! *in-scope* nil)

        ; Do the program
        ,program))))

(define-integrable (!inttype) nil)
(define-integrable (!booltype) nil)

; Declarative actions.
```

```
(define-integrable (!nulldecl) nil)

; Perform the declaration actions in sequence.
(macro !declseq
  (lambda (e)
    (let ((decl1 (cadr e))
          (decl2 (caddr e)))
      '(begin ,decl1 ,decl2))))

; Bind the name to a procedure denotation.
(define-integrable (!bindproc pname proc)
  (set! *procs* (cons (cons pname proc) *procs*)))

; Allocate the parameter, pass the argument value.
(define (!bindvalparam pname type)
  ; Add the parameter name to the list of allocated variables.
  (set! *in-scope* (cons pname *in-scope*))

  ; Allocate the parameter, store the address on its p-list.
  (let ((addrs (getprop pname 'address)))
    (putprop pname (cons *next-free* addrs) 'address)

    ; Pass the argument value.
    (vector-set! *memory* *next-free* (car *args*))
    (set! *args* (cdr *args*))

    ; Bump up the next free pointer.
    (set! *next-free* (1+ *next-free*))))

; Allocate the simple variable.
(define (!declsimplevar vname type)
  ; Add the variable name to the list of allocated variables.
  (set! *in-scope* (cons vname *in-scope*))

  ; Allocate the variable, store the address on its p-list.
  (let ((addrs (getprop vname 'address)))
    (putprop vname (cons *next-free* addrs) 'address)
    (set! *next-free* (1+ *next-free*))))

; Allocate the array.
(define (!declarrayvar aname bounds type)
  ; Add the array name to the list of allocated variables.
  (set! *in-scope* (cons aname *in-scope*))

  ; Allocate the array, store the address on its p-list.
  (let ((addrs (getprop aname 'address)))
    (putprop aname (cons *next-free* addrs) 'address)
    (set! *next-free* (+ (car bounds) *next-free*))))

; Imperative actions.

; Do nothing.
(define-integrable (!nullstmt) nil)
```

```
; Perform the actions in sequence.
(macro !stmtseq
  (lambda (e)
    (let ((stmt1 (cadr e))
          (stmt2 (caddr e)))
      `(begin ,stmt1 ,stmt2))))

; Elaborate the declarations, perform the imperative action,
; then undo the declarations.
(macro !block
  (lambda (e)
    (let ((decls (cadr e))
          (body (caddr e)))
      ; Save state before entering the block
      `(let ((old-next-free *next-free*)
             (old-in-scope *in-scope*))

         ; Do the block
         ,decls
         ,body

         ; Deallocate the block's variables
         (set! *next-free* old-next-free)

         ; Pop the address stacks for each of the block's variables
         (do ((vars *in-scope* (cdr vars)))
             ((eq? vars old-in-scope)
              (set! *in-scope* old-in-scope))
           (putprop (car vars)
                    (cdr (getprop (car vars) 'address))
                    'address))))))

; Elaborate the parameter binding, then perform the body action.
(macro !proc
  (lambda (e)
    (let ((paramBinders (cadr e))
          (procBody (caddr e)))
      `(lambda (args)
         (set! *args* args)
         (!block ,paramBinders ,procBody)))))


(define (!initialize) nil)
(define (!finalize) nil)

; Assign the value into the given address.
(define-integrable (!assign address value)
  (vector-set! *memory* address value))

; Conditionally execute one of the actions
(macro !test
  (lambda (e)
    (let ((test (cadr e))
          (then (caddr e))
```

```
          (else (cadddr e)))
      '(if ,test ,then ,else)))))

; Loop while the condition is true.
(macro !while
  (lambda (e)
    (let ((test (cadr e))
          (body (caddr e)))
      '(do ()
           ((not ,test))
           ,body)))))

; Call the named procedure, passing the given argument value.
(define (!call pname args)
  (let ((proc (cdr (assq pname *procs*))))
    (proc args)))

; Read an integer from the input file and store it into the
; given address.
(define-integrable (!readint address)
  (vector-set! *memory* address (read *input*)))

; Write the integer to the output file.
(define-integrable (!writeint n)
  (begin
    (display n)
    (display " ")))

; Value-producing actions.

; Construct the sequence of values.
(define-integrable (!exprseq val vals) (cons val vals))
(define-integrable (!nullexpr) nil)

; Fetch the contents of memory at the given address.
(define-integrable (!rvalue address) (vector-ref *memory* address))

; Retrieve the address of the variable/value parameter.
(define-integrable (!var vname type) (car (getprop vname 'address)))
(define-integrable (!valparam pname type) (car (getprop pname 'address)))

; Retrieve the base address of the array.
(define-integrable (!array aname bounds type)
  (car (getprop aname 'address)))

; Compute the address of the array element by adding the index to
; the base address of the array.
(define-integrable (!index array idxs) (+ array (car idxs)))

; Arithmetic and relational operations.

(define-integrable !add +)
(define-integrable !sub -)
(define-integrable !mult *)
```

```
(define-integrable !divi quotient)
(define-integrable !equal =?)
(define-integrable !less <?)
(define-integrable !booland and)
(define-integrable !boolnot not)

(define-integrable (!integer n) n)
(define-integrable (!boolean b) b)
```

C.4 Code Generator Microsemantics (excerpts)

The following are excerpts from a microsemantics given as a code generator specification for the Intel iAPX8086 microprocessor. The code generation model allocates registers on a statement by statement basis. All expression values are computed in register **ax**, and all L-values in register **bx**. Registers **cx**, **si**, and **di** are used as a stack for spilling the contents of **ax**, and when all of **cx**, **si**, **di** are in use, **ax** is spilled onto the machine stack. Register **dx** is involved in multiplication and division, and also contains the result of popping the machine stack.

A fair amount of case analysis is done in order to avoid extraneous move instructions. Constant expressions are folded as much as possible, and superfluous branches are always elided. Global variables are allocated statically, whereas parameters and local variables are allocated on the runtime stack and are addressed through the **bp** register. Call and return follow the usual C conventions, with argument values of type char or bool always occupying two bytes when pushed on the stack. The argument list in a call is evaluated from right to left.

The layout of an activation record for a procedure with n parameters and k locals is as follows:

...	
$-2*k$ [bp]	sp (top of stack)
...	
...	
-2 [bp]	first local variable
old bp	bp (dynamic link)
return address	two bytes (intra-segment call)
4 [bp]	argument 1
6 [bp]	argument 2
...	
...	
$2*(n+1)$ [bp]	argument n

Data objects are represented as follows. Reference parameters are represented as two-byte pointers. Integers are signed 16-bit values, and booleans are stored as 8-bit bytes with false being represented by 0, and true by 1.

```
(* FILE:          cg86.mes
 * CONTENTS:      Sol/C code generator microsemantics
 * AUTHOR:        Uwe Pleban
 *)


LEVEL   = union localL | globalL.


INTLIST = INT list.


(*
 * Register data base.
 *)
REGISTER = union
   ax | al | bx | cx | cl | dx | si | di | sp | bp.


STACKELEM = union
   reg of REGISTER |       (* element in register *)
   pop.                    (* element on machine stack *)


AVAIL   = REGISTER list.   (* currently available registers *)


STACK   = STACKELEM list.  (* stacked temporary values *)


UNUSED  = REGISTER list.   (* registers available for spilling *)


REGBASE = union
   rb of (AVAIL * STACK * UNUSED).  (* register data base *)


VALUEINREGISTER = union
   cont of NAME |          (* variable *)
   unknown.                (* too complex to keep track of *)


(*
 * Abstract operators
 *)
ADDOP       = union Add_  | Sub_.
DIVOP       = union Divi_ | Mod_.
RELOP       = union Equal_ | Nequal_ | Less_ | Greater_ |
                    LessEq_ | GreaterEq_.
ARRAYKIND   = union Array_ | RefArrayParam_.


(*
 * Encodings of operands for 8086 instructions.
 *)
```

```
OPERAND = union
   regOp of REGISTER |
   indRegOp of REGISTER |
   byteIndRegOp of REGISTER |
   wordIndRegOp of REGISTER |
   charOp of CHAR |
   intOp of INT |
   byteOp of (NAME * ENV) |
   wordOp of (NAME * ENV) |
   offsetOp of (NAME * ENV) |
   memoryOp of (NAME * ENV) |
   labelOp of NAME |
   globalLabelOp of NAME.

(*
 * Code generator environment
 *)
ASSOC        = NAME -> LEVEL.
REGCONTENTS  = REGISTER -> VALUEINREGISTER.
PARAMOFFSET  = INT.
LOCALOFFSET  = INT.
ENV          = ASSOC * LEVEL * REGCONTENTS *
               PARAMOFFSET * LOCALOFFSET.

LABELNUMBER  = INT.
LABEL        = NAME.
RETURNLABEL  = LABEL.
EXITLABEL    = LABEL.
PROGRAMNAME  = NAME.
ROUTINENAME  = NAME.
STRINGTABLE  = (NAME * STRING) list.
LABELENV     = LABELNUMBER * RETURNLABEL * EXITLABEL *
               PROGRAMNAME * ROUTINENAME * STRINGTABLE.

(*****************************************************************
 *          INPUT LANGUAGE AS SEEN BY THE CODE GENERATOR        *
 *****************************************************************)

DACTION = union
   BindProc of (NAME * IACTION) |
   BindValParam of (NAME * STYPE) |
   BindRefParam of (NAME * STYPE) |
   BindRefArrayParam of (NAME * DACTION * STYPE) |
   DeclSimpleVar of (NAME * STYPE) |
```

```
     DeclArrayVar of (NAME * INTLIST * STYPE) |
     DeclSeq of (DACTION * DACTION) |
     NullDecl.

IACTION = union
     Prog of (STRING * STRING * IACTION) |
     Block of (DACTION * IACTION) |
     Proc of (DACTION * IACTION) |
     LabelDef of (NAME * IACTION) |
     Jump of NAME |
     Assign of (VACTION * VACTION) |
     Test of (VACTION * IACTION * IACTION) |
     While of (VACTION * IACTION) |
     StmtSeq of (IACTION * IACTION) |
     Call of (NAME * VACTION) |
     ReadInt of VACTION |
     ReadChar of VACTION |
     WriteInt of VACTION |
     WriteChar of VACTION |
     Initialize |
     Finalize |
     NullStmt |
     ExitLoop |
     Return |
     ReadLine |
     WriteLine.

VACTION = union
     Rvalue of VACTION |
     Var of (NAME * STYPE) |
     Array of (NAME * VACTION * STYPE) |
     ValParam of (NAME * STYPE) |
     RefParam of (NAME * STYPE) |
     RefArrayParam of (NAME * VACTION * STYPE) |
     Index of (VACTION * VACTION) |
     Neg of VACTION |
     Add of (VACTION * VACTION) |
     Sub of (VACTION * VACTION) |
     Mult of (VACTION * VACTION) |
     Divi of (VACTION * VACTION) |
     Modulo of (VACTION * VACTION) |
     Equal of (VACTION * VACTION) |
     Less of (VACTION * VACTION) |
     Greater of (VACTION * VACTION) |
```

```
      BoolAnd of (VACTION * VACTION) |
      BoolOr of (VACTION * VACTION) |
      BoolNot of (VACTION) |
      IntToChar of VACTION |
      CharToInt of VACTION |
      Integer of INT |
      Character of CHAR |
      CharString of STRING |
      Boolean of NAME |
      ExprSeq of (VACTION * VACTION) |
      NullExpr.

STYPE    = union
      IntType | CharType | BoolType.
```

etc...

```
                     (****************************************)
                     (*            Register allocation        *)
                     (****************************************)

(* Initial values for 'avail', 'stack', and 'unused'. *)
val initRegbase: REGBASE = rb ([ax], [], [cx, si, di]).

stack (r: REGISTER, regbase as rb (avail, stack, unused)): REGBASE =
   (*
    * If register is still available, it need not be stacked.
    *)
   if member r avail then regbase
   else
      case unused of
         r1 :: rest =>
         (*
          * Otherwise, it is already busy, so its contents are moved
          * to another register, and the register is freed ...
          *)
            ( eMoveRegReg ((* to *) r1, (* from *) r).
              rb (r :: avail, reg (r1) :: stack, rest) ) |

         (* ... or the contents are moved on the machine stack,
          *     when the list of unused registers is exhausted
          *)
         nil =>
            ( ePushReg (r).
              rb (r :: avail, pop :: stack, unused) ).
```

```
(* unstack (REGBASE): (REGISTER * REGBASE) *)

unstack (rb (avail, reg (r) :: stack, unused)) =
    (r, rb (avail, stack, unused)) |

unstack (rb (avail, pop :: stack, unused)) =
    (* Always pop into register dx. *)
    ( ePopReg (dx)
      (dx, rb (avail, stack, unused)) ) |

unstack (regbase as rb (avail, nil, unused)) =
    ( print ("cannot unstack").
      putComment ("cannot unstack; ax returned").
      (ax, regbase) ).

(* makeBusy (REGISTER * REGBASE): REGBASE. *)

makeBusy (r: REGISTER, regbase as rb (avail, stack, unused)): REGBASE =
    (*
     * Mark register as busy.
     *)
    if member r avail then rb (remove (r, avail), stack, unused)
    else
        ( print ("ERROR: attempt to make register busy: ").
          print (registerName (r)).
          putString ("ERROR: attempt to make register busy: ").
          putReg (r).
          newLine ().
          regbase ).

(* mkAvail (REGISTER * REGBASE): REGBASE. *)

(* Make register 'r' available. *)
mkAvail (r: REGISTER, regbase as rb (avail, stack, unused)): REGBASE =
    if member r avail then
        ( print ("ERROR: register already available: ").
          print (registerName (r)).
          putString ("ERROR: register already available: ").
          putReg (r).
          newLine ().
          regbase )
    else
        rb (r :: avail, stack, unused).
```

```
(* mkUnused (REGISTER * REGBASE): REGBASE. *)

(* Make register 'r' unused. *)
mkUnused (dx, regbase: REGBASE) =
    (* Register dx is not part of the register data base.
     * It will be released after popping the machine stack into it. *)
    regbase |

mkUnused (r: REGISTER, rb (avail, stack, unused)) =
    rb (avail, stack, r :: unused).


                        (*****************************************)
                        (*             Register tracking        *)
                        (*****************************************)
(*
 * Remember that register 'r' contains the value of variable 'name'.
 *)
postValueOfName (r: REGISTER, name: NAME,
                 (assoc, level, regContents, p, l): ENV) : ENV =
    (assoc, level, [r => cont (name)] regContents, p, l).


(*
 * Remember that register 'r' contains an unknown value.
 *)
postUnknownValue (r: REGISTER, (assoc, level, regContents, p, l): ENV)
 : ENV =
    (assoc, level, [r => unknown] regContents, p, l).


(*
 * Load register 'r' with contents of word sized variable
 * with name 'name', if necessary.
 *)
loadWValueOfName (r: REGISTER, name: NAME,
                  env as (_, _, regContents, _, _): ENV) =
    case regContents (r) of
       unknown =>
          (* Must load register. *)
          eMoveWRegName (r, name, env) |
       cont (name1) =>
          if name1 = name then eSkip ()
          else eMoveWRegName (r, name, env) |
       _ => eSkip ().
```

```
(*
 * Make contents of all registers unknown.
 *)
forgetRegisterContents (env: ENV): ENV =
    (*
     * So far, only contents of ax is tracked.
     *)
    postUnknownValue (ax, env).
```

etc...

```
                    (***************************)
                    (*           R-values        *)
                    (***************************)

genRvalue (lvalue: VACTION, regBase: REGBASE, env: ENV, lEnv: LABELENV)
 : (REGISTER * REGBASE * ENV * LABELENV) =

case lvalue of
    (*
     * Contents of variable.
     *)
    Var (name, typ) =>
       let regbase = makeBusy (ax, stack (ax, regBase))
       in ( loadValueOfName (ax, name, typ, env).
            (ax, regBase, postValueOfName (ax, name, env), lEnv) )
       end |

    (*
     * Contents of general L-value.
     *)
    _ => (* Compile L-value into bx. *)
       let (r, regBase, env, lEnv) = genAddr (lvalue, regBase, env, lEnv).
           regbase = makeBusy (ax, stack (ax, regbase))
       in ( (*
             * Store [bx] into ax or al.
             *)
            if isIntType (exprType (lvalue)) then
               eMoveWRegInd ((* to *) ax, (* from *) r)
            else
               eMoveBRegInd ((* to *) al, (* from *) r).
            (ax, regBase, postUnknownValue (ax, env), lEnv) )
       end
and
```

```
(*****************************)
(*      Multiplication      *)
(*****************************)

genMultExpr (expr1: VACTION, expr2: VACTION, regBase: REGBASE,
             env: ENV, lEnv: LABELENV)
 : (REGISTER * REGBASE * ENV * LABELENV) =

case (expr1, expr2) of

   (_, Integer (2)) =>
      (*
       * Compile left subexpression into ax; then shift left 1 bit.
       *)
      let (r, regBase, env, lEnv) = genExpr (expr1, regBase, env, lEnv)
      in ( eShiftLeft1 (r).
           (r, regBase, postUnknownValue (r, env), lEnv) )
      end |

   (_, Integer (int)) =>
      (*
       * Compile left subexpression into ax.
       *)
      let (r, regBase, env, lEnv) = genExpr (expr1, regBase, env, lEnv)
      in
         ( (*
            * Load constant into bx.  Note that bx never holds a
            * relevant L-value or constant.
            *)
           eMoveWRegInt (bx, int).
           (*
            * Perform signed multiply, leaving result in <dx,ax>;
            * upper 16 bits in dx are ignored.
            *)
           eMultReg (bx).
           (r, regBase, postUnknownValue (r, env), lEnv) )
      end |

   (_, Rvalue (Var (name, IntType))) =>
      let (r, regBase, env, lEnv) = genExpr (expr1, regBase, env, lEnv)
      in
         ( (*
            * NOTE: r = ax holds.
            *)
```

```
          eMultName (name, env).
          (r, regBase, postUnknownValue (r, env), lEnv) )
      end |


  _ =>
    let (_, regBase, env, lEnv) =
          genExpr (expr2, regBase, env, lEnv).
        (r1, regBase, env, lEnv) =
          genExpr (expr1, regBase, env, lEnv).
        (*
        * r1 = ax holds; top of register stack contains right operand.
        *)
        (r2, regBase) = unstack (regBase)
    in ( (* Perform signed multiply, leaving result in <dx,ax>;
        * upper 16 bits in dx are ignored.
        *)
        eMultReg (r2).
        (*
        * Mark register r2 as unused.
        *)
        (r1, mkUnused (r2, regBase),
        postUnknownValue (r1, env), lEnv) )
      end
and

(*
 * For addition/subtraction operations.
 *)

genAddSubOp (opr: ADDOP, expr1: VACTION, expr2: VACTION,
            regBase: REGBASE, env: ENV, lEnv: LABELENV)
 : (REGISTER * REGBASE * ENV * LABELENV) =

case (expr1, expr2) of

    (_, Integer (int)) =>
      let (r, regBase, env, lEnv) = genExpr (expr1, regBase, env, lEnv)
      in ( eOpRegInt (opr, r, int).
          (r, regBase, postUnknownValue (r, env), lEnv) )
      end |

    (_, Rvalue (Var (name, IntType))) =>
      let (r, regBase, env, lEnv) = genExpr (expr1, regBase, env, lEnv)
      in ( eOpRegName (opr, r, name, env).
```

```
                  (r, regBase, postUnknownValue (r, env), lEnv) )
          end |


   _ =>
      let (_, regBase, env, lEnv) = genExpr (expr2, regBase, env, lEnv).
          (r1, regBase, env, lEnv) = genExpr (expr1, regBase, env, lEnv).
          (*
           * r1 = ax holds; top of regBase stack contains right operand.
           *)
          (r2, regBase) = unstack (regBase)
      in ( (*
            * Add/subtract operands.
            *)
           eOpRegReg (opr, r1, r2).
           (*
            * Mark register r2 as unused.
            *)
           (r1, mkUnused (r2, regBase),
            postUnknownValue (r1, env), lEnv) )
      end
```

etc...

```
(****
 * genIntAssign       (type of operand in assignment is IntType)
 ****)

genIntAssign (Var (name, _), expr: VACTION,
               env: ENV, lEnv: LABELENV)
 : (ENV * LABELENV) =
   let (r, _, env, lEnv) = genExpr (expr, initRegBase, env, lEnv)
   in ( putComment ("store result").
        eMoveWNameReg ((* to *) name, (* from *) r, env).
        (postValueOfName (r, name, env), lEnv) )
   end |

genIntAssign (lhs, expr, env, lEnv) =
   (*
    * Compile rhs into ax, and lhs into bx.
    *)
   let (_, regBase, env, lEnv) =
         genExpr (expr, initRegBase, env, lEnv).
       (lhsReg, regBase, env, lEnv) =
         genAddr (lhs, regBase, env, lEnv).
       (rhsReg, _) = unstack (regBase)
```

```
      in ( putComment ("store result indirect").
           eMoveWIndReg ((* through *) lhsReg, rhsReg).
           (env, lEnv) )
      end.

(*
 * General Assignments:
 * - Assign integer constant to simple variable.
 *)

genAssign (lhs: VACTION, rhs: VACTION, env: ENV, lEnv: LABELENV)
 : (ENV * LABELENV) =

case (lhs, rhs) of

   (Var (name, IntType), Integer (int)) =>
      ( eMoveWNameInt ((* to *) name, int, env).
        (env, lEnv) ) |

   (_, Integer (int)) =>
      (*
       * Compile lhs into bx.
       *)
      let (r, _, env, lEnv) = genAddr (lhs, initRegBase, env, lEnv)
      in ( eMoveWIndInt ((* through *) r, int).
           (env, lEnv) )
      end |

   (*
    * Incrementation/decrementation of variable.
    *)
   (Var (name1, IntType),
    Add (Rvalue (Var (name2, IntType)), Integer (int))) =>
      if name1 = name2 then
         ( if int = 1 then
              eIncWName (name1, env)
           else
              eAddWNameInt (name1, int, env).
           (env, lEnv) )
      else
         genIntAssign (lhs, rhs, env, lEnv) |

   (Var (name1, IntType),
    Add (Rvalue (Var (name2, IntType)), expr)) =>
```

```
          if name1 = name2 then
              let (r, _, env, lEnv) = genExpr (expr, initRegBase, env, lEnv)
              in ( eAddWNameReg (name1, r, env).
                    (env, lEnv) )
              end
          else
              genIntAssign (lhs, rhs, env, lEnv) |
```

etc...

```
genBlock (decl: DACTION, stmt: IACTION, env as (_, level, _, _, _): ENV,
          lEnv: LABELENV)
 :  (ENV * LABELENV) =

   if level = globalL then
      (*
       * Process declarations for the program block.
       *)
      ( dseg ().
        let (globalSize, env, lEnv) = genDecl (decl, env, lEnv).
            procName = getProgOrProcName (globalL, lEnv)
        in ( putString ("; size of global storage: ").
             putInt (globalSize).
             putString (" bytes.").
             newLine ().

             (* Emit program or procedure name as label. *)
             cseg ().
             eNameLabel (procName).

             (* Emit code for program entry. *)
             procEntry (0).

             (* Generate code for the body. *)
             let env = forgetRegisterContents (env).
                 (env, lEnv) = genStmt (stmt, env, lEnv)
             in ( (* Emit code for program exit. *)
                  procExit (0).
                  (env, lEnv) )
             end )
        end )
   else
      ( (* Process declarations for the block. *)
        dseg ().
        let env = initLocals (env).
```

```
                (lSize, env, lEnv) = genDecl (decl, env, lEnv).
                localSize = alignBlockSize (lSize).
                env = endLocals (env).
                procName = getProgOrProcName (localL, lEnv)
        in ( putString ("; aligned size of local storage: ").
             putInt (localSize).
             putString (" bytes.").
             newLine ().

             (* Emit procedure name as label. *)
             cseg ().
             eNameLabel (procName).

             (* Emit code for procedure entry. *)
             procEntry (localSize).

             (* Generate code for the body. *)
             let env = forgetRegisterContents (env).
                 (env, lEnv) = genStmt (stmt, env, lEnv).
                 returnLabel = getReturnLabel (lEnv)
             in ( (* Emit code for procedure exit.
                     *)
                  eLabel (returnLabel).
                  procExit (localSize).
                  (env, lEnv) )
             end )
        end )
and

genProc (decl: DACTION, stmt: IACTION, env: ENV, lEnv: LABELENV)
  : (ENV * LABELENV) =
    ( (* Process parameter declarations for the procedure. *)
      dseg ().
      let env = initParameters (env).
          (paramSize, env, lEnv) = genDecl (decl, env, lEnv).
          env = endParameters (env)
      in ( putString ("; size of parameter storage: ").
           putInt (paramSize).
           putString (" bytes.").
           newLine ().

           (* Set up for handling return statements. *)
           let (returnLabel, lEnv) = makeLabel (lEnv).
               lEnv = saveReturnLabel (returnLabel, lEnv).
```

```
                env = forgetRegisterContents (env).
                (env, lEnv) = genStmt (stmt, env, lEnv)
            in
                (env, deleteReturnLabel (lEnv))
            end )
      end )
and

genTest (expr: VACTION, stmt1: IACTION, stmt2: IACTION,
         env: ENV, lEnv: LABELENV)
 : (ENV * LABELENV) =

   let (thenLabel, lEnv) = makeLabel (lEnv).
       (elseLabel, lEnv) = makeLabel (lEnv).
       (endIfLabel, lEnv) = makeLabel (lEnv)
   in ((*
        * Process condition.
        *)
       putComment ("if").
       let (env, lEnv) =
              gonBoolExpr (expr, thenLabel, elseLabel, thenLabel,
                           env, lEnv)
       in ( (* Compile "then" branch. *)
            putComment ("then").
            eLabel (thenLabel).
            let (env, lEnv) = genStmt (stmt1, env, lEnv)
            in ( (* Jump to "endif" label only if "else" branch
                  * is not empty. *)
                 jumpOrSkip (stmt2, endIfLabel).

                 (* Compile "else" branch. *)
                 putComment ("else").
                 eLabel (elseLabel).
                 let (env, lEnv) =
                        genStmt (stmt2, forgetRegisterContents (env),
                                 lEnv)
                 in ( putComment ("end if").
                      eLabel (endIfLabel).
                      (forgetRegisterContents (env), lEnv) )
                 end )
            end )
        end )
   end
and
```

```
genWhile (expr: VACTION, stmt: IACTION, env: ENV, lEnv: LABELENV)
 : (ENV * LABELENV) =

   (* NOTE: expr is in canonical form. *)
   let (whileLabel, lEnv) = makeLabel (lEnv).
       (bodyLabel, lEnv) = makeLabel (lEnv).
       (endWhileLabel, lEnv) = makeLabel (lEnv).
       lEnv = stackExitLabel (endWhileLabel, lEnv)
   in ( eJump (whileLabel).

           (* Compile loop body. *)
           eLabel (bodyLabel).
           putComment ("body of while").

           let (env, lEnv) =
                 genStmt (stmt, forgetRegisterContents (env), lEnv)
           in ( (* Process condition. *)
               putComment ("while test").

               eLabel (whileLabel).

               let (env, lEnv) =
                   genBoolExpr (expr, bodyLabel, endWhileLabel,
                                endWhileLabel,
                                forgetRegisterContents (env), lEnv)
               in ( putComment ("end while").
                   eLabel (endWhileLabel).
                   (forgetRegisterContents (env),
                    unstackExitLabel (lEnv)) )
               end )
           end )
   end
```

etc...

```
genBindProc (procName: NAME, stmt:IACTION, env: ENV, lEnv: LABELENV)
 : (INT * ENV * LABELENV) =
   ( (* Compile parameter declarations and procedure body;
      * save name of procedure in order to generate a label later. *)
     putComment (" ").
     putString ("; -> procedure ").
     write (asf,  procName).
     newLine ().
     putComment (" ").
```

```
          let lEnv = saveProcName (procName, lEnv).
              env = forgetRegisterContents (env).
              (env, lEnv) = genStmt (stmt, localLevel (env), lEnv)
          in ( putComment (" ").
               putString ("; <- end procedure ").
               write (asf, procName).
               newLine ().
               putComment (" ").
               (0, globalLevel (env), deleteProcName (lEnv)) )
          end )
and

genBindValParam (name: NAME, typ: STYPE, env: ENV, lEnv: LABELENV)
  : (INT * ENV * LABELENV) =
    (*
     * Allocate a new slot on the stack
     *)
    let loc = currentParameter (env).
        env = addName (name, env).
        size = paramSizeOf (typ)
    in ( equate (name, loc).
         (size, nextParameter (size, env), lEnv) )
    end
and

genDeclArrayVar (name: NAME, boundsList: INTLIST, typ: STYPE,
                 env as (_, level, _, _, _): ENV, lEnv: LABELENV)
  : (INT * ENV * LABELENV) =
    let size = arraySize (boundsList) * sizeOf (typ).
        env = if level = globalL then env else nextLocal (size, env)
    in ( if level = globalL then
             (*
              * Reserve global storage for the array.
              *)
             reserveStorage (name, size)
         else
             (*
              * Reserve local storage for the array.
              *)
             equate (name, currentLocal (env)).
         (size, addName (name, env), lEnv) )
    end
  and
```

```
genDeclSimpleVar (name: NAME, typ: STYPE,
                  env as (_, level, _, _, _): ENV, lEnv: LABELENV)
 : (INT * ENV * LABELENV) =
   (*
    * Reserve global storage according to size requirements of type.
    *)
   let size = sizeOf (typ).
       env = if level = globalL then env else nextLocal (size, env)
   in ( if level = globalL then
            reserveStorage (name, size)
         else
            equate (name, currentLocal (env)).
         (size, addName (name, env), lEnv) )
   end
```

D A Compiler for HypoPL

The compiler

The following are fragments of the Scheme code generated by the MESS system
from the HypoPL macrosemantics given in Appendix B.

```
(DEFINE (!D AST)
  (LET* ((NODE (CAR AST))
         (ARGS (IF (GETPROP NODE 'LEAF?) AST (CDR AST))))
    (CASE NODE

(|DECL1 ";" DECL2|
  (APPLY
    (LAMBDA (!DECL1 !DECL2)
      (LAMBDA (!ENV)
        ((LAMBDA (!ENV)
           (LET ((V ((!D !DECL1) !ENV)))
             (LET ((!ENV1 (CAR V))
                   (!DA1 (CADR V)))
               (LET ((V ((!D !DECL2) !ENV1)))
                 (LET ((!ENV2 (CAR V))
                       (!DA2 (CADR V)))
                   (LIST !ENV2 (LIST '!DECLSEQ !DA1 !DA2)))))))
         !ENV)))
    ARGS))

(NIL (LAMBDA (!ENV)
       ((LAMBDA (!ENV)
          (LIST !ENV '!NULLDECL))
        !ENV)))

(|"int" ID|
  (APPLY
    (LAMBDA (!ID)
      (LAMBDA (!ENV)
        ((LAMBDA (!ENV)
           (!DECLAREVAR (CADR !ID) (!SIMPLET !INT_TYPE) !ENV !ID))
         !ENV)))
    ARGS))

(|"procedure" ID1 "(" ID2 ")" "is" BLOCK|
  (APPLY
    (LAMBDA (!ID1 !ID2 !BLOCK)
      (LAMBDA (!ENV)
```

```
      ((LAMBDA (!ENV)
        (IF (!NOTDECLARED (CADR !ID1) !ENV)
          (LET* ((!PROCNAME (!NAME (CADR !ID1)))
                 (!PARAMNAME (!MKALPHANAME (CADR !ID2)))
                 (!PARAMACTION (LIST '!BINDVALPARAM
                                     !PARAMNAME
                                     !INTEGERTYPE))
                 (!PROCMODE (!PROCM (LIST !PROCNAME !PARAMNAME)))
                 (!PARAMMODE (!PARAMM
                               (LIST !PARAMNAME
                                     (!SIMPLET !INT_TYPE))))
                 (!PROCENV (!ADDASSOC (CADR !ID1) !PROCMODE !ENV))
                 (!BODYENV (!ADDASSOC (CADR !ID2) !PARAMMODE
                                      (!ENTERPROC !PROCENV)))
                 (!BODYACTION ((!BR !BLOCK) !BODYENV)))
            (LIST !PROCENV
                  (LIST '!BINDPROC
                        !PROCNAME
                        (LIST '!PROC !PARAMACTION !BODYACTION))))
          (((!DECLERROR !ENV) !ID1)
           "Procedure already declared.")))
        !ENV)))
    ARGS))
```

etc...

```
(DEFINE (!S AST)
  (LET* ((NODE (CAR AST))
         (ARGS (IF (GETPROP NODE 'LEAF?) AST (CDR AST))))
    (CASE NODE

(|STMT1 ";" STMT2|
  (APPLY
    (LAMBDA (!STMT1 !STMT2)
      (LAMBDA (!ENV)
        ((LAMBDA (!ENV)
          (LIST '!STMTSEQ
                ((!S !STMT1) !ENV)
                ((!S !STMT2) !ENV)))
        !ENV)))
    ARGS))

(NIL (LAMBDA (!ENV)
      ((LAMBDA (!ENV) '!NULLSTMT) !ENV)))
```

```
(|LVAR ":=" EXPR|
  (APPLY
    (LAMBDA (!LVAR !EXPR)
      (LAMBDA (!ENV)
        ((LAMBDA (!ENV)
           (LET ((V ((!E !EXPR) !ENV)))
             (LET ((!RTYPE (CAR V))
                   (!RA (CADR V)))
               (LET ((V ((!L !LVAR) !ENV)))
                 (LET ((!LTYPE (CAR V))
                       (!LA (CADR V)))
                   (IF (EQUAL? !LTYPE !RTYPE)
                       (LIST '!ASSIGN !LA !RA)
                       ((!STMTERROR !LVAR)
                        "Type mismatch in assignment.")))))))
         !ENV)))
    ARGS))

etc...

(DEFINE (!E AST)
  (LET* ((NODE (CAR AST))
         (ARGS (IF (GETPROP NODE 'LEAF?) AST (CDR AST))))

(ID ((LAMBDA (!ID)
       (LAMBDA (!ENV)
         ((LAMBDA (!ENV)
            ((LAMBDA (V)
               (COND ((EQ? '!CONSTM (CAR V))
                      (LET ((!N (CADR V)))
                        (LIST (!SIMPLET !INT_TYPE)
                              (LIST '!INTEGER !N))))
                     (ELSE (LET ((V ((!L AST) !ENV)))
                            (LET ((!T (CAR V))
                                  (!LA (CADR V)))
                              (LIST !T (LIST '!RVALUE !LA)))))))
             (!LOOKUP (CADR !ID) !ENV)))
          !ENV)))
     ARGS))

etc...
```

Microsemantic implementation

Below are a few fragments from the Scheme code generated by the MESS system from the continuation-style microsemantic specification for HypoPL given in Appendix C.

```
(DEFINE !EXECUTE
  (REC !EXECUTE
    (LAMBDA (|v34|)
      ((LAMBDA (!PROGRAM) ((!PROGRAM !FINALCONT) !INITIALDENV))
       |v34|)))))

(DEFINE !DECLSEQ
  (REC !DECLSEQ
    (LAMBDA (|v59| |v60|)
      (LET (((|v57| (LIST |v59| |v60|))))
        ((LAMBDA (|v58|)
          (LET ((!DA1 (CAR |v58|))
                (!DA2 (CADR |v58|)))
            (LAMBDA (!DCONT)
              (LAMBDA (!DENV)
                ((!DA1 (LAMBDA (!DENV1)
                         ((!DA2 (LAMBDA (!DENV2) (!DCONT !DENV2)))
                          !DENV1)))
                 !DENV))))))
         |v57|))))))

(DEFINE !WHILE
  (REC !WHILE
    (LAMBDA |v101| |v102|)
      (LET (((|v99| (LIST |v101| |v102|))))
        ((LAMBDA (|v100|)
          (LET ((!TESTA (CAR |v100|))
                (!BODYA (CADR |v100|)))
            (LAMBDA (!CONT)
              (!TESTA
                (LAMBDA (V)
                  (COND ((AND (EQ? '!RVAL (CAR V))
                              (EQ? '!BOOLVALUE (CADR V)))
                         (LET ((!TESTVAL (CDDR V)))
                           (IF !TESTVAL
                               (!BODYA ((!WHILE !TESTA !BODYA) !CONT))
                               !CONT)))
                        (ELSE (RAISE-EXCEPTION !!MATCH '!!MATCH V))))))))
         |v99|))))
```

E The HypoPL Bubble-Sort Program

This appendix presents the bubble-sort program written HypoPL is used in Chapter 6. Excerpts of the POT and object code generated from this program are also presented.

```
program bubbleSort ( "stdin", "stdout" ) is
/*
 * This HypoPL program performs a sorting exercise for timing purposes.
 *
 * input:  an integer n, n <= 1000
 * action: sorts 0 ... n-1 into descending order using bubble-sort
 * output: original array: 0 ... n-1
 *         marker          : -999
 *         sorted array  : n-1 ... 0
 */
const max_size = 1000;
array num [1000];       /* The array to sort */

   procedure sort (numElts) is
   /*
    * This procedure uses a bubble sort to arrange the 0..numElts-1
    * elements of the "num" array.
    */
   int last;
   int current;
   int temp;

   begin
      last := numElts - 1;
      while 0 < last do
         current := 0;

         while current < last do
            if num [current] < num [current + 1] then
               temp := num [current];
               num [current] := num [current + 1];
               num [current + 1] := temp
            else
               skip
            endif;
            current := current + 1
         endwhile;

         last := last - 1
      endwhile
   end; /* sort */
```

```
   procedure printNums (size) is
   /*
    * Print out the "num" array, 0 .. size-1.
    */
   int i;

   begin
      i := 0;
      while i < size do
         write num [i];
         i := i + 1
      endwhile
   end; /* printNums */

/*
 * Main program
 */

int i;
int numSort;       /* The number of integers to sort */

begin
   read numSort;

   if max_size < numSort
   then skip
   else
      i := 0;

      while i < numSort do
         num [i] := i;
         i := i + 1
      endwhile;

      printNums (numSort);
      write 0 - 999;
      sorL (numSort);
      printNums (numSort)
   endif
end
```

The following is the POT generated for the procedure, `sort`.

```
(!DECLSEQ
  (!BINDPROC
    (NAME SORT)
    (!PROC
      (!BINDVALPARAM (NAME NUMELTS1) !INTTYPE)
      (!BLOCK
        (!DECLSEQ
          (!DECLSIMPLEVAR (NAME LAST1) !INTTYPE)
          (!DECLSEQ
            (!DECLSIMPLEVAR (NAME CURRENT1) !INTTYPE)
            (!DECLSEQ
              (!DECLSIMPLEVAR (NAME TEMP1) !INTTYPE)
              !NULLDECL)))
        (!STMTSEQ
          (!ASSIGN
            (!VAR (NAME LAST1) !INTTYPE)
            (!SUB (!RVALUE (!VALPARAM (NAME NUMELTS1) !INTTYPE))
                  (!INTEGER 1)))
          (!STMTSEQ
            (!WHILE
              (!LESS (!INTEGER 0)
                     (!RVALUE (!VAR (NAME LAST1) !INTTYPE)))
              (!STMTSEQ
                (!ASSIGN
                  (!VAR (NAME CURRENT1) !INTTYPE)
                  (!INTEGER 0))
                (!STMTSEQ
                  (!WHILE
                    (!RVALUE (!VAR (NAME CURRENT1) !INTTYPE))
                    (!RVALUE (!VAR (NAME LAST1) !INTTYPE)))
                  (!STMTSEQ
                    (!TEST
                      (!LESS
                        (!RVALUE
                          (!INDEX
                            (!ARRAY (NAME NUM0)
                                    (!EXPRSEQ (!INTEGER 1000)
                                              !NULLEXPR)
                                    !INTTYPE)
                            (!EXPRSEQ
                              (!RVALUE (!VAR (NAME CURRENT1) !INTTYPE))
                              !NULLEXPR)))
                        (!RVALUE
```

```
(!INDEX
  (!ARRAY (NAME NUM0)
          (!EXPRSEQ (!INTEGER 1000)
                    !NULLEXPR)
          !INTTYPE))
  (!EXPRSEQ
    (!ADD
      (!RVALUE (!VAR (NAME CURRENT1) !INTTYPE))
      (!INTEGER 1))
    !NULLEXPR))))
(!STMTSEQ
  (!ASSIGN
    (!VAR (NAME TEMP1) !INTTYPE)
    (!RVALUE
      (!INDEX
        (!ARRAY (NAME NUM0)
                (!EXPRSEQ (!INTEGER 1000)
                          !NULLEXPR)
                !INTTYPE)
        (!EXPRSEQ
          (!RVALUE (!VAR (NAME CURRENT1) !INTTYPE))
          !NULLEXPR))))
  (!STMTSEQ
    (!ASSIGN
      (!INDEX
        (!ARRAY (NAME NUM0)
                (!EXPRSEQ (!INTEGER 1000)
                          !NULLEXPR)
                !INTTYPE)
        (!EXPRSEQ
          (!RVALUE (!VAR (NAME CURRENT1) !INTTYPE))
          !NULLEXPR))
      (!RVALUE
        (!INDEX
          (!ARRAY (NAME NUM0)
                  (!EXPRSEQ (!INTEGER 1000)
                            !NULLEXPR)
                  !INTTYPE)
          (!EXPRSEQ
            (!ADD
              (!RVALUE (!VAR (NAME CURRENT1)
                            !INTTYPE))
              (!INTEGER 1))
            !NULLEXPR))))
```

```
                              (!STMTSEQ
                                (!ASSIGN
                                  (!INDEX
                                    (!ARRAY (NAME NUM0)
                                            (!EXPRSEQ (!INTEGER 1000)
                                                      !NULLEXPR)
                                            !INTTYPE)
                                    (!EXPRSEQ
                                      (!ADD
                                        (!RVALUE (!VAR (NAME CURRENT1)
                                                      !INTTYPE))
                                        (!INTEGER 1))
                                      !NULLEXPR))
                                    (!RVALUE (!VAR (NAME TEMP1) !INTTYPE)))
                                  !NULLSTMT))
                        (!STMTSEQ
                          !NULLSTMT
                          !NULLSTMT))
                      (!STMTSEQ
                        (!ASSIGN
                          (!VAR (NAME CURRENT1) !INTTYPE)
                          (!ADD (!RVALUE (!VAR (NAME CURRENT1) !INTTYPE))
                                (!INTEGER 1)))
                        !NULLSTMT))
                (!STMTSEQ
                  (!ASSIGN
                    (!VAR (NAME LAST1) !INTTYPE)
                    (!SUB (!RVALUE (!VAR (NAME LAST1) !INTTYPE))
                          (!INTEGER 1)))
                  !NULLSTMT))))
            !NULLSTMT)))))
!(DECLSEQ
    ...
```

Finally, the 8086 assembly code produced for the sort procedure by the code generator specified in Appendix C is as follows.

```
NUM_1   rb   2000
;
; -> procedure SORT
;
    dseg
NUMELTS_2   equ   4
; size of parameter storage: 2 bytes.
    dseg
LAST_3   equ   -2
CURRENT_4   equ   -4
TEMP_5   equ   -6
; aligned size of local storage: 6 bytes.
    cseg
SORT_:
    push  bp
    mov   bp, sp
    sub   sp, 6
    mov   ax, WORD [bp + NUMELTS_2]
    dec   ax
; store result
    mov   WORD [bp + LAST_3], ax
    jmp   _L1002
_L1003:
; body of while
    mov   WORD [bp + CURRENT_4], 0
    jmp   _L1005
_L1006:
; body of while
; if
    mov   ax, WORD [bp + CURRENT_4]
    inc   ax
    shl   ax, 1
    lea   bx, OFFSET NUM_1
    add   bx, ax
    mov   ax, WORD [bx]
    mov   cx, ax
    mov   ax, WORD [bp + CURRENT_4]
    shl   ax, 1
    lea   bx, OFFSET NUM_1
    add   bx, ax
    mov   ax, WORD [bx]
    cmp   ax, cx
```

```
        jge    _L1009
; then
_L1008:
        mov    ax, WORD [bp + CURRENT_4]
        shl    ax, 1
        lea    bx, OFFSET NUM_1
        add    bx, ax
        mov    ax, WORD [bx]
; store result
        mov    WORD [bp + TEMP_5], ax
        mov    ax, WORD [bp + CURRENT_4]
        inc    ax
        shl    ax, 1
        lea    bx, OFFSET NUM_1
        add    bx, ax
        mov    ax, WORD [bx]
        mov    cx, ax
        mov    ax, WORD [bp + CURRENT_4]
        shl    ax, 1
        lea    bx, OFFSET NUM_1
        add    bx, ax
; store result indirect
        mov    WORD [bx], cx
        mov    ax, WORD [bp + TEMP_5]
        mov    cx, ax
        mov    ax, WORD [bp + CURRENT_4]
        inc    ax
        shl    ax, 1
        lea    bx, OFFSET NUM_1
        add    bx, ax
; store result indirect
        mov    WORD [bx], cx
; skip
; else
_L1009:
; end if
_L1010:
        inc    WORD [bp + CURRENT_4]
; while test
_L1005:
        mov    ax, WORD [bp + CURRENT_4]
        cmp    ax, [bp + LAST_3]
        jl     _L1006
; skip
```

```
; end while
_L1007:
    dec    WORD [bp + LAST_3]
; while test
_L1002:
    mov    ax, 0
    cmp    ax, WORD [bp + LAST_3]
    jl     _L1003
; skip
; end while
_L1004:
_L1001:
    add    sp, 6
    pop    bp
    ret
;
; <- end procedure SORT
;
```

F A Macrosemantics for SOL/C

This appendix gives a macrosemantic specification for the SOL/C programming language. This is the actual specification used to generate the SOL/C compiler discussed in Chapter 7.

```
(* FILE:          solc.mes
 * CONTENTS:      MESS semantics for Sol/C
 * AUTHORS:       U. Pleban / P. Lee
 *)

(*
 * Naming conventions:
 *
 * - Domain names are in uppercase, e.g. MODE.
 * - Microsemantic operators start with an uppercase character.
 *)

semantics SolC

interface        "SolC"
microsemantics "SC86"

semantic domains

    (*
     * Static environments keep track of the statically-determined
     * information (the MODE) for each declared identifier.  In
     * addition to mapping identifiers to modes, the current block
     * number and scope level are maintained here.  Also, the environment
     * remembers whether a loop or a procedure is being processed
     * in order to check for the legality of exit and return statements.
     *)
    ENV          = ASSOC * BLOCK_INFO.
    ASSOC        = ID -> (MODE * LEVEL).
    BLOCK_INFO   = LEVEL * INLOOP * INPROC.
    LEVEL        = union  global_L | local_L of NAME.
    INLOOP       = BOOL.
    INPROC       = BOOL.

    (*
     * MODE: Identifier modes.
     * The denotations for identifiers in the static environment
     * are as follows:
     *
     *    0 - noneM:      undeclared
     *    1 - labelM:     labels
```

```
*    2 - constM:        constants
*    3 - varM:          variables
*    4 - procM:         procedures
*    5 - refParamM:     reference parameters
*    6 - valParamM:     value parameters
*    7 - constParamM:   constant parameters (array bounds)
*)
MODE = union
   noneM |
   labelM of NAME |
   constM of CONST |
   varM of VAR |
   procM of (NAME * NUM_PARAMS * MODELIST) |
   refParamM of PARAM |
   valParamM of PARAM |
   constParamM of PARAM.

CONST = union
   intC of INT |
   charC of CHAR |
   stringC of STRING.

VAR = NAME * TYPE.

TYPE = union
   noneT |
   simpleT of SIMPLE_TYPE |
   arrayT of (UPPERBOUND * TYPE) |
   openArrayT of (MODE * TYPE).

SIMPLE_TYPE = union
   int_type |
   bool_type |
   char_type.

UPPERBOUND = INT.

PARAM = VAR.

NUM_PARAMS = INT.

MODELIST = MODE list.
ID_MODE = ID * MODE.
ID_MODELIST = ID_MODE list.   (* used to simulate assoc mappings *)
```

```
(* -------------------------------------------------------------- *)

auxiliary functions

    (*
     * *** Name handling ***
     *)
    mkAlphaName (id: ID): NAME =  alphaName ("", id, "").

    mkAlphaLabel (id: ID): NAME = alphaName ("L_", id, "_").

    (*
     * *** Error handling ***
     *)
    declError env id msg =
        error (env, NullDecl) id msg.

    exprError exp msg =
        error (simpleT (int_type), NullExpr) exp msg.

    constError exp msg =
        error (intC (1)) exp msg.

    boundsError exp msg =
        constError exp msg.

    argError exp msg =
        error NullExpr exp msg.

    bindError (ims, _) exp msg =
        error (ims, NullDecl) exp msg.

    stmtError stm msg =
        error (NullStmt) stm msg.

    (*
     * ***** Mode Handling *****
     *)

    (*
     * Find the mode associated with an identifier in a given
     * ID_MODE list.
     *)
```

```
findIdMode (id: ID, ims: ID_MODELIST): MODE =
   case ims of
      nil => noneM |
      (id1, model) :: imRest =>
         if id = id1 then
            model
         else
            findIdMode (id, imRest).

(*
 * Check if an identifier occurs in an ID_MODE list.
 *)
infix occursIn.

op occursIn (id: ID, ims: ID_MODELIST): BOOL =
   case ims of
      nil => false |
      (id', _) :: imRest => (id = id') orelse (id occursIn imRest).

(*
 * Convert an ID_MODELIST into a MODELIST.  Note that
 * all constant parameters are skipped.
 *)
extractParamModes (ims: ID_MODELIST): MODELIST =
   case ims of
      nil => nil |
      (_, constParamM (_)) :: imRest =>
         extractParamModes (imRest) |
      (_, mode) :: imRest =>
         mode :: extractParamModes (imRest).

(*
 * Check the two ID_MODELISTs, making sure there are no
 * duplicates of the first in the second.
 *)
checkModeLists (ims: ID_MODELIST, ims': ID_MODELIST): BOOL =
   case ims of
      nil => true |
      im :: ims =>
         let (id, _) = im in
            if id occursIn ims' then false
            else checkModeLists (ims, im :: ims')
         end.
```

```
(*
 * ***** Environment Handling *****
 *)

(*
 * The initial environment.
 * NOTE: could add definitions of library functions laters.
 *)

val emptyAssoc: ASSOC = fn id. (noneM, global_L).

val initialBlockInfo: BLOCK_INFO = (
   global_L,        (* program block at global level *)
   false,           (* not inside a loop *)
   false).          (* not inside a procedure *)

val emptyEnv: ENV = (emptyAssoc, initialBlockInfo).

(*
 * Retrieve the mode of the given identifier from the
 * given environment.
 *)
lookup (id: ID, (assoc, (currentLevel, _, _)): ENV): MODE =
    let (mode, declLevel) = assoc id
    in
       if (declLevel = currentLevel) orelse (declLevel = global_L) then
          mode
       else
          noneM
    end.

(*
 * Check that an identifier is not yet declared in the
 * current block.
 *)
notDeclared (id: ID, (assoc, (currentLevel, _, _)): ENV): BOOL =
    let (mode, declLevel) = assoc id
    in
       (mode = noneM) orelse not (currentLevel = declLevel)
    end.

(*
 * Add a new association pair to the environment.
 *)
```

```
addAssoc (id: ID, mode: MODE,
           (assoc, info as (level, _, _))): ENV): ENV =
    ([id => (mode, level)] assoc, info).

(*
 * Add entries in an ID_MODE list to an association mapping.
 *)
addAssocList (ims: ID_MODELIST, (assoc, info as (level, _, _))): ENV)
  : ENV =
    let newAssoc =
        fn id.
            case findIdMode (id, ims) of
                noneM => assoc id |
                mode => (mode, level)
    in
        (newAssoc, info)
    end.

(*
 * Reflect that a loop is being processed.
 *)
enterLoop ((assoc, (level, _, inProc))): ENV): ENV =
    (assoc, (level, true, inProc)).

(*
 * Retrieve the current loop status indicator.
 *)
withinLoop ((_, (_, inLoop, _))): ENV): BOOL = inLoop.

(*
 * Reflect that a procedure is being processed.
 *)
enterProc (procName: NAME, (assoc, (_, inLoop, _))): ENV): ENV =
    (assoc, (local_L (procName), inLoop, true)).

(*
 * Retrieve the current procedure status indicator.
 *)
withinProc ((_, (_, _, inProc))): ENV): BOOL = inProc.

(*
 * ***** Type Handling *****
 *)
```

```
(*
 * Return the type-producing microsemantic operation corresponding
 * to the given simple type.
 *)
runtimeType (st:SIMPLE_TYPE) : TACTION =
   case st of
      int_type  => IntType |
      char_type => CharType |
      bool_type => BoolType.

(*
 * integerType: TACTION.
 *)
val integerType = runtimeType (int_type).

(*
 * Extract the upper bounds from an array type specification.
 *)
extractBounds (t:TYPE) : UPPERBOUND list =
   case t of
      arrayT (ub, t') => ub :: extractBounds (t') |
      _ => nil.

(*
 * Determine the number of dimensions of an array type.
 *)
numDimensions (t:TYPE) : INT =
  case t of
     arrayT (_, t')     => 1 + numDimensions (t') |
     openArrayT (_, t') => 1 + numDimensions (t') |
     _ => 0.

(*
 * Check that the list of types determined for a list
 * of index expressions contains only integer types,
 * and that the number of index types is identical to the
 * number of array bounds.
 *)
matchingBounds (ts: TYPE list, arrayType: TYPE): BOOL =
   let
      fun checkBounds (ts) =            (* TYPE list -> INT *)
         let minusInfinity = ~9999
         in
            case ts of
```

```
                    nil => 0 |
                    simpleT (int_type) :: tRest => 1 + checkBounds (tRest) |
                    _ => minusInfinity
            end
      in
         checkBounds (ts) = numDimensions (arrayType)
      end.

(*
 * Extract the simple component type of a given array type.
 *)
componentType (arr: TYPE): SIMPLE_TYPE =
   case arr of
      arrayT (_, t)      => componentType (t) |
      openArrayT (_, t)  => componentType (t) |
      simpleT (st)       => st.

(*
 * Evaluate the bounds of an array.
 *)
evalBounds (t: TYPE): VACTION =
   (*
    * t is either an array or an open array.
    *)
   case (t) of
      arrayT (ub, t') =>
         ExprSeq (Integer (ub), evalBounds (t')) |

      openArrayT (constParamM (name, t1), t') =>
         let vA = Rvalue (ValParam (name, integerType))
         in
            ExprSeq (vA, evalBounds (t'))
         end |

      _ => NullExpr.

(*
 * Two types t and t' are assignment compatible if
 *
 * (1) t and t' are identical simple types, or
 * (2) both are one-dimensional character array types;
 *     if the sizes of both arrays are known, that of t'
 *     may not exceed that of t.
 *)
```

```
assignmentCompatible (t: TYPE, t': TYPE): BOOL =
   case (t, t') of
      (simpleT (t1), simpleT (t1')) => t1 = t1' |

      (arrayT (ub, simpleT (char_type)),
       arrayT (ub', simpleT (char_type))) => ub >= ub' |

      (openArrayT (_, simpleT (char_type)),
       arrayT (_, simpleT (char_type))) => true |

      _ => false.

(*
 * Two types are parameter compatible if
 *
 * (1) they are identical simple types, or
 * (2) they are matching array types.
 *
 * Note that parameter compatibility is more general than
 * assignment compatibility.
 *)
parameterCompatible (t: TYPE, t': TYPE): BOOL =
   case (t, t') of
      (simpleT (t1), simpleT (t1')) => t1 = t1' |

      (openArrayT (_, t1), arrayT (_, t1')) =>
         parameterCompatible (t1, t1') |

      (openArrayT (_, t1), openArrayT (_, t1')) =>
         parameterCompatible (t1, t1') |

      _ => false.

(*
 * *** Other auxiliary functions ***
 *)
infix memberOf.

op memberOf (st: SIMPLE_TYPE, sts: SIMPLE_TYPE list): BOOL =
   case sts of
      nil => false |
      st' :: stRest => (st = st') orelse (st memberOf stRest).
```

```
(*
 * Return a tuple with the action components of the second and
 * third arguments if they are both simple types, and that simple
 * type occurs in the given list of valid simple types.
 *)
checkTypes (ast: AST, sts: SIMPLE_TYPE list,
            (t1: TYPE, vA1: VACTION), (t2: TYPE, vA2: VACTION))
  : VACTION * VACTION =
    let
        fun err () = error (NullExpr, NullExpr) ast
                        "Mismatched types in expression."
    in
        case (t1, t2) of
           (simpleT (st1), simpleT (st2)) =>
               if (st1 = st2) andalso (st1 memberOf sts) then
                   (vA1, vA2)
               else
                   err () |
           _ => err ()
    end.


(* ------------------------------------------------------------ *)


semantic functions

    Mm:    AST -> OUTPUTFILE.                    (* program meanings *)

    Dd:    AST -> ENV -> (ENV * DACTION).        (* declarations *)

    Cc:    AST -> ENV -> ENV.                    (* constant definitions *)
    CcV:   AST -> ENV -> CONST.                  (* constant values *)

    Vv:    AST -> ENV -> TYPE -> (ENV * DACTION). (* variable declarations *)
    VvT:   AST -> ENV -> TYPE -> TYPE.           (* array types *)

    Tt:    AST -> TYPE.                          (* simple types *)

    Pp:    AST -> (ID_MODELIST * DACTION).       (* parameters *)
    PpA:   AST -> TYPE -> (TYPE * ID_MODELIST * DACTION).
                                                 (* array param bounds *)

    BbP:   AST -> ENV -> IACTION.                (* program blocks *)
    BbR:   AST -> ENV -> IACTION.                (* routine blocks *)
```

```
Jj:    AST -> ENV -> ENV.                  (* labels *)
Ss:    AST -> ENV -> IACTION.              (* statements *)

Ll:    AST -> ENV -> (TYPE * VACTION).     (* l-value expressions *)
Ee:    AST -> ENV -> (TYPE * VACTION).     (* expressions *)
EeX:   AST -> ENV -> (TYPE list * VACTION).  (* index expressions *)
EeA:   AST -> ENV -> MODELIST -> VACTION.  (* argument expressions *)
EeN:   AST -> INT.                         (* length of expr lists *)
```

semantic equations

```
(* ------------------------------------------------------------- *)
(* ---                      programs                       --- *)
(* ------------------------------------------------------------- *)

Mm [[ "program" id "(" string1 "," string2 ")" "is" body ]] =
   (*
    * the program identifier is ignored.
    * string1, string2 are the names of the input and output files
    *)
   let programBody = BbP [[ body ]] emptyEnv
   in
      execute (Prog (string1, string2, programBody))
   end.

(* ------------------------------------------------------------- *)
(* ---                   program blocks                    --- *)
(* ------------------------------------------------------------- *)

BbP [[ decls "begin" stmts "end" ]] env =
   (*
    * Process declarations, then labels.
    *)
   let (env1, dAs) = Dd [[ decls ]] env.
       env2 = Jj [[ stmts ]] env1
   in
      Block (dAs,
         StmtSeq (Initialize,
            StmtSeq (Ss [[ stmts ]] env2,
                     Finalize)))
   end.
```

```
BbP [[ "begin" stmts "end" ]] env =
   (*
    * Process labels.
    *)
   let env1 = Jj [[ stmts ]] env
   in
      Block (NullDecl,
         StmtSeq (Initialize,
            StmtSeq (Ss [[ stmts ]] env1,
                     Finalize)))
   end.


(* ---------------------------------------------------------------- *)
(* ---                       routine blocks                   --- *)
(* ---------------------------------------------------------------- *)


BbR [[ decls "begin" stmts "end" ]] env =
   (*
    * Process declarations, then labels.
    *)
   let (env1, dAs) = Dd [[ decls ]] env.
       env2 = Jj [[ stmts ]] env1
   in
      Block (dAs, Ss [[ stmts ]] env2)
   end.

BbR [[ "begin" stmts "end" ]] env =
   (*
    * Process labels.
    *)
   let env1 = Jj [[ stmts ]] env in
      Block (NullDecl, Ss [[ stmts ]] env1)
   end.


(* ---------------------------------------------------------------- *)
(* ---                       declarations                     --- *)
(* ---------------------------------------------------------------- *)


Dd [[ decl ";" decls ]] env =
   let (env1, dA1) = Dd [[ decl ]] env.
       (env2, dA2) = Dd [[ decls ]] env1
   in
      (env2, DeclSeq (dA1, dA2))
   end.
```

```
Dd [[ ]] env = (env, NullDecl).

Dd [[ Type vars ]] env =
    let t = Tt [[ Type ]] in
        Vv [[ vars ]] env t
    end.

Dd [[ "const" constAssocs ]] env =
    (Cc [[ constAssocs ]] env, NullDecl).

Dd [[ "proc" id "(" ")" "is" body ]] env =
    if notDeclared (id, env) then
        let
            procName = name (id).
            (*
             * Build the environment in which to process the body.
             * Since the binding for the procedure identifier id
             * is visible, it may be called recursively.
             *)
            mode = procM (procName, 0, nil).
            procEnv = addAssoc (id, mode, env).
            bodyEnv = enterProc (procName, procEnv).
            (*
             * Process the routine body.
             *)
            bodyAction = BbR [[ body ]] bodyEnv
        in
            ( procEnv,
              BindProc (procName, Proc (NullDecl, bodyAction)) )
        end
    else
        declError env [[ id ]] "Procedure already declared.".

Dd [[ "proc" id "(" params ")" "is" body ]] env =
    if notDeclared (id, env) then
        let
            procName = name (id).
            (*
             * Determine static denotations of parameters.
             *)
            (ims, bindingActions) = Pp [[ params ]].
            paramList = extractParamModes (ims).
            numParams = length (paramList).
```

```
           (*
            * Build the environment in which to process the body.
            *
            * The existing environment is extended with
            * - the binding for the procedure identifier, and
            * - the bindings for the parameter identifiers.
            *
            * Since the binding for the procedure identifier id
            * is visible inside the body, the procedure may be
            * called recursively.
            *)
           mode = procM (procName, numParams, paramList).
           procEnv = addAssoc (id, mode, env).
           bodyEnv = addAssocList (ims, enterProc (procName, procEnv)).
           (*
            * Process the body.
            *)
           bodyAction = BbR [[ body ]] bodyEnv
       in
          ( procEnv,
            BindProc (procName, Proc (bindingActions, bodyAction)) )
       end
     else
       declError env [[ id ]] "Procedure already declared.".

(* -------------------------------------------------------------- *)
(* ---                      parameters                      --- *)
(* -------------------------------------------------------------- *)

Pp [[ param ","·params ]] =
   let (ims, dAs)  = Pp [[ param ]].
       ps as (ims', dAs') = Pp [[ params ]]
   in
      if checkModeLists (ims, ims') then
         (ims @ ims', DeclSeq (dAs, dAs'))
      else
         bindError ps [[ param ]] "Parameter will be redeclared."
   end.

Pp [[ ]] = (nil, NullDecl).

Pp [[ "val" Type id ]] =
   let t as simpleT (st) = Tt [[ Type ]]
   and name = mkAlphaName (id)
   in
```

```
        ( [ (id, valParamM (name, t)) ],
          BindValParam (name, runtimeType (st)) )
     end.

Pp [[ "ref" Type id ]] =
     let t as simpleT (st) = Tt [[ Type ]]
     and name = mkAlphaName (id)
     in
        ( [ (id, refParamM (name, t)) ],
          BindRefParam (name, runtimeType (st)) )
     end.

Pp [[ "ref" Type id "[" uboundids "]" ]] =
     let componentType as simpleT (st) = Tt [[ Type ]].
         name = mkAlphaName (id).
         (arrayType, ims, dAs) = PpA [[ uboundids ]] componentType.
         im = (id, refParamM (name, arrayType))
     in
        ( im :: ims,
          BindRefArrayParam (name, dAs, runtimeType (st)) )
     end.

(* ------------------------------------------------------------- *)
(* ---              open array parameter bounds           --- *)
(* ------------------------------------------------------------- *)

PpA [[ id "," uboundIds ]] componentType =
     let name = mkAlphaName (id).
         (*
          * Determine the mode for this identifier.
          *)
         param = constParamM (name, simpleT (int_type)).
         (subArrayType, idModes, dAs) = PpA [[ uboundIds ]] componentType
     in
        ( openArrayT (param, subArrayType),
          (id, param) :: idModes,
          DeclSeq (BindValParam (name, runtimeType (int_type)), dAs)
        )
     end.

PpA [[ ]] componentType =
     (componentType, nil, NullDecl).
```

```
(* ---------------------------------------------------------------- *)
(* ---                    constant associations                 --- *)
(* ---------------------------------------------------------------- *)

Cc [[ constAssoc "," constAssocs ]] env =
   let env1 = Cc [[ constAssoc ]] env
   in
      Cc [[ constAssocs ]] env1
   end.

Cc [[ ]] env = env.

Cc [[ id "=" const ]] env =
   if notDeclared (id, env) then
      let mode = constM (CcV [[ const ]] env)
      in
         addAssoc (id, mode, env)
      end
   else
      error env [[ id ]] "Constant already declared.".

(* ---------------------------------------------------------------- *)
(* ---                      constant values                     --- *)
(* ---------------------------------------------------------------- *)

CcV [[ int ]] env = intC (int).

CcV [[ char ]] env = charC (char).

CcV [[ string ]] env = stringC (string).

CcV [[ id ]] env =
   case lookup (id, env) of

      noneM => constError [[ id ]] "Constant not declared." |

      constM (constant) => constant |

      _ => constError [[ id ]] "Does not denote a compile time constant." .

(* ---------------------------------------------------------------- *)
(* ---                       simple types                       --- *)
(* ---------------------------------------------------------------- *)
```

```
Tt [[ "int" ]] = simpleT (int_type).

Tt [[ "bool" ]] = simpleT (bool_type).

Tt [[ "char" ]] = simpleT (char_type).

(* ---------------------------------------------------------------- *)
(* ---                       variables                       --- *)
(* ---------------------------------------------------------------- *)

Vv [[ var "," vars ]] env t =
   let (env1, dA1) = Vv [[ var ]] env t.
       (env2, dA2) = Vv [[ vars ]] env1 t
   in
      (env2, DeclSeq (dA1, dA2))
   end.

Vv [[ ]] env t = (env, NullDecl).

Vv [[ id ]] env t =
   if notDeclared (id, env) then
      let name = mkAlphaName (id).
          mode = varM (name, t).
          newEnv = addAssoc (id, mode, env).
          simpleT (st) = t
      in
         (newEnv, DeclSimpleVar (name, runtimeType (st)))
      end
   else
      declError env [[ id ]] "Identifier multiply declared.".

Vv [[ id "[" ubounds "]" ]] env t =
   if notDeclared (id, env) then
      let name = mkAlphaName (id).
          arrayType = VvT [[ ubounds ]] env t.
          mode = varM (name, arrayType).
          newEnv = addAssoc (id, mode, env).
          upperBounds = extractBounds (arrayType).
          simpleT (st) = t
      in
         (newEnv, DeclArrayVar (name, upperBounds, runtimeType (st)))
      end
   else
      declError env [[ id ]] "Identifier multiply declared.".
```

```
(* ------------------------------------------------------------- *)
(* ---                      array types                     --- *)
(* ------------------------------------------------------------- *)

VvT [[ ubound "," ubounds ]] env t =
   let intC (ub) =
      case CcV [[ ubound ]] env of
         intC (i) => intC (i) |
         _ => boundsError [[ ubound ]] "Illegal array bound."
   in
      arrayT (ub, VvT [[ ubounds ]] env t)
   end.

VvT [[ ]] env t = t.

(* ------------------------------------------------------------- *)
(* ---                        labels                        --- *)
(* ------------------------------------------------------------- *)

Jj [[ stmt ";" stmts ]] env =
   let env1 = Jj [[ stmt ]] env in
      Jj [[ stmts ]] env1
   end.

Jj [[ ]] env = env.

Jj [[ id ":" stmt ]] env =
   if notDeclared (id, env) then
      let name = mkAlphaLabel (id)
      in
         addAssoc (id, labelM (name), env)
      end
   else
      error env [[ id ]] "Label already declared.".

Jj [[ _ ]] env = env.

(* ------------------------------------------------------------- *)
(* ---                      statements                      --- *)
(* ------------------------------------------------------------- *)

Ss [[ stmt ";" stmts ]] env =
   StmtSeq (Ss [[ stmt ]] env, Ss [[ stmts ]] env).
```

```
Ss [[ ]] env = NullStmt.

Ss [[ id ":" stmt ]] env =
    let labelM (name) = lookup (id, env)
    in
        LabelDef (name, Ss [[ stmt ]] env)
    end.

Ss [[ "goto" id ]] env =
    (*
     * Only local gotos are allowed.
     *)
    case lookup (id, env) of
        labelM (name) -> Jump (name) |
        _ => stmtError [[ ... ]] "Illegal label reference.".

Ss [[ lvar ":=" expr ]] env =
    let (ltype, lA) = Ll [[ lvar ]] env
    and (rtype, rA) = Ee [[ expr ]] env
    in
        if assignmentCompatible (ltype, rtype) then
            Assign (lA, rA)
        else
            stmtError [[ lvar ]] "Type mismatch in assignment."
    end.

Ss [[ "if" expr "then" stmts "endif" ]] env =
    let (t, predicateAction) = Ee [[ expr ]] env.
        thenAction = Ss [[ stmts ]] env
    in
        case t of
            simpleT'(bool_type) =>
                Test (predicateAction, thenAction, NullStmt) |
            _ =>
                stmtError [[ expr ]] "IF expression must be Boolean."
    end.

Ss [[ "if" expr "then" stmts1 "else" stmts2 "endif"]] env =
    let (t, predicateAction) = Ee [[ expr ]] env.
        thenAction = Ss [[ stmts1 ]] env.
        elseAction = Ss [[ stmts2 ]] env
    in
        case t of
```

```
          simpleT (bool_type) =>
             Test (predicateAction, thenAction, elseAction) |
          _ =>
             stmtError [[ expr ]] "IF expression must be Boolean."
      end.


Ss [[ "loop" "while" expr stmts "endloop" ]] env =
   let (t, conditionAction) = Ee [[ expr ]] env.
      bodyAction = Ss [[ stmts ]] (enterLoop env)
   in
      case t of
         simpleT (bool_type) =>
            While (conditionAction, bodyAction) |
         _ =>
            stmtError [[ expr ]] "WHILE expression must be Boolean."
      end.


Ss [[ "loop" stmts "until" expr "endloop" ]] env =
   let bodyAction = Ss [[ stmts ]] (enterLoop env).
      (t, conditionAction) = Ee [[ expr ]] env
   in
      case t of
         simpleT (bool_type) =>
            While (Boolean (true),
               StmtSeq (bodyAction,
                     Test (conditionAction, ExitLoop, NullStmt))) |
         _ => stmtError [[ expr ]] "UNTIL expression must be Boolean."
      end.


Ss [[ "exit" ]] env =
   if withinLoop (env) then
      ExitLoop
   else
      stmtError [[ ... ]] "EXIT may not occur outside a loop.".


Ss [[ "call" id "(" ")" ]] env =
   case lookup (id, env) of
      procM (name, 0, nil) =>            (* procedure without parameters *)
         Call (name, NullExpr) |
      _ =>
         stmtError [[ id ]] "Unknown parameterless procedure.".


Ss [[ "call" id "(" exprs ")" ]] env =
   case lookup (id, env) of
```

```
       procM (name, numParams, ps) =>    (* procedure with parameters *)
          let argsAction = EeA [[ exprs ]] env ps
          in
              if EeN [[ exprs ]] = numParams then
                 Call (name, argsAction)
              else
                 stmtError [[ id ]] "Wrong number of procedure arguments."
          end |
       _ =>
          stmtError [[ id ]] "Unknown procedure.".

Ss [[ "return" ]] env =
   if withinProc (env) then
      Return
   else
      stmtError [[ ... ]] "RETURN may not occur outside a procedure.".

Ss [[ "read" lvar ]] env =
   let (t, lA) = Ll [[ lvar ]] env in
      case t of
         simpleT (int_type)  => ReadInt (lA) |
         simpleT (char_type) => ReadChar (lA) |
         _ => stmtError [[ lvar ]]
                     "READ argument must be of type int or char."
   end.

Ss [[ "readln" ]] env = ReadLine.

Ss [[ "write" expr]] env =
   let (t, vA) = Ee [[ expr ]] env in
      case t of
         simpleT (int_type)  => WriteInt (vA) |
         simpleT (char_type) => WriteChar (vA) |
         _ => stmtError [[ expr ]]
                     "WRITE argument must be of type int or char."
   end.

Ss [[ "writeln" ]] env = WriteLine.

Ss [[ "skip" ]] env = NullStmt.

(* ------------------------------------------------------------ *)
(* ---                      L-values                      --- *)
(* ------------------------------------------------------------ *)
```

```
Ll [[ id ]] env =
   case lookup (id, env) of

      noneM =>
         exprError [[ id ]] "Variable not declared." |

      varM (name, t as simpleT (st)) =>
         ( t, Var (name, runtimeType (st))) |

      varM (name, t as arrayT (_)) =>
         ( t,
           let compType = runtimeType (componentType (t))
           and vAs = evalBounds (t)
           in
               Array (name, vAs, compType)
           end
         ) |

      valParamM (name, t as simpleT (st)) =>
         ( t, ValParam (name, runtimeType (st)) ) |

      refParamM (name, t as simpleT (st)) =>
         ( t, RefParam (name, runtimeType (st)) ) |

      refParamM (name, t as openArrayT (_)) =>
         ( t,
           let compType = runtimeType (componentType (t))
           in
               RefArrayParam (name, evalBounds (t), compType)
           end
         ) |

      _ => exprError [[ id ]] "Object has no L-value.".

Ll [[ id "[" exprs "]" ]] env =
   let (ts, vAs) = EeX [[ exprs ]] env
   and (t, lA) = Ll [[ id ]] env
   in
      if matchingBounds (ts, t) then
         let st = componentType (t)
         in
            (simpleT (st), Index (lA, vAs))
         end
```

```
          else
              exprError [[ id ]] "Illegal array reference."
      end.

Ll [[ _ ]] env =
    exprError [[ ... ]] "Expression has no Lvalue.".

(* ------------------------------------------------------------ *)
(* ---            number of expressions in expression list      --- *)
(* ------------------------------------------------------------ *)

EeN [[ expr "," exprs ]] = 1 + EeN [[ exprs ]].

EeN [[ ]] = 0 .

(* ------------------------------------------------------------ *)
(* --               indexing expression lists                  --- *)
(* ------------------------------------------------------------ *)

EeX [[ expr "," exprs ]] env =
    let (t, vA) = Ee [[ expr ]] env
    and (ts, vAs) = EeX [[ exprs ]] env
    in
        (t :: ts, ExprSeq (vA, vAs))
    end.

EeX [[ ]] env = (nil, NullExpr).

(* ------------------------------------------------------------ *)
(* --               argument expressions lists                 --- *)
(* ------------------------------------------------------------ *)

EeA [[ expr "," exprs ]] env paramList =
    let
        fun evArg (param: MODE): VACTION =
            let (paramType, (argType, vA)) =
                case param of
                    valParamM (_, t)   => (t, Ee [[ expr ]] env) |
                    constParamM (_, t) => (t, Ee [[ expr ]] env) |
                    refParamM (_, t)   => (t, Ll [[ expr ]] env)
            in
                if parameterCompatible (paramType, argType) then
                    vA
                else
                    (print (paramType).
```

```
                    print (argType).
                    argError [[ expr ]] "Incorrect argument type."
                )
          end
    in
       case paramList of
          nil =>
             argError [[ ... ]] "Too many actual arguments." |
          param :: paramList' =>
             ExprSeq (evArg (param), EeA [[ exprs ]] env paramList')
    end.

EeA [[ ]] env paramList = NullExpr.

(* ------------------------------------------------------------- *)
(* ---                      expressions                     --- *)
(* ------------------------------------------------------------- *)

Ee [[ "-" expr ]] env =
   let (t, vA) = Ee [[ expr ]] env
   in
      case t of
         simpleT (int_type) => (t, Neg (vA)) |
         _ => exprError [[ expr ]] "Can't negate a non-integer."
   end.

Ee [[ expr1 "+" expr2 ]] env =
   let (vA1, vA2) = checkTypes ([[ ... ]], [int_type],
                                Ee [[ expr1 ]] env, Ee [[ expr2 ]] env)
   in
      (simpleT (int_type), Add (vA1, vA2))
   end.

Ee [[ expr1 "-" expr2 ]] env =
   let (vA1, vA2) = checkTypes ([[ ... ]], [int_type],
                                Ee [[ expr1 ]] env, Ee [[ expr2 ]] env)
   in
      (simpleT (int_type), Sub (vA1, vA2))
   end.

Ee [[ expr1 "*" expr2 ]] env =
   let (vA1, vA2) = checkTypes ([[ ... ]], [int_type],
                                Ee [[ expr1 ]] env, Ee [[ expr2 ]] env)
   in
```

```
        (simpleT (int_type), Mult (vA1, vA2))
    end.

Ee [[ expr1 "/" expr2 ]] env =
    let (vA1, vA2) = checkTypes ([[ ... ]], [int_type],
                            Ee [[ expr1 ]] env, Ee [[ expr2 ]] env)
    in
        (simpleT (int_type), Divi (vA1, vA2))
    end.

Ee [[ expr1 "mod" expr2 ]] env =
    let (vA1, vA2) = checkTypes ([[ ... ]], [int_type],
                            Ee [[ expr1 ]] env, Ee [[ expr2 ]] env)
    in
        (simpleT (int_type), Modulo (vA1, vA2))
    end.

Ee [[ expr1 "=" expr2 ]] env =
    let (vA1, vA2) = checkTypes ([[ ... ]], [int_type, char_type],
                            Ee [[ expr1 ]] env, Ee [[ expr2 ]] env)
    in
        (simpleT (bool_type), Equal (vA1, vA2))
    end.

Ee [[ expr1 "!=" expr2 ]] env =
    let (vA1, vA2) = checkTypes ([[ ... ]], [int_type, char_type],
                            Ee [[ expr1 ]] env, Ee [[ expr2 ]] env)
    in
        (simpleT (bool_type), BoolNot (Equal (vA1, vA2)))
    end.

Ee [[ expr1 "<" expr2 ]] env =
    let (vA1, vA2) = checkTypes ([[ ... ]], [int_type, char_type],
                            Ee [[ expr1 ]] env, Ee [[ expr2 ]] env)
    in
        (simpleT (bool_type), Less (vA1, vA2))
    end.

Ee [[ expr1 ">" expr2 ]] env =
    let (vA1, vA2) = checkTypes ([[ ... ]], [int_type, char_type],
                            Ee [[ expr1 ]] env, Ee [[ expr2 ]] env)
    in
        (simpleT (bool_type), Greater (vA1, vA2))
    end.
```

```
Ee [[ expr1 "<=" expr2 ]] env =
   let (vA1, vA2) = checkTypes ([[ ... ]], [int_type, char_type],
                                 Ee [[ expr1 ]] env, Ee [[ expr2 ]] env)
   in
      (simpleT (bool_type), BoolNot (Greater (vA1, vA2)))
   end.

Ee [[ expr1 ">=" expr2 ]] env =
   let (vA1, vA2) = checkTypes ([[ ... ]], [int_type, char_type],
                                 Ee [[ expr1 ]] env, Ee [[ expr2 ]] env)
   in
      (simpleT (bool_type), BoolNot (Less (vA1, vA2)))
   end.

Ee [[ expr1 "and" expr2 ]] env =
   let (vA1, vA2) = checkTypes ([[ ... ]], [bool_type],
                                 Ee [[ expr1 ]] env, Ee [[ expr2 ]] env)
   in
      (simpleT (bool_type), BoolAnd (vA1, vA2))
   end.

Ee [[ expr1 "or" expr2 ]] env =
   let (vA1, vA2) = checkTypes ([[ ... ]], [bool_type],
                                 Ee [[ expr1 ]] env, Ee [[ expr2 ]] env)
   in
      (simpleT (bool_type), BoolOr (vA1, vA2))
   end.

Ee [[ "not" expr ]] env =
   let (t, vA) = Ee [[ expr ]] env in
      case t of
         simpleT (bool_type) => (t, BoolNot (vA)) |
         _ => exprError [[ expr ]] "Can't apply NOT to a non-Boolean."
   end.

Ee [[ "char" "(" expr ")" ]] env =
   let (t, vA) = Ee [[ expr ]] env in
      case t of
         simpleT (int_type) =>
            (simpleT (char_type), IntToChar (vA)) |
         _ =>
            exprError [[ expr ]] "Can't apply CHAR to a non-integer."
   end.
```

```
Ee [[ "int" "(" expr ")" ]] env =
   let (t, vA) = Ee [[ expr ]] env in
      case t of
         simpleT (char_type) =>
            (simpleT (int_type), CharToInt (vA)) |
         _ =>
            exprError [[ expr ]] "Can't apply INT to a non-character."
   end.


Ee [[ id ]] env =
   case lookup (id, env) of
      constM (intC (i)) =>
         (simpleT (int_type), Integer (i)) |

      constM (charC (c)) =>
         (simpleT (char_type), Character (c)) |

      constM (stringC (s)) =>
         (arrayT (size (s), simpleT (char_type)), CharString (s)) |

      constParamM (name, t as simpleT (st)) =>
         (t, Rvalue (ValParam (name, runtimeType (st)))) |

      _ =>
         let (t, lA) = Ll [[ ... ]] env in
            (t, Rvalue (lA))
         end.

Ee [[ id "[" exprs "]" ]] env =
   let (t, lA) = Ll [[ ... ]] env in
      (t, Rvalue (lA))
   end.

Ee [[ bool ]] env = (simpleT (bool_type), Boolean (bool)).

Ee [[ int ]] env = (simpleT (int_type), Integer (int)).

Ee [[ char ]] env = (simpleT (char_type), Character (char)).

Ee [[ string ]] env =
   (arrayT (size (string), simpleT (char_type)), charString (string)).

end semantics
```

G SOL/C Benchmark Programs

```
program Fibonacci ( "stdin", "stdout" ) is
/*
 * This is a SOL/C benchmark program.
 * It computes the 22nd Fibonacci number 50 times.
 *
 */

proc fib (ref int result, val int n) is
/*
 * Recursively compute the nth Fibonacci number into the
 * result parameter.
 */
int r1, r2;

begin
   if n <= 2 then
      result := 1
   else
      call fib (r1, n - 1);
      call fib (r2, n - 2);
      result := r1 + r2
   endif
end; /* fib */

/* Main program */

const
   num = 22,
   times = 50;

int i, result;

begin
   i := 0;
   loop while i < times
      call fib (result, num);
      i := i + 1
   endloop;
   write result
end
```

```
program bubbleSort ( "stdin", "stdout" ) is
/*
 * This is a SOL/C benchmark program.
 * It constructs an array 0 .. 999, and then bubble sorts
 * it into descending order.
 */

proc sort (ref int num [n]) is
/*
 * This procedure uses a bubble sort to arrange the 0..n-1
 * elements of the "num" array.
 */
int last, current, temp;

begin
   last := n - 1;
   loop while last > 0
      current := 0;
      loop while current < last
         if num [current] < num [current + 1] then
            temp := num [current];
            num [current] := num [current + 1];
            num [current + 1] := temp
         endif;
         current := current + 1
      endloop;
      last := last - 1
   endloop
end; /* sort */

/* Main program */

const numSort = 1000;
int i;
int nums [1000];      /* The array to sort */

begin
   i := 0;
   loop while i < numSort
      nums [i] := i;
      i := i + 1
   endloop;
   call sort (nums)
end
```

```
program sieve ("stdin", "stdout") is
/*
 * This is a SOL/C benchmark program.
 * It performs 30 iterations of the standard Sieve of
 * Erathosthenes prime number generator.
 */

proc primes (val int iterations, ref bool flags [size]) is
int i, prime, j, count, loops;

begin
   loops := 0;
   loop while loops < iterations
      count := 0;
      i := 0;
      loop while i < size
         flags [i] := true;
         i := i + 1
      endloop;
      i := 0;
      loop while i < size
         if flags [i] then
            prime := 2 * i + 3;
            j := i + prime;
            loop while j < size
               flags [j] := false;
               j := j + prime
            endloop;
            count := count + 1
         endif;
         i := i + 1
      endloop;
      loops := loops + 1
   endloop
end; /* primes */

/* Main program */
const iterations = 30;
bool flags [8191];

begin
   call primes (iterations, flags)
end
```

```
program matrixMultiply ( "stdin", "stdout" ) is
/*
 * This is a SOL/C benchmark program.
 * It constructs two N x N matrices and multiplies them.
 */

const N = 20;

int A [N, N], B [N, N], C [N, N];      /* The matrices */

const iter = 100;
int k;

proc initMatrix (ref int mat [n, m]) is

int i, j;

begin
   i := 0;
   loop while i < n
      j := 0;
      loop while j < m
         mat [i, j] := 2 * i - j;
         j := j + 1
      endloop;
      i := i + 1
   endloop
end; /* initMatrix */

proc matMult (ref int Z [zu1, zu2],
              ref int X [xu1, xu2],
              ref int Y [yu1, yu2])
is

int i, j, k, sum;

begin
   /*
    * It is assumed that xu2 = yu1, zu1 = xu1, zu2 = yu2
    */
   i := 0;
   loop while i < xu1
      j := 0;
      loop while j < xu2
```

```
        k := 0;
        sum := 0;
        loop while k < yu1
            sum := sum + X [i, k] * Y [k, j];
            k := k + 1
        endloop;
        Z [i, j] := sum;
        j := j + 1
     endloop;
     i := i + 1
   endloop
end; /* matMult */

/* Main program */
begin
   call initMatrix (A);
   call initMatrix (B);
   k := 0;
   loop while k < iter
      call matMult (C, A, B);
      k := k + 1
   endloop
end /* matrixMultiply */
```

H Using the MESS System

This appendix gives a few quick tips that might be helpful in getting started with the MESS system.

Syntactic extensions to ML

The semantic metalanguage used by MESS is based on a purely applicative subset of ML, so the standard core definition of ML [Harper 86] can be consulted for most of the ML-specific details. The syntax has been changed and extended in a few minor ways, as follows:

- The syntax, `[a => b]f`, expresses the perturbation of function `f` so that it maps `a` to `b`. In other words,

  $$[a => b]f \equiv fn\ x.\ if\ x=a\ then\ b\ else\ f\ x$$

- A period (".") may be used in place of ML's double right arrow ("⇒"). This allows `fn` expressions to look more like λ-expressions.

- A period is used in place of the semicolon (";") for sequencing.

- The `auxiliary functions` section is simply a list of ML declarations. The binding keyword (*e.g.*, `fun`, `val`, *etc.*) may be omitted, in which case `fun` is assumed.

Error handling

MESS provides a predefined function called `error`:

$$error\ :\ \ 'a\ ->\ AST\ ->\ STRING\ ->\ 'a$$

The first argument is returned as the result of this function. Before returning this value, however, the source text corresponding to the given abstract syntax tree is marked, and the given string issued to the user as a diagnostic message.

Semantic domains

The collection of domain equations in the `semantic domains` section is very much like a system of mutually recursive type declarations in ML. However, type abbreviations are allowed to participate in the system of declarations.

Types defining data constructors are written as follows:

$$dom = \text{union } constr_1 \text{ of } t_1\ |\ constr_2 \text{ of } t_2\ |\ ...$$

The keyword `union` is used instead of ML's `datatype`.

The structure of MESS specifications

The preceding appendices give complete examples of semantic specifications that have been processed by the MESS system.

Running MESS

To run the TI PC Scheme implementation of MESS, simply type

```
(mess)
```

to the Scheme reader. This causes Scheme to load in the MESS system. Then, to process a macrosemantics or microsemantics, type an expression of the form

(m *file-name option...*)

where *file-name* may be either a string or an unquoted symbol giving the name of the specification file. If no file-name extension is given, `.mes` is assumed. MESS describes the possible options after it is loaded.

Bibliography

ADJ (1978) (J. A. Goguen, J. W. Thatcher, and E. Wagner). An initial algebra approach to the specification, correctness, and implementation of abstract data types. *Current Trends in Programming Methodology IV*, R. T. Yeh, Ed., Prentice-Hall, Englewood Cliffs, New Jersey, 80–149.

A. V. Aho, R. Sethi, and J. D. Ullman (1986). *Compilers—Principles, Techniques, and Tools.* Addison-Wesley, Reading, Massachusetts.

A. Appel (1985). Compile-time evaluation and code generation for semantics-directed compilers. Ph.D. Dissertation, Department of Computer Science, Carnegie Mellon University.

H. P. Barendregt (1981). *The Lambda Calculus: Its Syntax and Semantics.* North-Holland, Amsterdam.

W. A. Barrett and J. D. Couch (1985). *Compiler Construction: Theory and Practice.* 2nd ed., Science Research Associates, Inc.

P. Bird (1982). An implementation of a code generator specification language for table driven code generators. *Proceedings of the SIGPLAN'82 Symposium on Compiler Construction; SIGPLAN Notices 17*, 6, 44–55.

J. Bodwin, L. Bradley, K. Kanda, D. Litle, and U. Pleban (1982). Experience with a compiler generator based on denotational semantics. *Proceedings of the SIGPLAN'82 Symposium on Compiler Construction; SIGPLAN Notices 17*, 6, 216–229.

I. Bohlbro and M. Schwartzbach (1982). Models for abstract semantic algebras. Technical Report DAIMI IR-44, Computer Science Department, Aarhus University, Aarhus, Denmark.

Borland International, Inc. (1985). *Turbo Pascal Reference Manual (version 3.0).*

R. M. Burstall and P. J. Landin (1969). Programs and their proofs: an algebraic approach. *Machine Intelligence 4*, B. Meltzer and D. Michie, Eds., Edinburgh University Press, Edinburgh, Scotland, 17–43.

J. W. Davidson and C. W. Fraser (1980). The design and application of a retargetable peephole optimizer. *ACM Transactions on Programming Languages and Systems 2*, 2, 191–202.

F. DeRemer (1969). Practical translators for LR(k) languages. Ph.D. Dissertation, Department of Electrical Engineering, MIT, Cambridge, Massachusetts.

DeSmet (1983). *DeSmet C Development Package Manual (version 1.7).* C Ware.

V. Donzeau-Gouge (1980). On the formal description of Ada. *Semantics-Directed Compiler Generation,* N. D. Jones, Ed., *Lecture Notes in Computer Science,* No. 94, Springer-Verlag, Berlin, West Germany, 475–489.

R. Farrow (1982). LINGUIST-86: Yet another translator writing system based on attribute grammars. *Proceedings of the SIGPLAN'82 Symposium on Compiler Construction; SIGPLAN Notices 17*, 6, 160–171.

_____ (1984). Generating a production compiler from an attribute grammar. *IEEE Software* (October), 77–93.

R. W. Floyd (1967). Assigning meanings to programs. *Proceedings of the Symposia in Applied Mathematics 19*, T. Schwartz, Ed., *Mathematical Aspects of Computer Science,* American Mathematical Society, Providence, Rhode Island, 19–32.

D. Friedman and D. S. Wise (1976). CONS should not evaluate its arguments. *Proceedings of the 3rd ICALP Conference*, S. Michaelson and R. Milner, Eds., Edinburgh, Scotland, 257–284.

M. Ganapathi (1980). Retargetable code generation and optimization using attribute grammars. Ph.D. Dissertation, Technical Report 406, Computer Science Department, University of Wisconsin, Madison, Wisconsin.

M. C. Gaudel (1981). Compiler generation from formal definition of programming languages: A survey. *Formalization of Programming Concepts*, J. Diaz and I. Ramos, Eds., *Lecture Notes in Computer Science*, No. 107, Springer-Verlag, Berlin, West Germany, 96–114.

R. S. Glanville and S. Graham (1978). A new method for compiler code generation. *Proceedings of the 5th Annual ACM Symposium on Principles of Programming Languages*, Tucson, Arizona, 231–239.

M. J. C. Gordon (1979). *The denotational description of programming languages: An introduction.* Springer-Verlag, Berlin, West Germany.

A. N. Habermann (1973). Critical comments on the programming language Pascal. *Acta Informatica* 3, 47–57.

R. Harper (1986). Standard ML. Technical Report ECS-LFCS-86-2, Laboratory for Foundations of Computer Science, Edinburgh University, Edinburgh, Scotland.

P. Henderson and J. M. Morris (1976). A lazy evaluator. *Proceedings of the 3rd Annual ACM Symposium on Principles of Programming Languages*, Atlanta, Georgia, 95–103.

W. Henhapl and C. Jones (1982). ALGOL 68. *Formal Specification and Software Development*, D. Bjorner and C. Jones, Eds., Prentice-Hall, Englewood Cliffs, New Jersey, 1982, 141–174.

J. R. Hindley, B. Lercher, and J. P. Selden (1972). *Introduction to Combinatory Logic.* Cambridge University Press, Cambridge, England.

C. A. R. Hoare (1969). An axiomatic basis for computer programming. *Communications of the ACM* 12, 10, 576–580.

C. A. R. Hoare and N. Wirth (1973). An axiomatic definition of the programming language Pascal. *Acta Inf. 2*, 335–355.

J. Hughes (1982). Super combinators: A new implementation method for applicative languages. *Proceedings of 1982 ACM Conference on LISP and Functional Programming*, Pittsburgh, Pennsylvania, 1–10.

M. Jazayeri, W. F. Ogden, and W. C. Rounds. The intrinsically exponential complexity of the circularity problem for attribute grammars. *Communications of the ACM 18*, 12, 697–706.

M. Jazayeri and K. G. Walter (1975). Alternating semantic evaluators. *Proceedings of the ACM National Conference*, New York, New York, 230–234.

S. C. Johnson (1975). YACC: Yet another compiler compiler. Technical Report 32, Bell Laboratories, Murray Hill, New Jersey.

N. D. Jones and H. Christiansen (1982). Control flow treatment in a simple semantics-directed compiler generator. *Formal description of programming concepts II*, IFIP IC-2 Working Conference, D. Bjorner, Ed., North Holland, Amsterdam.

N. D. Jones, P. Sestoft, and H. Sondergaard (1985). An experiment in partial evaluation: The generation of a compiler generator. *Rewriting Techniques and Applications*, J. Jouannaud, Ed., *Lecture Notes in Computer Science*, No. 202, Springer-Verlag, Berlin, West Germany, 125–140.

U. Kastens, B. Hutt, and E. Zimmerman (1982). GAG: A practical compiler generator. *Lecture Notes in Computer Science*, No. 141, Springer-Verlag, Berlin, West Germany.

K. Kennedy (1981). A survey of data flow analysis techniques. *Program Flow Analysis: Theory and Applications*, S. S. Muchnick and N. D. Jones, Eds., Prentice-Hall, Englewood Cliffs, New Jersey, 5–54.

B. W. Kernighan and D. M. Ritchie (1978). *The C Programming Language*. Prentice-Hall, Englewood Cliffs, New Jersey.

D. E. Knuth (1965). On the translation of languages from left to right. *Information and Control 8*, 6, 607–639.

D. Kranz, R. Kelsey, J. Rees, P. Hudak, J. Philbin, and N. Adams (1986). ORBIT: An optimizing compiler for Scheme. In *Proceedings of the SIGPLAN'86 Symposium on Compiler Construction; SIGPLAN Notices 21*, 7, 219–233.

P. J. Landin (1964). The mechanical evaluation of expressions. *Computer Journal 6*, 308–320.

O. Lecarme and P. Desjardins (1975). More comments on the programming language Pascal. *Acta Informatica 4*, 231–243.

P. Lee and U. F. Pleban (1986). On the use of LISP in implementing denotational semantics. *Proceedings of 1986 ACM Conference on LISP and Functional Programming*, Cambridge, Massachusetts, 233–248.

_____ (1987). A realistic compiler generator based on high-level semantics. *Proceedings of the 14th Annual ACM Symposium on Principles of Programming Languages*, Munich, West Germany, 284–295.

O. L. Madsen (1980). On defining semantics by means of extended attribute grammars. *Semantics-Directed Compiler Generation*, N. D. Jones, Ed., *Lecture Notes in Computer Science*, No. 94, Springer-Verlag, Berlin, West Germany, 259–299.

B. H. Mayoh (1978). Attribute grammars and mathematical semantics. Ph.D. Dissertation, Technical Report DAIMI PB-90, Computer Science Department, Aarhus University, Aarhus, Denmark.

J. McCarthy, P. W. Abrahams, D. J. Edwards, T. P. Hart, and I. L. Levin (1965). *LISP 1.5 Programmer's Manual*. MIT Press, Cambridge, Massachusetts.

W. M. McKeeman (1965). Peephole optimization. *Communications of the ACM 8*, 7, 443–444.

R. E. Milne and C. Strachey (1976). *A theory of programming language semantics*. Chapman and Hall, London, England.

F. L. Morris (1973). Advice on structuring compilers and proving them correct. *Proceedings of the 1st Annual ACM Symposium on Principles of Programming Languages*, Boston, Massachusetts, 144–152.

J. Moses (1970). The function of FUNCTION in LISP. AI Memo 199, Department of Electrical Engineering, MIT, Cambridge, Massachusetts.

P. D. Mosses (1974). The mathematical semantics of Algol 60. Technical Monograph PRG-12, Programming Research Group, Oxford University Computing Laboratory, Oxford, England.

____ (1975). Mathematical semantics and compiler generation. Ph.D. Dissertation, Oxford University, London, England.

____ (1979). SIS—Semantics Implementation System. Technical Report DAIMI MD-30, Computer Science Department, Aarhus University, Aarhus, Denmark.

____ (1982). Abstract semantic algebras! *Formal description of programming concepts II*, IFIP IC-2 Working Conference, D. Bjorner, Ed., North Holland, Amsterdam, 63–88.

____ (1984). A basic abstract semantic algebra. *Semantics of Data Types*, G. Kahn, D. B. MacQueen, G. Plotkin, Eds., *Lecture Notes in Computer Science*, No. 173, Springer-Verlag, Berlin, West Germany, 87–107.

P. D. Mosses and D. A. Watt (1986). The use of action semantics. Technical Report DAIMI PB–217, Computer Science Department, Aarhus University, Denmark; also, *Proceedings of the IFIP TC2 Working Conference on Formal Description of Programming Concepts III*, North-Holland, 1987.

____ (1987). Pascal: dynamic action semantics. Draft-Version 0.33, Computer Science Department, Aarhus University, Denmark.

S. S. Muchnick and U. F. Pleban (1982). A semantic comparison of LISP and Scheme. *Proceedings of 1982 ACM Conference on LISP and Functional Programming*, Stanford, California, 95–107.

P. Naur (1963). Revised report on the algorithmic language ALGOL 60. *Communications of the ACM* 6, 1, 1–17.

H. R. Nielson and F. Nielson (1986). Semantics directed compiling for functional languages. *Proceedings of 1986 ACM Conference on LISP and Functional Programming*, Cambridge, Massachusetts, 249–257.

L. Paulson (1981). A compiler generator for semantic grammars. Ph.D. Dissertation, Department of Computer Science, Stanford University, Stanford, California.

____ (1982). A semantics-directed compiler generator. *Proceedings of the Ninth Annual ACM Symposium on Principles of Programming Languages*, Albuquerque, New Mexico, 224–239.

U. F. Pleban (1984). Formal semantics and compiler generation. *Programmierumgebungen und Compiler*. H. Morgenbrod and W. Sammer, Eds., Teubner-Verlag, Stuttgart, 145–161.

____ (1987). User's Guide to FrEGe: the Front-End Generator. Unpublished manuscript, Applied Dynamics International, Ann Arbor, Michigan.

U. F. Pleban and P. Lee (1987). High-level semantics — An integrated approach to programming language semantics and the specification of implementations. *Proceedings of the Third Workshop on the Mathematical Foundations of Programming Language Semantics, Lecture Notes in Computer Science*, No. 298, Springer-Verlag, Berlin, West Germany.

____ (1988). An automatically generated, realistic compiler for an imperative programming language. *Proceedings of the SIGPLAN'88 Symposium on Programming Language Design and Implementation*, Atlanta, Georgia.

K. Raiha (1980). Experiences with the compiler writing system HLP. *Semantics-Directed Compiler Generation*, N. D. Jones, Ed., *Lecture Notes in Computer Science*, No. 94, Springer-Verlag, Berlin, West Germany, 350–362.

J. C. Reynolds (1972). Definitional interpreters for higher-order programming languages. *Proceedings of the ACM National Conference*, New York, New York, 717–740.

M. Richards and C. Whitby-Stevens (1979). *BCPL — The Language and its Compiler*. Cambridge University Press, Cambridge, Massachusetts.

D. M. Ritchie and K. Thompson (1974). The UNIX time-sharing system. *Communications of the ACM 17*, 7, 365–375.

D. A. Schmidt (1985). Detecting global variables in denotational specifications. *ACM Transactions on Programming Languages and Systems 7*, 2, 299–310.

____ (1986). *Denotational semantics—A methodology for language development*. Allyn and Bacon, Newton, Massachusetts.

D. S. Scott (1971). Outline of a mathematical theory of computation. Technical Monograph PRG-2, Programming Research Group, Oxford University Computing Laboratory, Oxford, England.

R. Sethi (1981). Control flow aspects of semantics directed compiling. Technical Report 98, Bell Laboratories, Murray Hill, New Jersey; Also *Proceedings of the SIGPLAN'82 Symposium on Compiler Construction; SIGPLAN Notices 17*, 6, 245–260.

G. L. Steele and G. J. Sussman (1978). The revised report on SCHEME. AI Memo 452, Department of Electrical Engineering, MIT, Cambridge, Massachusetts.

J. E. Stoy (1977). *Denotational semantics: The Scott-Strachey approach to programming language theory*. MIT Press, Cambridge, Massachusetts.

R. D. Tennent (1973). Mathematical semantics of SNOBOL4. *Proceedings of the 1st Annual ACM Symposium on Principles of Programming Languages*, Boston, Massachusetts, 95–107.

____ (1976). The denotational semantics of programming languages. *Communications of the ACM 19*, 8, 437–453.

____ (1977). A denotational definition of the programming language Pascal. Technical Report 77–47, Department of Computing Sciences, Queen's University, Kingston, Ontario.

Texas Instruments, Inc. (1985). *TI Scheme Language Reference Manual*

M. H. van Emden and R. A. Kowalski (1976). The semantics of predicate logic and a programming language. *Journal of the ACM 23*, 4, 733–743.

A. van Wijngaarden, B. J. Mailloux, J. L. Peck, C. H. A. Koster, M. Sintzoff, C. H. Lindsey, L. G. L. Meertens, and R. G. Fisker (1975). Revised report on the algorithmic language Algol 68. *Acta Informatica 5*, 1–236.

J. E. Vuilleman (1973). Proof Techniques for Recursive Programs. Memo AIM 318, STAN-CS-73-393, Computer Science Department, Stanford University, Stanford, California.

W. M. Waite and G. Goos (1984). *Compiler construction*. Springer-Verlag, New York, New York.

M. Wand (1982). Deriving target code as a representation of continuation semantics. *ACM Transactions on Programming Languages and Systems 4*, 3, 496–517.

____ (1984). A semantic prototyping system. *Proceedings of the SIGPLAN 84 Symposium on Compiler Construction; SIGPLAN Notices 19*, 6, 213–221.

D. A. Watt (1979). An extended attribute grammar for Pascal. *SIGPLAN Notices 14*, 2, 60–74.

____ (1984). Executable semantic descriptions. *Software—Practice and Experience 16*, 1, 13–43.

____ (1988). An action semantics of Standard ML. *Proceedings of the Third Workshop on the Mathematical Foundations of Programming Language Semantics, Lecture Notes in Computer Science*, No. 298, Springer-Verlag, Berlin, West Germany.

P. Wegner (1972). The Vienna Definition Language. *Computing Surveys 4*, 1, 5–63.

N. Wirth (1971). The programming language Pascal. *Acta Informatica 1*, 35–63.

Index

The MIT Press, with Peter Denning, general consulting editor, and Brian Randall, European consulting editor, publishes computer science books in the following series:

ACM Doctoral Dissertation Award and Distinguished Dissertation Series

Artificial Intelligence, Patrick Henry Winston and J. Michael Brady founding editors; J. Michael Brady, Daniel G. Bobrow, and Randall Davis, current editors

Charles Babbage Institute Reprint Series for the History of Computing Martin Campbell-Kelly, editor

Computer Systems, Herb Schwetman, editor

Exploring with Logo, E. Paul Goldenberg, editor

Foundations of Computing Michael Garey and Albert Meyer, editors

History of Computing I. Bernard Cohen and William Aspray, editors

Information Systems, Michael Lesk, editor

Logic Programming, Ehud Shapiro, editor; Fernando Pereira, Koichi Furukawa, and D. H. D. Warren, associate editors

The MIT Electrical Engineering and Computer Science Series

Research Monographs in Parallel and Distributed Processing, Christopher Jesshope and David Klappholz, editors

Scientific Computation, Dennis Gannon, editor

Technical Communication, Ed Barrett, editor